DATE DUE

SEP 0 6 2007	

QUALITATIVE RESEARCH FOR EDUCATION:
AN INTRODUCTION
TO
THEORY AND METHODS

ROBERT C. BOGDAN
Syracuse University

and

SARI KNOPP BIKLEN
The Education Designs Group

Allyn and Bacon, Inc.
Boston   London   Sydney   Toronto

Library of Congress Cataloging in Publication Data

Bogdan, Robert.
  Qualitative research for education.

  Bibliography: p.
  Includes index.
  1. Educational research. I. Biklen, Sari Knopp.
II. Title.
LB1028.B56   370'.7'8   81-10952
ISBN 0-205-07695-5   AACR2

Printed in the United States of America
18 17 16 15 14   92 91 90

To
Yinka, Meg, Chet, and Jono
and
Noah and Molly

CONTENTS

FOREWORD

The publication of this book is cause for celebration. During the past ten years there has been an explosion of interest in the application of qualitative methods to the study of education. Yet throughout this past decade, there has not existed a volume which explicitly linked this methodological approach to the study of education. With this present effort, *Qualitative Research for Education,* that linkage is now made. Those interested in education and who wish to study it from a qualitative vantage have available to them here an exceptional resource. This is all the more important given that it is the first book of its kind. It sets such a standard of excellence and completeness that other books to follow in this same area will be hard pressed to match, let alone surpass, it in quality and breadth of analysis.

What is remarkable about this book is that it educates readers in so many different ways. We are taken in a systematic fashion from the earliest stages of problem conceptualization and finding the appropriate site through modes of entree, data collection, data analysis, and presentation of findings. In a clear and definitive fashion we are told about the various strategies we might employ when the findings are to be written and then disseminated, be the findings those from either basic or applied research. Throughout this presentation, the authors do more than simply bring together what is currently known about qualitative research. They also break new ground with their discussions, for example, of the use of photography in data collection or the use of the constant comparative method as a means of data analysis.

There are also other, perhaps more subtle, ways in which we as readers are educated. Bogdan and Biklen provide us with countless rich examples of the diversity of the human condition, be this diversity reflected in the experiences of persons labeled as mentally retarded, of those who are desperately poor, or of those new parents who are experiencing the trauma that comes with learning that their child has been born with severe physical handicaps. By approaching the study of research methods as the authors have, we gain insights into the human condition—the goal of all good qualitative research.

Throughout this process of educating us about the logic and order of qualitative research, we are also educated about the authors. We learn about them as individuals and as scholars. The countless vignettes, descriptions of field experiences, and their own reactions to events provide us with an emphatic understanding of how it was that they responded to the world they were experiencing. This is extremely rare for academic researchers. The norm is the creation of a wall of depersonalized objectivity between writer and reader. In this instance, that wall has been broken down. The results are salutary. We not only gain insights into the beliefs and behaviors of the authors, but we are able to sharpen our own perceptions in juxtaposition to theirs. The human dimension of qualitative work comes through so strongly and so forcefully in this volume that the authors cannot help but share some of their own humanity with us.

It is in this context that the fundamental attraction of qualitative research in the study of education becomes apparent: qualitative research brings back into focus a concern of many who toil in the vineyard of educational research. This mode of research brings the study of human beings *as human beings* to center stage. It represents a fundamental rejection of the ultimately irrational pursuit to quantify all aspects of human belief and experience. We as human beings are more than simply the sum total of psychological measures, survey instrument responses, and bits of data on a laboratory checklist. That our experiences, fears, anxieties, emotions, beliefs, reactions, hopes, behaviors, and irrationalities are not well captured or explained by the rush to quantification is one reason that qualitative research is experiencing the renaissance it is.

One of the complaints of those who are not familiar with qualitative research, but who are interested in knowing more, is that there appears to be almost as many variations in conducting qualitative research as there are qualitative researchers. Does qualitative research, in fact, constitute a "method" if the variation is so great? The answer provided to us in this volume is "yes," though not for the reason we may think. Qualitative research does have an internal order and logic to it. What is seen from the outside is not these attributes, but rather the diversity of employing observations, interviews, document analysis, historical research, and constant reframing of the key areas of study. The authors of this book remind us that what we are witnessing are variations on a theme—much as in the same way a complex piece of music might not be immediately understood. The description of social reality is the description of a mosaic. Any method that would seek to do this must itself reflect and be open to the world as it is, not as we might wish it to be.

Bogdan and Biklen provide us with a systematic introduction to the qualitative method. They have not provided a cookbook that would answer every question nor prescribe a procedure for every situation. Instead, we have here a benchmark against which those doing qualitative work can judge their own procedures and gain insights on alternatives. There is no one-and-only way of conducting qualitative research, but there is a set of systematic research tools available. The task is one of learning when they are appropriately employed. Here the book makes a most significant contribution.

Qualitative Research for Education is lively and stimulating reading. The character of the book is defined both by the good spirits of the authors and their readily evident conviction that conducting qualitative research is an exhilarating, though demanding, experience. Their own enthusiasm and conviction come through time and again. Should those who read this book find those attributes of enthusiasm and conviction a bit contagious, they will not regret what has been passed on to them.

Ray C. Rist

PREFACE

Educational research is changing. A field once dominated by measurement, operationalized definitions, variables, and empirical fact has had to make room for a research approach gaining in popularity, one that emphasizes inductive analysis, description, and the study of people's perceptions. Generations of educational researchers trained to think of research in one dimension, the quantitative, have been asked to embrace a broader view. Approaches that a short time ago were peremptorily dismissed as prescientific or "fluff," have begun to play a role more central to educational research.

Qualitative research techniques such as participant observation and indepth interviewing are respected and regularly employed in the social sciences, particularly in sociology and anthropology. In the last decade their popularity has grown and now many courses incorporate the qualitative perspective or are exclusively devoted to teaching this research strategy.

Partly because of education's historical link with measurement and experimental design, research in education has not been as quick to embrace the new wave of interest in qualitative methods. But dependence on qualitative methods for studying various educational issues is growing. One has only to look at the funding patterns of government agencies and the recent programs of education research conventions to know that qualitative research in education has, or will soon, come of age. Some educational research courses focus entirely on the qualitative approach and general research courses regularly incorporate it into their curriculum. While journal articles on qualitative methods appear with increasing frequency, not a single book devotes itself to the application of qualitative research to educational settings. That is the purpose of this book: to provide a background for understanding the uses of qualitative research in education, to examine its theoretical underpinnings, and to discuss specific methods for conducting research.

The question might be raised, "Is such a book necessary?" After all, it could be said there are a number of books available on qualitative research; in fact, one of the authors has written one. Is education so unique that a special book is needed? Certain unique research issues and problems related to educational settings do exist that have not been addressed elsewhere. Though schools have much in common with other organizations, they have a particular hierarchical structure and they shape interpersonal relationships that require special investigative strategies. Observing in classrooms offers special problems, as does the study of interactions between administrators and parents. A second adult in a classroom can be very obtrusive, something that a qualitative researcher wants to minimize. In addition, many of the subjects in educational studies are children. There are special considerations in establishing rapport with students. Discussions of these and other special problems posed by educational settings are absent in the present literature and are covered here. While the examples we have just used represent schools and children, the book deals with education, broadly conceived. It will be helpful not only to those doing research in primary and secondary schools but in preschool programs, adult education settings, inservice education, job training, and professional education, as well as in colleges and universities.

In addition to the nature of educational settings, other aspects of educational research call for a book devoted to that topic. While much of the research in education is "basic research," people in the field have a strong applied interest. They are interested in evaluation and in the practical implications of research findings. We have made this an important concern of our book.

While the qualitative approach has not been central in educational research, a rich tradition of this type of research has grown in other fields. Anthropologists and sociologists have successfully conducted qualitative studies of educational issues. This tradition and the vantage points from which disciplines approach education are discussed here. Lastly, students who take research courses in education have different backgrounds and concerns than students for whom existing qualitative books have been written. Books that are presently available are written for sociology or social science majors. They assume a certain background in social theory that those in education may not have. We have written a book that more explicitly lays out the theoretical underpinnings of the approach, yet we have not been so theoretical that it loses people with more substantive educational concerns.

We start the book with a broad discussion of what qualitative research is and its relationship to education, looking at both the theoretical and historical concepts. In the next four chapters we apply the concepts to actual practice, detailing design, data, fieldwork relationships, and data analysis. From there, we move in the next chapter to writing up the findings. In the last chapter, we zero in on a special set of cases in qualitative research in education—applied research. In this area we discuss evaluation, pedagogical, and action research.

We have many people to thank. The National Institute of Education (grant number 400-79-0052) supported the mainstreaming study we discuss in the book. The study of the neonatal unit in the teaching hospital was supported by a grant from the New York Bureau of Mental Retardation and Developmental Disabilities as well as Syracuse University's Senate Research Fund. People who read and commented on earlier drafts include Judy Kugelmass, Susan Foster, Margaret Ksander, Mary Alice Brown, Jerry Grant, Burton Blatt, Andrejs Ozolins, Michele Sokoloff, Paula Freedman, Diane Murphy, Janet Bogdan, and Douglas Biklen. Andrejs Ozolins wrote parts of the photography sections and helped choose the photographs in the book. Seymour Sarason provided general support and ideas. Mary Wolfskill at the Library of Congress helped locate pictures. Loraine Kotary, Helen Anderson, and Rosemary Alibrandi helped in various ways in preparing the manuscript. The staff at the Syracuse University Day Care Center provided excellent child care.

FOUNDATIONS OF
QUALITATIVE RESEARCH
IN EDUCATION:
AN INTRODUCTION

A RESEARCHER IN HIS EARLY THIRTIES STOOD ON AN ELEMENTARY school playground watching a busload of black children arrive on the first day of school. They were the first blacks ever to attend this school. He was conducting a study to explore the process of integration. The work brought him to the school regularly to observe what the children and teachers experienced. In addition, he informally interviewed teachers, the principal, children, parents, and attended meetings as well. This work continued for a full year and during this period he unobtrusively kept a detailed, written account of what he observed (Rist, 1978).

In another part of the United States a group of researchers were interested in exploring the meaning that test items have for children who take them. They queried first graders about their responses. One test question, for example, asked the children to choose the one picture from three that "goes best with" the word that accompanied the pictures. Many of the children had responded to the word *fly,* represented by pictures of an elephant, a bird, and a dog, by circling the bird and the elephant or even just the elephant (the "right" answer was the bird). When probed about their choices, the children told the researchers that the elephant was "Dumbo," Walt Disney's flying elephant. The students had understood the concept the test question attempted to illicit, but answered from a framework different from the one the testmakers had in mind. The study was investigating students' reasoning (Mehan, 1978).

In a large city a researcher interviewed female teachers in an attempt to understand the relationship between their out-of-school lives and their lives as teachers. Her sample was small, less than ten. She had gotten to know these women well because her interviews were long and intense, and she conducted them for over a year in their homes and classrooms. The researcher sifted through this case study data, looking for patterns of perspectives that these women hold about their lives as teachers (Hall, 1979).

1

These are examples of people conducting *qualitative research* for education. They exhaust neither the variety of strategies nor the range of topics. Other qualitative researchers look through fairy tales and textbooks to see how people with handicaps are presented (Biklen and Bogdan, 1977); scrutinize pictures of children in family photo albums to understand how members portray themselves (Musello, 1979); and take and pour over videotapes of students doing ''school work'' in an attempt to understand children's assumptions about order (Florio, 1978; McDermott, 1976). The educational experiences of people of all ages (as well as material that expands our knowledge of these experiences), in schools as well as out, can be the subject matter. Qualitative research for education takes many forms and is conducted in many settings.

We use *qualitative research* as an umbrella term to refer to several research strategies that share certain characteristics. The data collected has been termed *soft,* that is, rich in description of people, places, and conversations, and not easily handled by statistical procedures. Research questions are not framed by operationalizing variables; rather, they are formulated to investigate in all their complexity, in context. While people conducting qualitative research may develop a focus as they collect data, they do not approach the research with specific questions to answer or hypotheses to test. They are concerned as well with understanding behavior from the subject's own frame of reference. External causes are of secondary importance. They tend to collect their data through sustained contact with people in settings where subjects normally spend their time.

The best known representatives of qualitative research and those that most embody the characteristics we just touched upon are *participant observation* and *indepth interviewing.* The man watching black children get off the bus was starting a participant observation study. The researcher enters the world of the people he or she plans to study, gets to know, be known and trusted by them, and systematically keeps a detailed written record of what is heard and observed. This material is supplemented by other data such as school memos and records, newspaper articles, and photographs.

The woman studying female teachers is an example of the use of indepth interviewing. Sometimes termed ''unstructured'' (Maccoby and Maccoby, 1954), or ''open-ended'' (Jahoda, Deutsch, and Cook, 1951), ''non-directive'' (Meltzer and Petras, 1970), or ''flexibly structured'' (Whyte, 1979), the researcher is bent on understanding, in considerable detail, how people such as teachers, principals, and students think and how they came to develop the perspectives they hold. This goal often leads the researcher to spend considerable time with subjects in their own environs, asking open-ended questions such as ''what is a typical day like for you?'', ''what do you like best about your work?'' and recording their responses. The open-ended nature of the approach allows the subjects to answer from their own frame of reference rather than from one structured by prearranged questions. In this type of interviewing, questionnaires are not used; while loosely-structured interview guides may sometimes be employed, most often the researcher is the only instrument, and works at getting the subjects to freely express their thoughts around particular topics. Because of the detail sought, most studies have small samples. In some studies, the researcher draws an indepth portrait of only one subject. When the intent is to capture one person's interpretation of his or her life, the study is called a *life history*.

We use the phrase *qualitative research,* but others use different terms and conceptualize the brand of research we present in this book slightly differently. *Field research* is a term that is sometimes used by anthropologists and sociologists, and its use derives from the fact that data tend to be collected *in the field* as opposed to laboratories or other researcher-controlled sites (see Junker, 1960).[1] In education, qualitative research is frequently called *naturalistic* because the researcher hangs around where the events he or she is interested in naturally occur. And the data is gathered by people engaging in natural behavior: talking, visiting, looking, eating, and so on. (Guba, 1978; Wolf, 1979). *Ethnographic* is a phrase that is applied to the approach as well. While some use it in a formal sense to refer to a particular type of qualitative research, one in which most anthropologists engage and which is directed at describing culture, it is also used more generally—sometimes synonymously—with qualitative research as we are defining it.

Other phrases are associated with qualitative research. They include *symbolic interactionist, inner perspective, the Chicago School, phenomenological, case study, interpretive, ethnomethodological, ecological,* and *descriptive.* The exact use and definition of these terms, as well as words like *field work* and *qualitative research* varies from user to user and from time to time. We do not mean to suggest that they all mean the same thing, nor to imply that some do not have very exact meanings when used by particular people. We prefer to use the term *qualitative research* to include the range of strategies that we call "qualitative." We will clarify some of the phrases we have just mentioned as we proceed with our discussion.

At this point we have merely introduced our subject matter. We will return in this chapter to discuss in more detail the characteristics of qualitative research as well as its theoretical underpinnings, but first we set our subject in historical context.

TRADITIONS OF QUALITATIVE RESEARCH IN EDUCATION

Chroniclers of traditional educational research cite 1954 as a watershed year (Travers, 1978; Tyler, 1976). Congress passed the Cooperative Research Act that year which for the first time provided for grants to be made to institutions in support of educational research.[2] If federal funding is any indicator, educational research had come of age. For qualitative methodologists whose work then lay at the edge of the mainstream, their breakthrough was yet to come. For these scholars, 1954 passed much like other years of low-profile work. For reasons we shall explore in these next pages, it was not until the late sixties that qualitative research in education flowered.

Though qualitative research has only lately gained recognition in the field of education, it harbors a long and rich tradition. The particulars of this heritage help qualitative educational researchers to understand the methodology in historical context.[3] The roots of qualitative research lie in more than one discipline, so our historical sketch transcends disciplinary boundaries. We offer one perspective on the development of qualitative research methods in education.

Nineteenth-Century Roots

Several features of nineteenth century American life gave rise to social investigation. Urbanization and the impact of mass immigration created problems in cities: problems of sanitation, health, welfare, and education. Photographer Jacob Riis (1890) revealed the lives of the urban poor on the pages of *How the Other Half Lives*. Muckraking journalists like Lincoln Steffens (1904, 1931) and others, exposed in their articles corruption in city government, the "shame of the cities," and other blights. Between 1870 and 1890, paper became cheaper, newspaper circulation expanded enormously, and "yellow journalism" flourished (Taylor, 1919).

This publicity called attention to the deteriorating conditions of urban life in American society. The journalistic exposés of social problems demanded response, and one response was the social survey movement, a series of community-wide, coordinated studies of urban problems undertaken near the beginning of the twentieth century. These surveys embodied a particular form because the rise of the natural sciences stimulated disciplines like sociology to be perceived as scientific rather than simply as philosophical (Harrison, 1931; Riley, 1910–1911). They also followed surveys of the urban poor in Europe and England.

Jacob Riis.

Teacher and pupils, New York City, 1890s. *Museum of the City of New York.* (Courtesy of the Library of Congress)

During the late 1800s, the Frenchman Frederick LePlay studied working-class families through the method that social scientists writing in the 1930s labeled "participant observation" (Wells, 1939). LePlay himself called it "observation" (Zimmerman and Frampton, 1935), and employed it to seek a remedy for social suffering. As participant observers, LePlay and his colleagues lived with the families they studied, participated in their lives, carefully observing what they did at work, at play, at church, and in school. Published as *Les Ouvriers Europeans* (the first volume of which appeared in 1879), they described in detail the life of the working-class family in Europe.

The research of Charles Booth, a statistician who conducted social surveys of the poor in London beginning in 1886 (Webb, 1926), followed on the heels of a new urban literature. Henry Mayhew's *London Labour and the London Poor,* published in four volumes between 1851 and 1862 (Fried and Elman, 1968; Stott, 1973), consisted of reporting, anecdote, and description about conditions of workers and the unemployed. Mayhew presented life histories and the results of extensive, indepth interviews with the poor.

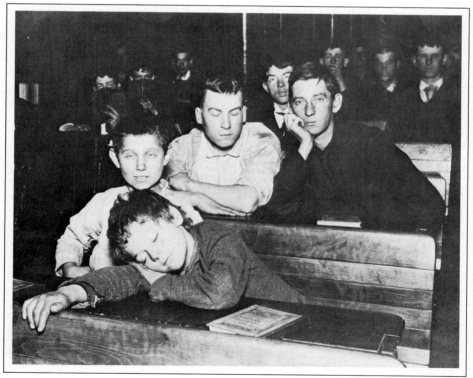

Jacob Riis.

Night school in 7th Avenue lodging house, early 1890s. *Children's Aid Society.* (Courtesy of the Library of Congress)

Booth's undertaking was of incredible proportions, lasting for seventeen years and filling as many volumes. His chief purpose was to discover how many poor there were in London and the condition of their lives. While his major concern was to quantitatively document the extent and nature of poverty in London, his work contained extensive and detailed descriptions of the people he studied. These descriptions were collected during the periods that Booth lived, anonymously, among the people he surveyed. His goal was to experience firsthand the lives of his subjects (see Taylor, 1919; Webb, 1926; Wells, 1939).

One of the workers on Booth's colossal project was Beatrice Webb (née Potter) who, along with her husband, went on to become a major figure in the Fabian socialist movement. A life-long investigator of the sufferings of the poor and of social institutions, Webb's sympathy, commitment, and understanding arose from her first fieldwork experience. For the first time, she then understood what another documentarian of the poor was later to write, "Individuals make up a people" (Stott, 1973):[4]

> I never visualized labor as separate men and women of different sorts and kinds. Right down to the time when I became interested in social science and began to train as a social investigator, labor was an abstraction, which seemed to denote an arithmetically calculable mass of human beings, each individual a repetition of the other, very much in the same way that the capital of my father's companies consisted, I imagined, of gold sovereigns identical with all other gold sovereigns in form, weight and color and also in value...(Webb, 1926, p. 41).

What were once abstractions became flesh and blood for Beatrice Webb through firsthand involvement with the subjects of her research. The Webbs later published a description of their methodology, which was widely read in the United States (Wax, 1971),[5] and appears to be the first practical discussion of the qualitative approach (Webb and Webb, 1932).[6]

On this side of the Atlantic, the first American social survey was the Pittsburgh Survey, undertaken in 1907. Leaders of hundreds of survey researchers to follow (Harrison, 1931) this group attempted to apply the "scientific method" to the study of social problems. While scholars of the survey movement tended to emphasize the statistical nature of these surveys (see, for example, Devine, 1906–1908; Kellogg, 1911–1912), the results of the Pittsburgh Survey, for instance, suggest that this emphasis may have reflected more on contemporary values which portrayed quantification as the symbol of the scientific approach than on the content of the actual reports. While the Pittsburgh Survey presents quantities of statistics on issues ranging from industrial accidents to weekly incomes, from the types and location of "water closets" to school attendance, it also bulges with detailed descriptions, interviews, portraits (sketched by artists in charcoal), and photographs.

This interweaving of the quantitative and the qualitative emerges clearly in *Charity and the Commons* (the journal later became *The Survey*), which published data from the Pittsburgh Survey in three large issues during 1908–1909. Description ranges from educational planning: "School buildings in this city," said one of the experienced school officials of Allegheny, "are first built, then thought about"

(North, 1909); to problems that "duller" children encountered in school because of a first-grade teacher's approach to tracking. This teacher:

> Had 128 pupils one year and 107 the next. She divided the children into two classes. The brighter children came in the morning and were allowed to go on as fast as they could, "getting through" six to nine books in a year; the backward, a smaller number, came in the afternoon. They were worn out with play, the teacher was also worn, and the afternoon session was but two hours; so these children usually got through but one book a year.

The students ended up dropping out to join the "ranks of uneducated industrial workers" (North, 1909). Other anecdotes abound.

The varieties of data in the social surveys related to the interdisciplinary nature of the research: social scientists, social workers, civic leaders, the knowledgeable outsider (our modern consultant), and journalists contributed to the efforts. Additionally, materials were discussed at public meetings and set up in displays for the community (Taylor, 1919).

Lewis Hine.

Breaker boys working in Ewen Breaker Mine in S. Pittston, Pennsylvania, January 10, 1911. Hine's photographic work contributed to the passage of child labor laws of the Progessive Era. *Records of the Children's Bureau.* (Courtesy of the National Archives)

The social survey carries particular importance for understanding the history of qualitative research in education because of its immediate relation to social problems and because of its peculiar position midway between the exposé and the scientific study. In 1904, for example, Lincoln Steffens introduced his *Shame of the Cities* with the following comments:

> This is all very unscientific, but then, I am not a scientist. I am a journalist. I did not gather with indifference all the facts and arrange them patiently for permanent pres- ervation and laboratory analysis. I did not want to preserve, I wanted to destroy the facts. My purpose was no more scientific than the spirit of my investigation and my reports; it was, as I said above, to see if the shameful facts, spread out in all their shame, would not burn through our civic shamelessness and set fire to American pride. That was the journalism of it. I wanted to move and to convince (Steffens, 1904, in Harrison, 1931, p. 21).

By his writing, Steffens hoped to precipitate actions to alleviate human suffering. Twenty-five years later, after countless social surveys across America, William Ogburn would make the following comments in his 1929 presidential address to the Amer- ican Sociological Society. How contrasting the scientific and journalistic methods ap- peared at the time. From the professional perspective, sociology would have to devel- op new habits to be scientific:

> One of these new habits will be the writing of wholly colorless articles, and the abandonment of the present habit of trying to make the results of science into liter- ature....Articles will always be accompanied by the supporting data, hence the text will be shorter and the records longer....The sociologist will of course work on prob- lems that tend to make sociology an organized systematic body of knowledge, but also he will choose for his researchers the study of those problems the solution of which will benefit the human race and its culture....But the scientific sociologist will attack these problems once chosen with the sole idea of discovering new knowledge (Harrison, 1931, p. 21).

The social survey fell between these two worlds. It was undertaken to encourage social change through research. Its methods portrayed the problems in human terms.

The Rise of Anthropology

The anthropological roots of qualitative research in education have been persuasively documented (see, particularly, Roberts,1976).[7] Boas was probably the first anthro- pologist to write on anthropology and education in an article published in 1898 on the teaching of anthropology at the university level. Boas and his co-researchers were also among the first anthropologists to spend time in the natural setting, although the time spent there was brief, and they relied on competent informers who spoke English as they did not learn the native language.

For our purposes here, Boas's most significant contribution to the development of qualitative research for education was his concept of culture. In contrast to earlier anthropologists, Boas was a "cultural relativist," believing that each culture studied had to be approached inductively. If ethnographers approached a culture expecting to understand it through a Western framework, they would distort what they saw. Boas believed that anthropologists should study cultures with the intent of learning how the culture was understood by its members (see Case, 1927).

Also in 1898, the year of Boas's article, Nina Vandewalker, who Roberts (1976) describes as an "unknown scholar," for the first time applied anthropology to education in "Some Demands of Education upon Anthropology," published in the *American Journal of Sociology*. She focused upon education and its relationship to culture (Vandewalker, 1898).

For the development of fieldwork techniques we must look first to anthropologists studying native cultures. Unlike Boas who had been drawn more to documents and informants than to extensive firsthand observation, Bronislaw Malinowski was the first social anthropologist to really spend long periods of time in a native village to observe what was going on (Wax, 1971). He was also the first professional anthropologist to descibe how he obtained his data and what the fieldwork experience was like. Malinowski insisted that a theory of culture had to be grounded in particular human experiences, based on observations and inductively sought (Malinowski, 1960). Malinowski's field approach, interestingly, seems to have developed accidentally. When he arrived in New Guinea with an extremely limited budget, World War I immediately broke out. His travel was curtailed, forcing him to remain in Australia and on the islands until the end of war in 1918. This shaped the direction "fieldwork" would take.

Perhaps the most substantive application of anthropology to American education was made by the anthropologist Margaret Mead (see, especially, Mead, 1942 and 1951). Concerned particularly with the school as an organization and the role of the teacher, she brought her experiences in less technological societies to bear on the fast-changing American educational scene. Mead examined how particular contexts—the kinds of schools she categorized as the little red schoolhouse, the city school, and the academy—called for particular kinds of teachers and how these teachers interacted with students. She argued that teachers needed to study, through observations and firsthand experiences, the changing contexts of their students' socialization and upbringing in order to become better teachers. While she did not conduct formal fieldwork in the United States, she reflected on education here, focusing on anthropological concepts rather than on method.

A major figure in the development of qualitative method, however, was Robert Redfield, an anthropologist who studied at the University of Chicago during the ascension of sociology. He was the son-in-law of Robert Park, a sociologist who, as we will discuss later, was a leader in the development of qualitative research in that discipline. The field research of the anthropologists was an important source of the model of what is known as *Chicago sociology* (Douglas, 1976). Redfields's ethnographic studies had an important influence on field research in communities (Faris, 1967). From the perspective of Wax, an anthropologist, the "Chicago sociologists" continued the anthropological fieldwork tradition. In her words: "By focusing upon 'participant observation,' the Chicago sociologists have emphasized their linkage to the tradition of ethnographic fieldwork from Malinowski onward" (Wax, 1971, P. 40).

Chicago Sociology

Albion Small founded the sociology department at the University of Chicago in 1892; it was the first as well as the largest in the world (Odum, 1951). The "Chicago School," a label applied to a group of sociological researchers teaching and learning at the sociology department in Chicago in the 1920s and 1930s, contributed enormously to the development of the research method we refer to as qualitative.

While the sociologists at Chicago differed from each other in important ways, they shared some common theoretical and methodological assumptions. Theoretically they all saw symbols and personalities emerging from social interaction (Faris, 1967). Methodologically, they relied on the study of the single case, whether it was a person, a group, a neighborhood, or a community (Wiley, 1979).

Of the numerous characteristics of the Chicago school methodology, several are most important for our understanding of qualitative research for education. First, the Chicago sociologists relied on firsthand data-gathering for their research. This technique rested on the work of two men: W. I. Thomas and Robert Park. Thomas was one of the earliest graduate students in the sociology department. His study with Florian Znaniecki, *The Polish Peasant in Europe and America* (Thomas and Znaniecki, 1927), has been called a "turning point in the history of sociological research" because it concentrated "upon the qualitative analysis of personal and public documents" and "introduced new elements into research and new techniques to study these elements which were not standard to empirical investigations in the traditional sense" (Bruyn, 1966). Thomas did not visualize data in quantitative terms. Interestingly, it is reported that he accidentally stumbled upon the use of letters as research data. It is said that as he was walking through the Polish ghetto of Chicago one day, he pulled back to avoid being struck by garbage hurled from a window. He saw a pack of letters in the pile, and, since he could read Polish he looked through them. He found an insider's perspective on immigrant life (Collins and Makowsky, 1978, p. 184). This accident, like Malinowski's being stranded during World War I, had a profound influence on the shape of social research. Thomas shared with the anthropologist Boas a commitment to the importance of understanding different people's grasp of reality and their points of view.[8]

After he had met Thomas at a conference on race relations, Robert Park came to the University of Chicago in 1916 (Hughes, 1971). Though Park became one of the leading figures in the Chicago school, it was not his first career. He had already been a newspaper reporter as well as Booker T. Washington's public relations man. Many historians of Chicago sociology have linked the department's push to have graduate students enter the social worlds they studied to Park's newspaper experiences (see, for example, Douglas, 1976; Faris, 1967; Matthews, 1977; Wax, 1971). Park sent his students to the streets of Chicago in the 1920s so that they could personally observe what happened.

The emphasis on city life is the second important characteristic of the Chicago sociologists. Whatever they studied, they did so against the backdrop of the community as a whole; what Becker has called "the scientific mosaic" (Becker, 1970b). Park "regularly encouraged his students to undertake general but intensive studies of particular communities, attempting to perceive a community as a whole" (Faris, 1967). Works of these students were later published and illustrate both the interest in different aspects of ordinary life and an orientation to the study of ethnicity. They studied the Jewish ghetto (Wirth, 1928), the taxi-dance hall (Cressy, 1932), the boys' gang (Thrasher, 1927), the professional thief (Sutherland, 1937), the hobo (Anderson, 1923), *The Gold Coast and the Slum* (Zorbaugh, 1929), and the delinquent (Shaw, 1966; first published in 1930). In this emphasis on the intersection of social context and biography lies the roots of contemporary descriptions of qualitative research as "holistic." As a Chicago sociologist put it, "Behavior can be studied profitably in terms of the situation out of which it arises" (Wells, 1939).

The Chicago sociologists, as we have said, took an interactionist approach to their research (Carey, 1975), emphasizing the social and interactional nature of reality. Park, for example, in his introduction to a study of the methodology of a race relations survey on Oriental-Occidental relationships in California, suggested that the study was important because of its recognition "that all opinions, public or private, are a social product" (Bogardus, 1926). Indeed, the researchers captured the perspectives of those they interviewed. Many of the subjects shared their views on the difficulties they faced as Oriental Americans:

> I thought I was American. I had American ideals, would fight for America, loved Washington and Lincoln. Then in high school I found myself called Jap, looked down on, ostracized. I said I did not know Japan, could not speak the language, and knew no Japanese history or heroes. But I was repeatedly told I was not American, could not be American, could not vote. I am heart sick. I am not Japanese and am not allowed to be American. Can you tell me what I am? (Bogardus, 1926, p. 164).

They emphasized the human dimension.

Though the Chicago sociologists studied social problems and conducted social investigations of city life, community problems, and deviant careers, they were not, foremost, advocates of reform. The earlier social survey movement had been undertaken at a time when sociology was not yet fully separated from the "organized charities movement" (what later took the name of social work). When sociology diverted sharply from social work, it left behind its overt reformist nature and took with it only the influence of the case study method. This approach was not simply a field method, but one which recognized the interrelatedness of social problems (Taylor, 1919). Sociology had indeed become scientific, but with this group of Chicago sociologists, what they wrote was not the dry material Ogburn described at the American Sociological Society meetings.

The Sociology of Education

One might expect that since the field of educational sociology developed at a time when the Chicago Sociology Department was reaching its zenith, qualitative research strategies might be strongly reflected in research designs in educational sociology. This was not the case, however.

Educational sociology officially began as a field in 1915 when the first "Sociology of Education" course was offered (Snedden, 1937), but the *Journal of Educational Sociology* did not appear until 1926. Originally, two out of three associate editors came from the Chicago school, Harvey Zorbaugh of *The Gold Coast and the Slum* fame, and Frederick Thrasher, author of *The Gang*. Among the contributing editors were three faculty members from the Chicago Sociology Department: Emory S. Bogardus, Ellsworth Faris, and Robert Park. In fact, early in the first volume, an editorial suggested that the *Journal of Educational Sociology* represented "the Chicago point of view" (1927, 1:4, p. 177).

Various issues in Volume One suggest that the Chicago perspective was present: Articles reviewed Thrasher's *The Gang,* followed the professional development of Professor Bogardus, mentioned the forthcoming publication of Shaw's *The Jack Roller,* and reported a speech by Faris. This perspective did not dominate the journal, but it was represented.

During the period covered by Volume Two (1928–1929), however, the always-present concern for the natural sciences and measurement mounted. In the third issue, for example, an editorial reflected on discussions over the past year on the question, "Is educational sociology a science or can it become a science?" To become scientific, the editorial explained, educational sociology must become experimental.

This view of the scientific school measurement movement reflects education's dominant concern of the times. This was "the heyday of empiricism"(Cronbach and Suppes, 1969). The "scientific method" in education became identified with quantification. Educational sociology as a whole (always the second cousin to educational psychology) and the *Journal* in particular, moved away from the Chicago perspective toward a quantitative, experimental approach.

This unwillingness to consider, for example, other material beside statistics as data is reflected in the *Journal* in articles such as "The Validity of Life Histories and Diaries" (Bain, 1929). The author suggested several reasons why life histories and diaries were suited for social work but not sociology: the documents were not scientific enough; researchers could not treat materials of life history documents statistically; and they could not be standardized. "They may be 'interesting and dramatic,'" said Bain, "but so are...the movies."[9] As educators became increasingly concerned with measurement, quantification, and prediction, qualitative strategies such as first-hand investigation, the use of personal documents, and the fieldworker's concern with social context were less influential on educators (Peters, 1937). Additionally, as we said, psychologists dominated educational research, and they were strongly experimentalist.

There is perhaps a second reason why Chicago sociology had little impact on the development of educational sociology. We discuss this reason tentatively, and hope that historians will later investigate this question more thoroughly. Between 1893 and 1935 over one hundred doctoral dissertations were completed under the Chicago Sociology Department. Only two, however, related to education (Faris, 1967).[10] While more masters theses concerned education,[11] they constitute only a small percentage of the topics. Socialization, community life, youth, work, and family appear more representative subjects. These topics may reflect education, broadly conceived, but the professional side of education went almost unnoticed.

In part, this lack of interest may reflect educational sociology's infant status. At the annual dinner of the American Sociological Society's meeting in 1927, Ellsworth Faris "took occasion to call the attention of the members present to the inportance of the fields of educational sociology and asked their support in directing the attention of sociologists to the various problems presented in this field" (*Journal of Educational Sociology,* 1927, 1:7). The words *education* and *sociology* had only recently been joined.

While quantification represented the dominant school of thought in educational sociology (Peters, 1937; Snedden, 1937), exceptions did appear, notably in the work of Willard Waller. Waller had studied for a masters degree under Ellsworth Faris in the Chicago Sociology Department, and his orientation to educational sociology was empirical but antiquantitative, based on firsthand involvement with the social world, and concerned with how parts related to the whole. Waller is particularly important for qualitative researchers in education because his classic *Sociology of Teaching* remains influential (Waller, 1932).

In *Sociology of Teaching,* Waller relied on indepth interviews, life histories, participant observation, case records, diaries, letters, and other personal documents to describe the social world of teachers and their students. For Waller, the starting point of his book was his belief that: "Children and teachers are not disembodied intelligences, not instructing machines and learning machines, but whole human beings tied together in a complex maze of social interconnections. The school is a social world because human beings live in it (Waller, 1932, p. 1). Waller called upon the methods of the "cultural anthropologist," the "realistic novelist," and what we would now describe as the qualitative researcher. His goal was to help teachers develop insight into the social realities of school life, and he felt to accomplish this goal he had to be realistic by being concrete:

> To be concrete is to present materials in such a way that characters do not lose the qualities of persons, nor situations their intrinsic human reality. Realistic sociology must be concrete. In my own case, this preference for concreteness had led to a relative distrust of statistical method, which has seemed, for my purposes, of little utility. Possibly the understanding of human life will be as much advanced by the direct study of social phenomena as by the study of numerical symbols abstracted from this phenomena.

For Waller, insight informed the scientific method, not the reverse (Waller, 1934).

The importance of Waller's discussion of the social life of schools and their participants rests not only on the strength and accuracy of his description, but also on the sociological concepts on which he depended. Among the foremost of these was W. I. Thomas's "definition of the situation" (Thomas, 1923), a clearly interactional concept that suggests people examine and "define" situations before they act on them. These "definitions" are what make situations real for us. Another important foundation for Waller's work was Cooley's idea that dramatic interplay is the distinctive trait of social knowledge. Using the metaphor of a tennis game, Cooley wrote that a player always needs someone on the other side of the net to return the ball; one cannot play tennis alone (Cooley, 1926). So is personal growth and social understanding dialectic.

The Thirties to the Fifties

With a few substantial exceptions, some scholars see research from the thirties to the fifties as a hiatus for the qualitative approach. There are many perspectives one might take on this assumption, depending on how one defines research, one's academic and political biases, and the historical sources one searches. Each field draws boundaries both to include and exclude. Historians of qualitative research have never, for instance, included Freud and Piaget as developers of the qualitative approach, yet both relied on case studies, observations and indepth interviews. There is something about the work of these men that spurs chroniclers of qualitative research to exclude them from their domain. Scholars from a different school, however, like psychology, might include these men in a discussion of qualitative psychology. From our perspective, while qualitative approaches were not popular research tools during these decades, the methodology developed and inproved. And in some ways, as we suggest, the tradition flourished; what essentially changed was who practiced it and where it was practiced (at least during the thirties and forties). As we go through the events of these years we have attempted to remain self-conscious about those historical aspects that are traditionally included by sociologists and anthropologists, and those that are not. What happened to qualitative research during the next several decades before it flowered again in the late sixties?

The influence of Chicago's sociology department waned in the thirties for a number of reasons. The Depression affected funding for their research projects; the Laura Spelman Rockefeller money which had helped to fund their studies of the Chicago community was no longer available. The Depression had another effect as well: It shifted the area of sociologists' concern from Americanizing immigrants and other ethnic issues on which the Chicago school had concentrated, to problems of mass unemployment. Political and methodological differences among American sociologists, as well as the retirement or death of many of the major figures at Chicago, played a role in this hiatus. (For an interesting discussion of these different issues, see Wiley, 1979.) But the students of the Chicago school continued to have a major effect. Everett C. Hughes, in particular, developed the field of the sociology of occupations and his students went on to become leaders in qualitative research in the fifties, many studying educational questions (Becker et al., 1961; Becker, Geer, and Hughes, 1968; Geer, 1973). Herbert Blumer coined the term *symbolic interactionism* in 1937 and brought the concept to fruition. The School also influenced the social anthropologists.

One widely recognized source for the continuing qualitative approach can be found in the work of the social anthropologists who took the field methods they had developed in their studies abroad and applied them to American culture. One of the earliest of these transplanted efforts was the famous Yankee City Series, carried out under the directorship of W. Lloyd Warner, recently returned from studying Aborigines in Australia (Warner and Lunt, 1941). An enormous undertaking, this study attempted to penetrate the culture and life of a modern community. The research commenced in 1930, although the findings, eventually published in six volumes, did not begin to appear until 1941. The Yankee City researchers proclaimed their debt to the Chicago sociologists (Warner and Lunt, 1941, P. 4), explaining that they had chosen a smaller community to study so that it would not take several generations of researchers to reach their goals: to understand the effect of the community on the individual, to explore how the community emerges through its individual members, and to describe in detail the nature of the community itself. Part of this study examined education in Yankee City, particularly the social aspects of schooling.

Other major studies of community conducted during this period which were wholly or partly qualitative included the Lynds' studies of Middletown (Lynd and Lynd, 1929, 1937) which have major sections on education, and Whyte's *Street Corner Society,* a study of life among poor Italian men in Boston (Whyte, 1955). Whyte's study, originally published in 1943, was reissued in 1955 to include an outstanding description of his methodology.[12]

These efforts, as well as other ethnographic studies of the period (Davis and Dollard, 1940; Davis, Gardner, and Gardner, 1941; Davis and Havighurst, 1947; Dollard, 1937; Hollingshead, 1949), carried forth what Charles Horton Cooley described as the ultimate purpose of the social sciences: "We are seeking, I presume, to get at the human meaning of our institutions' processes as they work out in the lives of men, women and children" (in Stott, 1973). It was not only academic sociologists and anthropologists who conducted qualitative research during this period, however.

Depression America created overwhelming and visible problems for a majority of citizens, and many people, including those hired by government agencies, turned to a qualitative approach to document the nature and extent of these problems. The Work Projects Administration (WPA), for example, produced informant narratives. *These Are Our Lives* were oral biographies, life histories of black and white southern workers in three states (Federal Writers' Project, 1939). The authors were not social scientists; they were writers who needed work, but the method is sociological. Other forerunners to what we now call oral history included a folk history of slavery, a series of interviews with former slaves, collected in the mid-thirties (Botkin, 1945); and an obscure pamphlet, "The Disinherited Speak: Letters from Sharecroppers," published in 1937 on behalf of the Southern Tenant Farmers' Union (Stott, 1973). This collection, consisting of letters from union members to their union officers, relied on the same kind of documents that Thomas and Znaniecki (1927) used for their mammoth study, *The Polish Peasant in Europe and America.*

Documentary photography attempting to examine the dimensions of suffering of dispossessed American people also flourished (see, for example, Evans, 1973; Gutman, 1974; and Hurley, 1972).[13] Americans were attracted to the naturalistic approach during this period, whether in literature, journalism, photography, or nonacademic research, because it documented in personal, particular detail what the Depression meant for most Americans—the southern sharecropper, the northern worker, the homeless Okie.[14]

Marion Post Walcott.

First grade near Montezuma, Georgia. *Farm Security Administration.* (Courtesy of the Library of Congress)

In the 1940s, Mirra Komarovsky, a sociologist who had published one of two well-known qualitative studies of the family and the Depression (Komarovsky, 1940; see also Angell, 1936), completed a study of women in higher education which was to become an important document of the feminist movement in the early seventies. Using a qualitative approach, she conducted eighty indepth interviews with women who were students at Barnard College and studied the effect of cultural values on women's sex-role attitudes, noting the difficulty women described in being both ''feminine'' and ''successful'' (Komarovsky, 1946).

For qualitative research, the fifties appear at first glance to continue to ebb; it was not, after all, qualitative researchers in education who benefited from the Co-operative Research Act. But in fact, a number of developments occurred that promoted and advanced qualitative research for education. While one could not call a qualitative approach a mainstream methodology in the fifties, a number of developments coalesced to give it a new voice.

Photographer Unknown.

A negro mother teaching her children the numbers and alphabet in her home, 1939. (Courtesy of the Library of Congress)

The work of the social anthropologists can be traced right through the fifties. Anthropologists' interest in education rose. Again, using qualitative methods, anthropologists studying education in the early fifties[15] wrote about what Philip Jackson (1968) was to label a decade later as "the hidden curriculum"—the implicit rather than explicit messages of socialization that schools give to children. Jules Henry brought the methods he had developed in Brazil, Argentina, and Mexico to the elementary schools of Chicago (Henry, 1955b, 1957) and combined them with his interest in how people communicate (Henry, 1955a). This research formed the basis for his well-known and popular book *Culture Against Man* (Henry, 1963). Anthropologists explored the relationships between the two disciplines during this period: they held conferences about it (Spindler, 1955), devoted special issues of journals to it, and lectured about it (Mead, 1951; Redfield, 1955; Spindler, 1959).

The fifties also furthered methodological and conceptual development of qualitative or fieldwork methods. During the period of "Chicago sociology," individual research experiences rarely merited description in published accounts. The process of fieldwork itself now became the subject of accounts as qualitative researchers became self-conscious and introspective about method (see Becker, 1958; Becker and Geer, 1960; Junker, 1960; Whyte, 1955). *Human Organization,* the publication of the Society for Applied Anthropology, undertook in 1957 to publish articles on field methods that had appeared in its journal over the past eighteen years (Adams and Preiss, 1960). Conceptual development was furthered by the publication of Erving Goffman's *The Presentation of Self in Everyday Life* in 1959, which examined the ways in which people try to manage how others will see them, and how this maneuvering affects social reality (Goffman, 1959). Goffman called his perspective "dramaturgical."

Another important methodological development was the evolution of the interview as a central qualitative research strategy. The *American Journal of Sociology* devoted an entire issue to it in 1956 (see, for example, Benney and Hughes, 1956; Dexter, 1956). How to use it in field research, its strengths and weaknesses, and its varied forms were examined (see Hyman, 1954; Jahoda, Deutsch, and Cook, 1951; Maccoby and Maccoby, 1954). Additionally, sociologists looked to the "nondirective interview" developed by the psychologist Carl Rogers for his client-centered therapy (Rogers, 1945, 1951; Whyte, 1960).

The most visible qualitative research in education undertaken during the fifties was produced by Howard S. Becker, a student of Everett C. Hughes at Chicago's sociology department. Becker interviewed Chicago schoolteachers in order to understand more clearly their career patterns and their views on their work. Three well-known and still frequently cited articles emerged from this dissertation research (Becker, 1951) which were published in the *Journal of Educational Sociology* (Becker, 1952b and 1953) and in the *American Journal of Sociology* (Becker, 1952a). A study of medical education that was to become a classic of the qualitative approach, *Boys in White* (Becker et al., 1961) was also undertaken in the fifties. In this portrait of medical student culture, the researchers paid serious attention to the notion of *perspective,* a term that is part of the key vocabulary of qualitative researchers. Their research became an attempt to understand what characterized the medical student's perspective on school.

While the qualitative approach could not be called "popular" among educational researchers during this period, it was alive and growing.

The Sixties: A Time of Social Change

The 1960s brought national focus to educational problems, revived interest in qualitative research, and opened up educational researchers to the qualitative approach. Up until this period most of the research that employed qualitative strategies to illuminate educational concerns had been undertaken by scholars trained in, and members of, other disciplines like sociology and anthropology. By the sixties, educational researchers themselves began to show interest in these strategies, as federal agencies started to fund research employing qualitative methods.

The sixties were also a time of upheaval and social change. Educators' focus turned to the experiences minority children encountered in schools. One reason for this was political: as cities burned and as leaders searched for ways to prevent future protests, they associated poor educational performance with black people's insistence that they receive inadequate services. Spokespeople within the civil rights movement insisted that the perspectives of those who suffered discrimination needed presentation.

People wanted to know what the schools were like for the children who were not "making it," and many educators wanted to talk about it. A number of autobiographical and journalistic accounts of life in ghetto schools appeared (for example, Decker, 1969; Haskins, 1969; Herndon, 1968; Kohl, 1967; Kozol, 1967). These accounts spoke from the "front lines," attempting to capture the quality of the daily lives of the children they taught.

Federal programs, recognizing how little we really knew about the schooling of different groups of children, funded some research on these issues which used what is now generically labeled *ethnographic* methods. Qualitative research methods began to catch people's imagination.

One of the largest of these federally funded studies was Project True, undertaken in 1963 at Hunter College to understand different aspects of life in urban classrooms. The researchers relied on interviews with principals, teachers, parents, members of the Board of Education, and the community to examine school integration (Fuchs, 1966). They also used indepth interviews to examine the experiences of new teachers in urban schools (Eddy, 1969; Fuchs, 1969). They used participant observation to examine individual classroom experiences (Roberts, 1971), elementary schools (Moore, 1967), and the urban school in the context of the community (Eddy, 1967). This group of sociologists and anthropologists saw their work as exploratory. As a group, they held the atttude that education had failed poor children, that the cities were in crisis, and that these old problems demanded to be studied in new ways.

Two major funded studies began in the sixties and used a qualitative approach. One included a comparative study of urban schools conducted by the well-known anthropologist, Eleanor Leacock (1969). This work, which has become a classic on the effect of schools and teacher expectations on the lives of children, is, like Becker's works a decade earlier, referenced by sociologists and anthropologists alike. The other major funded study on racial issues in education that used field work methods was a project directed by Jules Henry which studied elementary schools in St. Louis (see Gouldner, 1978; Rist, 1970, 1973). Through his involvement in this project, Ray Rist, one of the most influential contemporary qualitative researchers in education, began his research.

The audience for qualitative research in education grew in the 1960s. Not yet firmly established as a legitimate research paradigm, its status caused many graduate students to face major hurdles if they chose to study a problem from this perspective.

But qualitative approaches kindled excitement. Why did qualitative research begin to emerge from its long hibernation in education at this particular historical period? Several developments suggest reasons for this.

First, the social upheaval of the sixties indicated to many that we did not know enough about how students experienced school. Popular accounts exposed for education what nineteenth-century muckracking revealed about social welfare: we did not know how the other half lived. We needed description. Some researchers wanted to start at the beginning to observe daily life in schools and to interview teachers who had excellent reputations (Jackson, 1968). Another researcher undertook participant observation at a rural school to discover whether rural schools faced problems of urban settings (McPherson, 1972). The qualitative description of process was timely.

Second, qualitative methods gained popularity because of their recognition of the views of the powerless and the excluded—those on the "outside." The qualitative emphasis on understanding perspectives of all participants at a site challenges what has been called "the hierarchy of credibility" (Becker, 1970c): the idea that the opinions and views of those in power are worth more than those who are not. As part of their typical research process, qualitative researchers studying education solicited the views of those who had never felt valued or represented. Qualitative research methods represented the kind of democratic impetus on the rise during the sixties. The climate of the times renewed interest in qualitative methods, created a need for more experienced mentors of this research approach, and opened the way for methodological growth and development.

More than the political climate of the times was at play. The academic disciplines of sociology and anthropology were in transition as well. Anthropologists found fewer Third-World communities that were willing to allow them to conduct their research; funding for such studies diminished. The number of peoples that had not been significantly changed by contact with the Western world had declined, undermining the mandate anthropologists had operated under to describe the cultures of the world before they were "spoiled." Anthropologists increasingly turned to studying urban areas and their own culture.

During the sixties, the field of sociology, which had been dominated by the ideas of structural functionalist theory for twenty years, began to turn to the writings of phenomenologists. Groups of researchers began doing what they came to call *ethnomethodology*. Others organized around the more established symbolic interaction tradition. Interest in qualitative methods was kindled by the publication of a number of theory and methods books. *The Human Perspective in Sociology* (Bruyn, 1966) presented the philosophical and methodological underpinnings of participant observation, while *The Discovery of Grounded Theory* (Glaser and Strauss, 1967) set forth the process of collecting and analyzing descriptive data in order to develop theory, an effort which clearly illustrated that qualitative research was not merely a descriptive undertaking. Collections of articles discussing in more detail many specific issues were published (Filstead, 1970; McCall and Simmons, 1969). A reader-

ship developed for those who wrote from the qualitative perspective and the literature began to grow (Bogdan and Taylor, 1975; Carini, 1975; Denzin, 1978; Georges
and Jones, 1980; Schwartz and Jacobs, 1979; Wolf, 1979).

The Seventies: Qualitative Research in Education, The Great Diversity

If qualitative research had not yet come of age, it was practicing for its bar mitzvah.
Less suspect to educational researchers, participant observation and ethnography especially claimed an ever-growing following. In the sixties, the qualitative mode was
still marginal in education, practiced only by the more unconventional. While qualitative methods could not claim a central position in mainstream research and development in education in the early seventies, they could no longer be labeled fringe
efforts either. Federal funding agencies, such as the National Institute of Education,
expressed greater interest in receiving proposals employing qualitative approaches.
More papers using qualitative methods were presented at professional associations,
like the American Educational Research Association, and these methods also gained
greater prominence in fields such as evaluation research (see Guba, 1978; Patton,
1980).

Methodological debates, however, continued between quantitative and qualitative researchers. Conflicts over questions like "hard" vs. "soft" data, "journalism"
vs. "research," and "scientific" vs. "intuitive" approaches each had their followers.
The call came for quantitative researchers to change their attitude from "disdain" to
"detente" (Rist, 1977). Tensions between qualitative and quantitative researchers
diminished in hostility. In fact, greater dialogue between the two groups opened up.
Some researchers who held positions of great prominence in quantitative circles began exploring the perspective and advocating its use (i.e., Bronfenbrenner, 1976;
Campbell, 1978; Cronbach, 1975; Glass, 1975). Many researchers in education had
come to feel that the years of promise for what quantitative research would be able to
do (the problems it could solve) had caught up with it. Quantitative methods, relying on the hard science paradigm, had not delivered. As the vision widened, qualitative approaches caught people's imagination (see Scriven, 1972). And so, qualitative
research mushroomed in education. Reviewing the literature, once a relatively simple
task, grew more complex, partly because of the great diversity in method, style, and
subject.

Some qualitative researchers in education do "field work"—participant observation, indepth interviewing, or ethnography—by spending extended amounts of time
at the research site, with the research subjects, or with documents. They record their
notes on paper so that they have data to analyze and they write up their findings, including many descriptions, reports of conversations, and dialogues. Educational research presents many examples of this type. Observations in schools have resulted, for
example, in studies on racial integration (Metz, 1978; Rist, 1978), the life of a school
principal (Wolcott, 1973), the experiences of teachers in rural schools (McPherson,
1972), and school innovations (Sussmann, 1977; Wolcott, 1977). Educational re-

searchers also rely on the indepth interview and have learned about children excluded from school (Cottle, 1976a), busing (Cottle, 1976b), and women's roles in educational leadership (Schmuck, 1975).

Some educational researchers, however, feel that what they call conventional field studies are "too anecdotal" (Mehan, 1978), or that ethnographic research should take a more "empirical" approach to the study of schools (McDermott, 1976). These researchers belong to a group that advocate what might be called a more *empiricist* approach to the study of human interaction. "Constitutive ethnography," consequently, relies on videotape and film to capture people's acts and gestures (Mehan, 1978, 1979). Researchers using this approach feel that observers' descriptions often reflect more the observers' orientation than the participants', and they also worry that participants may not be able to tell the researcher enough (Florio, 1978). Consequently, they depend on mechanical equipment to record verbatim what is happening. Other researchers who work in this mode include Erickson (1975), and the sociolinguist Shuy (Shuy and Griffin, 1978; Shuy, Wolfram, and Riley, 1967). These approaches vary in degree of obtrusiveness and in how the research is structured.

The style with which people conduct and present their research also varies. One stylistic difference lies in what we might call the cooperative vs. the conflictual approach to research. Those researchers who belong to the cooperative school generally believe that field workers should be as truthful as possible with the subjects they study. They hold to the basic and optimistic assumption that people will grant access to a research site if they can. Followers of this perspective are those who tend to see themselves as descendants of the Chicago school (see Bogdan and Taylor, 1975). On the other hand, practitioners of the conflictual approach assume that many subjects want to cover up what they do; truthful and overt researchers will get less information. Particularly if one wants to penetrate the world of big business, organized crime, or groups that have been labeled deviant, a researcher should use covert means and not speak truthfully in explaining his or her presence. This perspective has been clearly articulated by Douglas (1976).

Another stylistic difference is reflected in the attitude of the researcher toward informants or subjects under investigation. One group, again descendants of the Chicago school, might be said to have an "empathetic" perspective; that is, they have sympathy and understanding toward those whom they study. Hence, many of their research publications have shown readers humanity in lives that at first glance seem to make little sense. Proponents of this perspective have, in fact, been charged with identifying too closely with those whom they study, whether they are deviants, outcasts, or powerbrokers. At the other end of this continuum are those whose position seems to reflect the view that "the sociology of everything is ridiculous." This perspective is reflected most clearly in the group called the ethnomethodologists (see, for example, Garfinkel, 1967; Mehan and Wood, 1975). Ethnomethodologists study how people negotiate the daily rituals of their lives, and in the process often put people's feelings on the sidelines.

W. I. Thomas.

Everett Hughes.

Robert Park.

Herbert Blumer.

Sociologists central to the qualitative research tradition. (Courtesy of the American Sociological Association)

Margaret Mead in Samoa, 1925, at age twenty-four with the daughter of a Samoan Chief. She was just beginning her celebrated field studies. (Courtesy of the Library of Congress)

Ethnomethodology is a relatively new orientation to qualitative research whose origins can be traced to phenomenological philosophers. Harold Garfinkel (1967) and colleagues and their work in the mid-fifties employed the orientation and coined the term. During the sixties and seventies the approach and term grew in popularity, but everyone was not sure he or she was talking about the same thing. Garfinkel, speaking about the confusion over the term in 1968, stated: "I think the term may, in fact, be a mistake. It has acquired a life of its own" (Hill and Crittenden, 1968).

Rosalie Wax on the Pine Ridge Reservation, South Dakota, 1963, with members of the Sioux family she discusses in *Doing Fieldwork*. (Courtesy of Murray and Rosalie Wax)

While growing in popularity it was also under attack. Academics debated whether it was any different from other approaches, like symbolic interaction. People who wrote from the approach were criticized for being obscure in their writing and displaying a cult-like style (Coser, 1979). In addition, some of the followers of ethnomethodology tended to use data-gathering techniques that were irreverent to others' sense of ethics and appeared unconcerned with the suffering of people. This struck an antagonistic note with some of the more traditional practitioners of qualitative research, many of whom were humanistic in their approach to research, and liberal in their politics.

This great diversity among qualitative researchers studying educational issues reflects the maturing and growing sophistication of this approach. Despite these real differences, however, certain common strains connect work in the qualitative mode. In the next section, we list these common characteristics.

Ray Rist. (Courtesy of Ray Rist)

CHARACTERISTICS OF QUALITATIVE RESEARCH

Some researchers "hang around" schools with spiral notepads in hand to collect their data. Others rely on video equipment in the classroom and would never conduct research without it. Still others draw charts and diagrams of student-teacher verbal communication patterns. All of them, though, have this in common: their work fits our definition of qualitative research and they study an aspect of educational life. In this section we elaborate on the common strands and show why, in spite of differences, their research fits in our category of qualitative research.

There are five features of qualitative research, as we define it. All studies that we would call qualitative do not exhibit all the traits with equal potency. Some, in fact, are almost completely barren of one or more. The question is not whether a particular piece of research is or is not absolutely qualitative; rather it is an issue of degree. As we mentioned earlier, participant observation and indepth interview studies tend to be exemplary.

1. *Qualitative research has the natural setting as the direct source of data and the researcher is the key instrument.* Researchers enter and spend considerable time in schools, families, neighborhoods, and other locales learning about educational concerns. Although some people use videotape equipment and recording devices, many go completely unarmed save for a pad and a pencil. Even when equipment is used, however, the data is collected on the premises and supplemented by the understanding that is gained by being on location. In addition, mechanically recorded materials are reviewed in their entirety by the researcher with the researcher's insight being the key instrument for analysis. In a major study in medical education, for example, researchers went to a mid-western medical school where they followed students to classes, laboratories, hospital wards, and the places where they gathered for social occasions as well: their cafeterias, their fraternities, and study halls (Becker et al., 1961). A study of educational stratification in California (Ogbu, 1974) took the author twenty-one months to complete the fieldwork of visiting, observing, and interviewing teachers, students, principals, families, and members of school boards.

Qualitative researchers go to the particular setting under study because they are concerned with context. They feel that action can best be understood when it is observed in the setting in which it occurs. The setting has to be understood in the context of the history of the institutions of which they are a part. When the data with which they are concerned is produced by subjects, as in the case of official records, they want to know where, how, and under what circumstances it came into being. Of what historical circumstances and movements are they a part? To divorce the act, word, or gesture from its context is, for the qualitative researcher, to lose sight of significance. As one anthropologist described it:

> If anthropological interpretation is constructing a reading of what happens, then to divorce it from what happens—from what in this time or that place specific people say, what they do, what is done to them, from the whole vast business of the

world—is to divorce it from its application and render it vacant. A good interpretation of anything—a poem, a person, a history, a ritual, an institution, a society—takes us to the heart of that of which it is the interpretation (Geertz, 1973, p. 18).

Whether the data are collected on classroom interaction by videotape machines (Florio, 1978; Mehan, 1979), on science education through interviewing (Denny, 1978a), or on desegregation by participant observation (Metz, 1978), qualitative researchers assume that human behavior is significantly influenced by the setting in which it occurs, and wherever possible, go there.

2. *Qualitative research is descriptive.*   The data collected is in the form of words or pictures rather than numbers. The written results of the research contain quotations from the data to illustrate and substantiate the presentation. The data include interview transcripts, field notes, photographs, videotapes, personal documents, memos, and other official records. In their search for understanding, qualitative researchers do not reduce the pages upon pages of narration and other data to numerical symbols. They try to analyze it with all its richness as closely as possible to the form in which it was recorded or transcribed.

Qualitative articles and reports have been described by some as "anecdotal." This is because they often contain quotations and try to describe what a particular situation or view of the world is like in narrative form. The written word is very important in the qualitative approach, both in recording data and disseminating the findings.

In collecting descriptive data, qualitative researchers approach the world in a nit-picking way. Many of us are locked into our "taken for granted" worlds, oblivious to the details of our environment, and to the assumptions under which we operate. We fail to notice such things as gestures, jokes, who does the talking in a conversation, the decorations on the walls, and the special words we use and to which those around us respond.

The qualitative research approach demands that the world be approached with the assumption that nothing is trivial, that everything has the potential of being a clue which might unlock a more comprehensive understanding of what is being studied. The researcher constantly asks such questions as: Why are these desks arranged the way they are? Why are some rooms decorated with pictures and others not? Why do certain teachers dress differently from others? Is there a reason for certain activities being carried out where they are? Why is there a television in the room if it is never used? Nothing is taken as given, and no statement escapes scrutiny. Description succeeds as a method of data gathering when details face accounting.

3. *Qualitative researchers are concerned with process rather than simply with outcomes or products.*   How do people negotiate meaning? How do certain terms and labels come to be applied? How do certain notions come to be taken as part of what we know as "common sense"? What is the natural history of the activity or events under study? In studies of mainstreaming and integration in schools, for in-

stance, the researchers examined teachers' attitudes toward certain kinds of children and then studied how these attitudes were translated into daily interactions with them, and how the daily interactions then in turn reified those taken-for-granted attitudes (Bruni, 1980; Rist, 1978). In interviews with school administrators and candidates for administrative positions, a researcher showed how attitudes that reflected lower expectations, sexual fears, and other stereotyped notions toward women were integrated into the hiring process (Schmuck, 1975).

The qualitative emphasis on process has been particularly beneficial in educational research in clarifying the self-fulfilling prophecy, the idea that students' cognitive performance in school is affected by teachers' expectations of them (Rosenthal and Jacobson, 1968). Quantitative techniques have been able to show by means of pre- and posttesting that changes occur. Qualitative strategies have suggested just how the expectations are translated into daily activities, procedures, and interactions. A particularly brilliant rendition of the self-fulfilling prophecy in a kindergarten classroom can be found in a participant observation study of an all-black kindergarten class in St. Louis. The children were divided into groups based on essentially social and economic criteria within the first few days of school. The teacher interacted more with her top group, allowed the top group more privileges, and even permitted them to discipline members of the lower group. The day-to-day process of interaction is richly portrayed (Rist, 1970). This kind of study focuses on how definitions (teacher's definitions of students, student's definitions of each other and themselves) are formed.

4. *Qualitative researchers tend to analyze their data inductively.* They do not search out data or evidence to prove or disprove hypotheses they hold before entering the study; rather, the abstractions are built as the particulars that have been gathered are grouped together.

Theory developed this way emerges from the bottom up (rather than from the top down), from many disparate pieces of collected evidence that are interconnected. It is called *grounded theory* (Glaser and Strauss, 1967). As a qualitative researcher planning to develop some kind of theory about what you have been studying, the direction you will travel comes after you have been collecting the data, after you have spent time with your subjects. You are not putting together a puzzle, whose picture you already know. You are constructing a picture which takes shape as you collect and examine the parts. The process of data analysis is like a funnel: things are open at the beginning (or top), and more directed and specific at the bottom. The qualitative researcher plans to use part of the study to learn what the important questions are. He. or she does not assume that enough is known to recognize important concerns before undertaking the research.

5. *"Meaning" is of essential concern to the qualitative approach.* Researchers who use this approach are interested in the ways different people make sense out of their lives. In other words, qualitative researchers are concerned with what are called *participant perspectives.* They focus on questions like: What assumptions do people

make about their lives? What do they take for granted? In one educational study, for example, the researcher focused part of his work on parent perspectives on their children's education. He wanted to know what parents thought about why their children were not doing well in school. He found that the parents he studied felt that the teachers did not value their insights about their own children because of their poverty and their lack of education. The parents also blamed teachers who assumed that this very poverty and lack of education meant the children would not be good students (Ogbu, 1974). He also studied the teachers' and the children's perspectives on the same issues in hopes of finding some intersections in perspective, and to explore the implications for schooling. By learning the perspectives of the participants, qualitative research illuminates the inner dynamics of situations—dynamics that are often invisible to the outsider.

Qualitative researchers are concerned with making sure they capture perspectives accurately. Some researchers who use videotape show the completed tapes to the participants in order to check their own interpretations with those of the informants (Mehan, 1978). Other researchers may show drafts of articles or interview transcripts to key informants. Still others may verbally check out perspectives with subjects. Although there is some controversy over such procedures, they reflect a concern with capturing the people's own way of interpreting significance as accurately as possible.

Qualitative researchers in education can continually be found asking questions of the people they are learning from to discover "what *they* are experiencing, how *they* interpret their experiences, and how *they* themselves structure the social world in which they live" (Psathas, 1973).

THEORETICAL UNDERPINNINGS

The concern qualitative researchers have for "meaning," as well as other features we have described as characteristic of qualitative research, leads us to a discussion of the theoretical orientation of the approach. There are many ways people use the word *theory*. Among quantitative researchers in education its use is sometimes restricted to a systematically stated and testable set of propositions about the empirical world. Our use of the phrase is much more in line with its use in sociology and anthropology and similar to the term *paradigm* (Ritzer, 1975). A paradigm is a loose collection of logically held-together assumptions, concepts, or propositions that orient thinking and research. When we refer to a "theoretical orientation" or "theoretical perspective," we are talking about a way of looking at the world, the assumptions people have about what is important, and what makes the world work. Whether stated or not, all research is guided by some theoretical orientation. Good researchers are aware of their theoretical base and use it to help collect and analyze data. Theory helps data cohere and enables research to go beyond an aimless, unsystematic piling up of accounts. In this section, we briefly examine the theoretical underpinnings of qualitative approaches.

Most other research approaches trace their roots to positivism and the great social theorist, Auguste Comte. They emphasize facts and causes of behavior. While there are theoretical differences between qualitative approaches and even within single schools (Meltzer, Petras, and Reynolds, 1975), all qualitative researchers in some way reflect a phenomenological perspective. There are many debates concerning the use of the word *phenomenology* and we use it in the most general sense. We start our discussion of theory by presenting the phenomenological perspective and clarifying some issues it raises. Next we discuss symbolic interactionism, a well-established particular type of phenomenological framework. "Culture" as an orientation, the interpretation of which is the undertaking of many anthropologists, is next on our agenda. Then we briefly introduce a newer approach to the qualitative scene, ethnomethodology. Our discussion does not exhaust the types. We have picked the most widely used and those most closely aligned with phenomenology.

Phenomenological Approach

At the scene of a car accident a conversation occurred which illustrates two approaches people use to understand what happens around them. At an intersection where all the roads faced stop signs, two cars collided. The drivers were discussing what had happened when a police officer arrived on the scene. One driver took the position that the other had not made a full stop, while the other driver said that he had indeed stopped and that he had the right of way anyway. A reluctant witness was drawn into the debate who, when asked by one of the drivers for her account of the incident, said that it was hard to tell what exactly had happened from where she was standing. Phrases such as, "How could you say that?" "It happened right before your eyes." "Facts are facts. You didn't stop!" "You were looking the other way." were bantered about. The police officer was asked how she reconciled conflicting accounts. Her response was that contradictions occur all the time and that the parties involved were not necessarily lying since "it all depends on where you are sitting, how things look to you." The approach the police officer took to understand the situation is reflective of qualitative approaches that depend on a phenomenological point of view. They require a set of assumptions that are different from those used when human behavior is approached with the purpose of finding "facts" and "causes."

Researchers in the phenomenological mode attempt to understand the meaning of events and interactions to ordinary people in particular situations. Phenomenological sociology has been particularly influenced by the philosophers Edmund Husserl and Alfred Schutz. It is also located within the Weberian tradition which emphasizes "verstehen," the interpretive understanding of human interaction. Phenomenologists do not assume they know what things mean to the people they are studying (Douglas, 1976). "Phenomenological inquiry begins with silence" (Psathas, 1973). This "silence" is an attempt to grasp what it is they are studying. What phenomenologists emphasize, then, is the subjective aspects of people's behavior. They attempt to gain entry into the conceptual world of their subjects (Geertz, 1973) in order to understand how and what meaning they construct around events in their daily lives. Phenomenologists believe that for human beings multiple ways of inter-preting experiences are available to each of us through interacting with others, and that it is the meaning of our experiences that constitutes reality (Greene, 1978). Reality, consequently, is "socially constructed" (Berger and Luckmann, 1967).

While there are various brands of qualitative research, all share to some degree this goal of understanding the subjects from their own point of view. When we ex-amine this proposition carefully, though, the phrase "from their own point of view" presents a problem. And that is the rather fundamental concern that "their point of view" is not an expression that subjects use themselves; it may not represent the way they think of themselves. "Their point of view" is a way that people who do this kind of research approach their work. "Point of view" is thus a research construct. Looking at subjects in terms of this idea may, consequently, force subjects' exper-ience of the world into a mode that is foreign to them. This kind of intrusion of the researcher on the subject's world, however, is inevitable in research. After all, the re-searcher is making interpretations, and must have some conceptual scheme to do this. Qualitative researchers believe that approaching people with a goal of trying to understand their point of view, while not perfect, distorts the subject's experience the least. There are differences in the degree to which qualitative researchers are con-cerned with this methodological and conceptual problem as well as differences in how they come to grips with it. Some researchers attempt to do "immaculate phe-nomenological description"; others show less concern and attempt to build abstrac-tions by interpreting from the data on "their point of view." Whatever one's posi-tion, qualitative analysis has to be self-conscious in regard to this theoretical and methodological issue.

While qualitative researchers tend to be phenomenological in their orientation, most are not radical idealists. They emphasize the subjective, but they do not neces-sarily deny a reality "out there" that stands over and against human beings, capable of resisting action toward it (Blumer, 1980). A teacher may believe he can walk through a brick wall, but it takes more than thinking to accomplish it. The nature of the wall is unyielding, but the teacher does not have to perceive "reality" as it is. He may still believe that he can walk through the wall, but not at this time, or that he had a curse put on him, and therefore, cannot walk through the wall. Thus reality comes to be understood to human beings only in the form in which it is perceived. Qualitative researchers emphasize subjective thinking because, as they see it, the world is dominated by objects less obstinate than walls. And human beings are much more like "The Little Engine that Could." We live in our imaginations, settings more symbolic than concrete.

Symbolic Interaction

As a review of history suggests, symbolic interaction has been around a while. It was present in the Chicago school approach to research in the early part of this century. John Dewey, the pragmatist philosopher and educator, was at Chicago during the formulative years of this theoretical perspective, and his writings and personal contact with such people as Charles Horton Cooley, Robert Park, Florian Znanicki, and, most important, George Herbert Mead contributed to its development. Mead's formulation in *Mind, Self, and Society* (Mead, 1934)[16] is the most cited, early source of what is now called symbolic interaction. No agreement exists among social scientists about the use or importance of various concepts of it. Most use it synonymously with qualitative research, but there are a few social scientists calling themselves symbolic interactionists who do quantitive research (i.e., the Iowa School of symbolic interaction). In our discussion we draw heavily on students of Mead's work: Herbert Blumer and Everett Hughes, and their students, Howard S. Becker and Blanche Geer.

Compatible with the phenomenological perspective and basic to the approach is the assumption that human experience is mediated by interpretation (Blumer, 1969). Objects, people, situations, and events do not possess their own meaning; rather, meaning is conferred on them. Where the educational technologist, for instance, will define a sixteen-millimeter projector as a device to be used by the teacher to show instructional films relevant to educational objectives, the teacher may define it as an object to entertain students when she runs out of work for them to do or when she is tired. Or, place the projector with a nonwestern tribal group, and it may be defined as a religious icon to be worshipped (until the A.V. specialist arrives bringing, perhaps, new perceptions and possibly influencing some definitions). The meaning people give to their experience and their process of interpretation is essential and constitutive, not accidental or secondary to what the experience is. To understand behavior, we must understand definitions and the process by which they are manufactured. Human beings are actively engaged in creating their world; understanding the intersection of biography and society is essential (Gerth and Mills, 1953). People act, not on the basis of predetermined responses to predefined objects, but rather as interpreting, defining, symbolic animals whose behavior can only be understood by having the researcher enter into the defining process through such methods as participant observation.

Interpretation is not an autonomous act, nor is it determined by any particular force, human or otherwise. Individuals interpret with the help of others—people from their past, writers, family, television personalities, and persons they meet in settings in which they work and play—but others do not do it for them. Through interaction the individual constructs meaning. People in a given situation (for example, students in a particular class) often develop common definitions (or "share perspectives" in the symbolic interactionist language) since they regularly interact and share experiences, problems, and background; but consensus in not inevitable. While some take "shared definitions" to indicate "truth," meaning is always subject to negotiation. It can be influenced by people who see things differently. When acting on the basis of a particular definition, things may not go well for a person. People have problems and these problems may cause them to forge new definitions, to discard old ways—in short, to change. How such definitions develop is the subject matter for investigation.

Interpretation, then, is essential. Symbolic interaction becomes the conceptual paradigm rather than "internal drives," "personality traits," "unconscious motives," "needs," "socioeconomic status," "role obligations," "cultural prescriptions," "social control mechanisms," or the physical environment. These factors are some of the constructs that social scientists draw upon in their attempts to understand and predict behavior. The symbolic interactionist does not deny the fact that these theoretical constructs might be useful; however, they are relevant to understanding behavior only to the degree that they enter in and affect the defining process. A proponent of the theory would not deny, for example, that there is a drive for food and that there are certain cultural definitions of how, what, and when one should eat. They would deny, however, that eating can be understood solely in terms of drives and cultural definitions. Eating can be understood by looking at the interplay between how people come to define eating and the specific situations in which they find themselves. Eating comes to be defined in different ways: the process is experienced differently, and people exhibit different behaviors while eating in different situations. Teachers in a school come to define the proper time to eat, what to eat, and how to eat very differently from students in the same location. Eating lunch can be a break from work, an annoying intrusion, a chance to do some low-key business, a time to diet, or a chance to get the answers to questions on an examination. (We are not suggeting that these are mutually exclusive.) Some people's meals, for example, may serve as benchmarks for specific developments in their day. Here, eating takes on significance by providing an event by which one can measure what has or has not been accomplished, how much the day he or she may still have to endure, or how soon one will be forced to end an exciting day.

Eating lunch has symbolic meaning with which concepts like drives and rituals cannot deal. The theory does not deny that there are rules and regulations, norms, and belief systems in society. It does suggest that they are important in understanding behavior only if people take them into account. Further, it is suggested that it is not the rules, regulations, norms, or whatever that are crucial in understanding behavior, but how these are defined and used in specific situations. A high school may have a grading system, an organizational chart, a class schedule, a curriculum, and an official motto that suggests the prime purpose is the education of the "whole person." People act, however, not according to what the school is supposed to be, or what administrators say it is, but rather, according to how they see it. For some, high school is primarily a place to meet friends, or even a place to get high; for most, it is a place to get grades and amass credits so they can graduate—tasks they define as leading to college or a job. The definitions they have determine their actions, although the rules and the credit system may set certain limits and impose certain costs, and thus affect their behavior. Organizations vary in the extent to which they provide fixed meanings and the extent that alternative meanings are available and created.

Another important part of symbolic interaction theory is the construct of the "self." The self is not seen lying inside the individual like the ego or an organized body of needs, motives, and internalized norms or values. The self is the definition people create (through interacting with others) of who they are. In constructing or defining self, people attempt to see themselves as others see them by interpreting gestures and actions directed toward them and by placing themselves in the role of the other person. In short, we come to see ourselves in part as others see us. The self is thus also a social construction, the results of persons perceiving themselves and then developing a definition through the process of interaction. This loop enables people to change and grow as they learn more about themselves through this interactive process. This way of conceptualizing the self has led to studies of the self-fulfilling prophecy and provided the background for what has come to be called the "labelling approach" to deviant behavior (Becker, 1963; Erickson, 1962; Rist, 1977).

Culture

Many anthropologists operate from a phenomenological perspective in their studies of education (see, for example, Wolcott, 1973). The framework for these anthropological studies is the concept of culture. The attempt to describe culture or aspects of culture is called *ethnography*. While anthropologists often disagree on a definition of culture, they all count on it for a theoretical framework to inform their work. Several definitions help expand our understanding of how it shapes research. Some anthropologists define culture as "the acquired knowledge people use to interpret experience and generate behavior" (Spradley, 1980, p. 6). In this scheme, *culture* embraces what people do, what people know, and things that people make and use (Spradley, 1980, p. 5). To describe culture from this perspective a researcher might think about events in the following way: "At its best, an ethnography should account for the behavior of people by describing what it is that they know that enables them to behave appropriately given the dictates of common sense in their community" (McDermott, 1976, p. 159). Researchers in this tradition say that an ethnography succeeds if it teaches readers how to behave appropriately in the cultural setting, whether it is among families in a black community (Stack, 1974), in the school principal's office (Wolcott, 1973), or in the kindergarten class (Florio, 1978).

Another definition of culture emphasizes semantics, and insists that there is a difference between knowing the behavior and lingo of a group of people and being able to do it oneself (Geertz, 1973). From this perspective, culture looks a bit more complicated and a bit different:

> As interworked systems of construable signs (what, ignoring provincial usages, I would call symbols), culture is not a power, something to which social events, behaviors, institutions, or processes can be causally attributed; it is a context, something within which they can be intelligibly—that is, *thickly*—described (Geertz, 1973, p. 14).

In this sense, there is interaction between culture and the meanings people attribute to events. The phenomenological orientation of this definition is clear.

Geertz has borrowed the term "thick description" from the philosopher Gilbert Ryle to describe the task of ethnography. Geertz uses Ryle's example of a person blinking one eye, and examining all the different levels on which such an act can be analyzed. Some of the levels include: the person blinking might have a twitch, or might be winking, or might be pretending to be winking (and so putting the audience on), or might be learning to wink and practicing this in front of a mirror and hence rehearsing. How and at what level one analyzes these behaviors constitutes the difference between thin and thick description:

> Between the..."thin description" of what the rehearser (parodist, winker, twitcher...) is doing ("rapidly contracting his right eyelid") and the "thick description" of what he is doing ("practicing a burlesque of a friend faking a wink to deceive an innocent into thinking a conspiracy is in motion"), lies the object of ethnography: a stratified hierarchy of meaning structures in terms of which twitches, winks, fake winks, parodies, rehearsals of parodies are produced, perceived, and interpreted, and without which they would not (not even the zero-form twitches, which *as a cultural category* are as much non-winks as winks are non-twitches), in fact exist, no matter what anyone did or didn't do with his eyelids (Geertz, 1973, p. 7).

Ethnography, then, is "thick description." What the ethnographer is faced with when culture is examined from this perspective is a series of interpretations of life, common-sense understandings, which are complex and difficult to separate from each other. The ethnographer's goals are to share in the meanings that the cultural participants take for granted and then to depict the new understanding for the reader and for outsiders.

A third and last conceptual handle on culture we take from the anthropologist Rosalie Wax (Wax, 1971). In a discussion of the theoretical presuppositions of field work, Wax discusses the tasks of ethnography in terms of understanding. Understanding, according to Wax, is not some "mysterious empathy" between people; rather, it is a phenomenon of "shared meaning." And so the anthropologist begins *outside,* both literally in terms of his or her social acceptance and figuratively in terms of understanding:

> Thus, a field worker who approaches a strange people soon perceives that these people are saying and doing things which they understand but he does not understand. One of the strangers may make a particular gesture, whereupon all the other strangers laugh. They share in the understanding of what the gesture means, but the field worker does not. When he does share, he begins to "understand." He possesses a part of the "insider's view" (Wax, 1971, p. 11).

A recent ethnographic study of a kindergarten class (Florio, 1978) examines how children entering kindergarten become insiders, i.e., how they learn kindergarten culture and develop appropriate responses to teachers' and classroom expectations.

It is the framework of culture, whatever the specific definitions, as the principal organizational or conceptual tool to interpret data that characterizes ethnography. Ethnographic procedures, while similar if not identical to those employed in participant observation, do rely on a different vocabulary and have developed in different academic specialities. Recently, educational researchers have used the term *ethnography* to refer to any qualitative study, even within sociology. While people do not agree on the appropriateness of using ethnography as the generic word for qualitative studies (see, for example, Wolcott, 1975), there is some evidence to suggest the sociologist and the anthropologist are coming closer in the ways they conduct their research and the theoretical orientation that underlies their work. A well-known ethnographer has, in fact, declared that "the concept of culture as acquired knowledge has much in common with symbolic interaction" (Spradley, 1980).

Ethnomethodology

Ethnomethodology does not refer to the methods that researchers employ to collect their data; rather, it points to the subject matter to investigate. As Harold Garfinkel tells the story, the term came to him while he was working with the Yale cross-culture area files which contained words like *ethnobotany, ethnophysics, ethnomusic,* and *ethnoastronomy.* Terms like these refer to how members of a particular group (usually tribal groups in the Yale files) understand, use, and order aspects of their environment; in the case of ethnobotany, the particular subject is plants. Ethnomethodology thus refers to the study of how individuals create and understand their daily lives—their method of accomplishing everyday life. Subjects for ethnomethodologists are not members of primitive tribes; they are people in various situations in our own society.

Garfinkel, giving what he calls a shorthand definition of the work of ethnomethodologists, says: "I would say we are doing studies of how persons, as parties to their ordinary arrangements, use the features of the arrangements to make for members the visibly organized characteristics happen (Garfinkel, in Hill and Crittenden, 1968, p. 12)." Ethnomethodologists try to understand how people go about seeing, explaining, and describing order in the world in which they live.

A number of people in education have been influenced by the approach. While their work is sometimes difficult to separate from the work of other qualitative researchers, it tends to deal more with micro-issues, with the specifics of conversation and vocabulary, and with details of action and understanding. Researchers in this mode use such phrases as "common-sense understanding," "everyday life," "practical accomplishments," "routine grounds for social action," and "accounts." The researchers described in the first pages of this book asking children about their responses to tests are associated with the ethnomethodological approach (see Mehan and Woods, 1975; Turner, 1974).

It is too early developmentally to comment on the contribution of ethnomethodology to educational research. One issue to which ethnomethodologists have sensitized researchers is that research itself is not a uniquely scientific enterprise; rather, it can be studied as "a practical accomplishment." They have suggested that we look carefully at the common-sense understandings under which data collectors operate. They push researchers working in the qualitative mode to be more sensitive to the need to "bracket" or suspend their own common-sense assumptions, their own world view, instead of taking it for granted.

A Story

To sum up our discussion of theory we end with an anecdote. If we had to give it a title, we would call this story "Forever."

One night at a dinner party a group of university faculty, including the Dean of the law school, a physics professor, and a geology professor, all distinguished in their fields, began discussing the concept of "forever." The conversation began with someone making reference to the practice of having property leases drawn up in periods of ninety-nine years. Someone asked the Dean of the law school whether the phrase wasn't the convention of the legal profession to refer to "forever." The Dean said, "Yes, more or less, that's what it means." The geology professor suggested that in her field, "forever" refers to something quite different—the concept had more to do with how long the earth was expected to exist. The physics professor chimed in with the comment that in his field, "forever" really meant "forever."

Many children's stories end with the phrase, "And they lived happily for ever after," another interpretation. Sometimes when children are waiting for their parents to take them some place, they complain that they have been waiting "forever." We have not exhausted all the possibilities, but the point is clear. Looked at from a number of perspectives, the word is rich in connotations. Each person referred to uses the idea of "forever" in a very different world view. The child who says, "I have been waiting forever," finds it difficult to see the world from the point of view of a physicist, and the physicist dismisses the child's use of the concept with a knowing adult smile.

Some might attempt to resolve the discrepancy between the views of various users of the concept by calling for a more precise definition of the term—in other words, to create consensus by "deciding on" "real" definitions of the term. In discussion groups or in board meetings, this method might forestall misunderstanding, but qualitative researchers attempt to expand rather than confine understanding. They do not attempt to resolve such ambiguity by seeing the differences as a "mistake," and so attempt to establish a standard definition. Rather, they seek to study the concept as it is understood in the context of all those who use it. Similarly, when going to study an organization, one does not attempt to resolve the ambiguity that occurs when varied definitions arise of what the word *goal* means, or when people have different goals. The subject of the study focuses instead on how various participants see and experience goals. It is multiple realities rather than a single reality which concern the qualitative researcher.

EIGHT COMMON QUESTIONS ABOUT QUALITATIVE RESEARCH

Hearing about qualitative research for the first time usually causes a number of questions to come to mind. We address eight questions others have raised that you may also have.

1. *Can qualitative and quantitative approaches be used together?* Some people do use them together. It is common, for example, in designing questionnaires to do open-ended interviews first. You can use indepth observations in discovering why two variables which are shown to be statistically related are related. There are studies that have qualitative and quantitative components. Most often, descriptive statistics and qualitative findings have been presented together (Mercurio, 1979). While it is possible, and in some cases desirable, to use the two approaches together, the same person attempting to carry out a sophisticated quantitative study while doing an indepth qualitative study simultaneously is likely to produce a big headache. Researchers, especially novices, trying to combine good quantitative design and good qualitative design have a difficult time pulling it off, and rather than producing a superior hybrid, usually produce a piece of research that does not meet the criteria for good work in either approach. The two approaches are based on different assumptions. While it is useful to have an interplay of competing data, often such studies turn out to be studies in method rather than in the topic you originally started out to study.

2. *Is qualitative research really scientific?* Educational researchers have in the past modeled their research after what they saw the so-called ''hard scientists'' doing. Some saw measurement as synonomous with science and anything straying from this mode was suspect. The irony of it is that scientists in the hard sciences (physics and chemistry, for example) do not define science as narrowly as some of those who emulate them. Nobel Prize-winning physicist P. W. Bridgeman has this to say of the scientific method: ''There is no scientific method as such.... The most vital feature of the scientist's procedure has been merely to do his utmost with his mind, no holds barred'' (Dalton, 1967, p. 60). Dalton says:

> ...many eminent physicists, chemists, and mathematicians question whether there is a reproducible method that all investigators could or should follow, and they have shown in their research that they take diverse, and often unascertainable steps in discovering and solving problems'' (Dalton, 1967, p. 60).

Some people may use an extremely narrow definition of science, calling only research which is deductive and hypothesis-testing scientific. But part of the scientific attitude, as we see it, is to be open-minded about method and evidence. Scientific research, to us, involves rigorous and systematic empirical inquiry; that is, which is data-based. Qualitative research meets these requirements, and in this book we describe some of the conventions in this scientific tradition that define what rigorous and systematic investigation entails.

3. *How does qualitative research differ from what other people like teachers, reporters, or artists do?* Let us take teachers first. Many intelligent laypeople are astute observers of their world, do systematic inquiries, and come to conclusions. Good teachers do this consistently. What they do is like qualitative research, but it is different in a number of ways. First, the observer's primary duty is to the research; he or she does not have to devote time to developing curriculum, teaching lessons, and disciplining students. The researcher can thus devote full time and energy to taking it all in. Also, researchers are rigorous about keeping detailed records of what they find. They keep data. Teachers keep records too, but these are much less extensive and of a different sort. Further, researchers do not have as much of a personal stake in having the observations come out one way or the other. The teacher's life, career, and self-concept are always intimately tied to seeing what he or she is doing in a particular way. This is not to say that teachers cannot transcend this to do research or that researchers do not also have a stake in their studies. But for the researchers, success is defined by doing what certain others define as good research, not seeing what the teacher does in any particular way. Another way that the researcher and the teacher differ is that the researcher has been trained in the use of a set of procedures and techniques developed over the years to collect and analyze data. Many of these are described in this book. Last, the researcher is well-grounded in theory and research findings. These provide a framework and clues to direct the study and place what is generated in a context.

What about reporters? Some people link qualitative research with journalism disparagingly. We do not. As the short history we presented suggests, some traditions of qualitative research are linked to journalism. Journalists share some of the goals and standards that social scientists have, and some produce research of greater social-science value than those who flaunt their academic credentials and titles (Levine, 1980a). While this is so, we do believe that academic researchers in general do work in a different way than journalists. Journalists tend to be more interested in particular events and issues and tend to have a bias toward the news makers. Journalists work under deadlines. Rather than spending years collecting data and carefully analyzing it, they usually write with less evidence; they shoot from the hip. They also tend to write for a different audience and their work is more directed at telling a story than analyzing it. Journalists also are not necessarily grounded in social theory. Therefore, they do not address their findings to theoretical questions. Of course, journalists also are interested in selling papers and this puts some constraints on what they can say and how they write. Sometimes, however, the line separating social-science research and good investigative journalism is nonexistent (see Douglas, 1976; Levine, 1980a).

What about artists? Some novelists and poets are very keen observers of the human scene. Again, they may not be as formal or as rigorous as qualitative researchers in their data-collecting techniques and they may take greater license with the data they do collect. Much of what they have to say, however, is of interest to social scientists. Some people fall between the cracks of social science and art. They write in a very involving style while drawing from social-science traditions in what they say

(Coles, 1964; Cottle, 1976a). Social scientists probably have a lot to learn from novelists and essayists. They'd best not set themselves apart, but rather try to understand what it is that they can learn from them to improve their own trade (see Eisner, 1980).

4. *Are qualitative findings generalizable?* When researchers use the term *generalizability,* they are usually referring to whether the findings of a study hold up beyond the specific research subjects and the setting involved. If you study a particular classroom, for example, people want to know whether other classrooms are like the one you studied. Not all qualitative researchers are concerned with the question of generalizability as we have just stated it. Those who are concerned are very careful to explicitly state that. If they do a case study of a classroom, for example, they do not mean to imply in reporting results of the study that all classrooms are like that one.

Others who are concerned with generalizability, as we have discussed it thus far, may draw upon other studies to establish the representativeness of what they have found, or they may conduct a larger number of less intense mini-studies to show the nonidiosyncratic nature of their own work. In a study of day-care centers, for example, after conducting intense observations in one setting for four months, a researcher we know visited three other centers to get a sense of the similarities and differences between the one studied and the others (Freedman, 1980).

Some qualitative researchers do not think of generalizability in the conventional way. They are more interested in deriving universal statements of general social processes rather than statements of commonality between similar settings such as classrooms. Here, the assumption is that human behavior is not random or idiosyncratic. They therefore concern themselves not with the question of whether their findings are generalizable, but rather with the question of to which other settings and subjects they are generalizable.

In the study of an intensive care unit at a teaching hospital we studied the ways professional staff and parents communicate about the condition of their children. As we concentrated on the interchanges, we noticed that the professional staff not only diagnosed the infants but sized up the parents as well. These parental evaluations formed the basis for judgments the professionals made about what to say to parents and how to say it. Reflecting about parent-teacher conferences in public schools and other situations where professionals have information about children to which parents might want access, we began to see parallels. In short, we began concentrating on a general social process which appeared clearly in one particular setting. One tack we are presently exploring is the extent to which the findings of the intensive care unit are generalizable not to other settings of the same substantive type, but to other settings in which professionals talk to parents, such as schools. The approach to generalizability as we have just described it is embraced more by researchers who are interested in generating what is called a *grounded theory.*

Another way some qualitative researchers approach generalizability is to think that if they carefully document a given setting or group of subjects, it is then someone else's job to see how it fits into the general scheme of things. Even a description of a deviant type is of value because theories have to account for all types. They see their work as having the potential to create anomalies that other researchers might have to explain. Some of the explanation might entail enlarging the conception of the phenomena under study.

Before gorillas were studied by detailed observation in their own environments, doing what they naturally do, they were considered to be extremely aggressive, dangerous to humans and other animals. George Schaller went out and studied gorillas in their own environments and found out that they did not resemble the profiles drawn of gorillas in captivity. He observed them to be timid and shy, preferring to flee or avoid people rather than to attack. They would, however, rear up and beat their chests in a ritualistic warning when challenged. Questions about whether all gorillas are like that and under what conditions they are the way they have been described cannot be answered by such limited case-study research, but Schaller's gorillas have to be reckoned with in future discussions about gorilla behavior (Schaller, 1965; Waldorf and Reinarman, 1975).

5. *What about the researcher's opinions, prejudices, and other biases and their effect on the data?*   Qualitative researchers, whether in the tradition of sociology or anthropology, have wrestled over the years with charges that it is too easy for the prejudices and attitudes of the researcher to bias the data. Particularly when the data must "go through" the researcher's mind before it is put on paper, the worry about subjectivity arises. Does perhaps the observer record only what he or she wants to see rather than what is actually there? Qualitative researchers are concerned with the effect their own subjectivity may have on the data they produce.

What qualitative researchers attempt to do, however, is to objectively study the subjective states of their subjects. While the idea that researchers can transcend some of their own biases may be difficult to accept at the beginning, the methods that researchers use aid this process. For one thing, qualitative studies are not impressionistic essays made after a quick visit to a setting or after some conversations with a few subjects. The researcher spends a considerable time in the empirical world laboriously collecting and reviewing piles of data. The data must bear the weight of any interpretation, so the researcher must constantly confront his or her own opinions and prejudices with the data. Besides, most opinions and prejudices are rather superficial. The data that are collected provides a much more detailed rendering of events than even the most creatively prejudiced mind might have imagined prior to the study.

Additionally, the researcher's primary goal is to add to knowledge, not to pass judgment on a setting. The worth of a study is the degree to which it generates theory, description, or understanding. For a study to blame someone for a particular state of affairs, or to label a particular school as "good" or "bad," or to present a pat prejudicial analysis can brand a study as superficial. Qualitative researchers tend to believe that situations are complex, so they attempt to portray many dimensions rather than to narrow the field.

Further, as we discuss in detail in Chapter 3, qualitative researchers guard against their own biases by recording detailed fieldnotes which include reflections on their own subjectivity. Some qualitative researchers work in teams and have their field-notes critiqued by a colleague as an additional check on bias. It should be noted that we are talking about *limiting* observers' biases, not eliminating them. Qualitative researchers attempt to seek out their own subjective states and their effects on data but they never think they are completely successful. All researchers are affected by observers' bias. Questions or questionnaires, for example, reflect the interests of those who construct them, as do experimental studies. Qualitative researchers try to acknowledge and take into account their own biases as a method of dealing with them.

6. *Doesn't the presence of the researcher change the behavior of the people he or she is trying to study?* Yes, and these changes are referred to as "observer effect." Almost all research is confounded by this problem. Take surveys that try to tap opinions. Asking people to sit down and fill out a questionnaire changes their behavior. Might not asking a person for their opinion create an opinion? Some experimental studies create a completely artificial world (in the laboratory) in which to observe people's behavior. Because other research approaches suffer from the problem does not mean that qualitative researchers take the issue of "observer effect" lightly. Throughout the history of qualitative methods practitioners have addressed themselves to this problem and have incorporated procedures to minimize it.

Qualitative researchers try to interact with their subjects in a natural, unobtrusive, and nonthreatening manner. The more controlled and obtrusive one's research, the greater the likelihood that one will end up studying the effects of one's methods (Douglas, 1976, p. 19). If you treat people as "research subjects," they will act as research subjects, which is different from how they usually act. Since qualitative researchers are interested in how people act and think in their own settings, they attempt to "blend into the woodwork," or to act so that the activities that occur in their presence do not differ significantly from those that occur in their absence. Similarly, since interviewers in this type of research are interested in how people think about their lives, their experiences, and particular situations, they model their interviews after a conversation between two trusting parties rather than on a formal question-and-answer session between a researcher and a respondent. It is only in this manner that they can capture what is important in the minds of the subjects themselves.

One can never eliminate all of one's own effects on subjects or obtain a perfect correspondence between what one wishes to study—the "natural setting"—and what one actually studies—"a setting with a researcher present." One can, however, understand one's effect on the subjects through an intimate knowledge of the setting, and use this understanding to generate additional insights into the nature of social life. Researchers learn to "discount" some of their data; that is, to interpret them in context (Deutscher, 1973). One often finds subjects' attempts to manage impressions of researchers and their activities especially during the early stages of the project (Douglas, 1976). Teachers, for example, might not yell at their students in front of you, or in other ways act more reserved. Knowing that you are seeing teachers' behavior before strangers is important to take into account. Principals may engage in behavior they consider principal-like, and in order to do this upset their normal routines. You can turn this to your advantage to learn what principals consider to be principal-like behavior (see Morris and Hurwitz, 1980). In their reaction to outsiders, people reveal as much as in their reactions to insiders, provided of course you know the difference.

7. *Will two researchers independently studying the same setting or subjects come up with the same findings?*   This question is related to the quantitative researchers' word *reliability.* Among certain research approaches, the expectation exists that there will be consistency in results of observations made by different researchers or the same researcher over time. Qualitative researchers do not share exactly this expectation.

Educational researchers come from a variety of backgrounds and have divergent interests. Some have studied psychology, others sociology, others child development, and still others anthropology or social work. The academic training one has had affects the questions one brings to an area of inquiry. In the study of a school, for example, social workers might be interested in the social background of the students; sociologists might direct their attention to the school's social structure; developmental psychologists might wish to study the self-concept of pupils in the early grades. As such, social workers, sociologists, and developmental psychologists who pursue their interests in different ways may spend more time in some parts of the school than others, or may speak more to certain people than others. They will collect different types of data and reach different conclusions. Similarly, theoretical perspectives specific to their fields will structure a study.

In qualitative studies, researchers are concerned with the accuracy and comprehensiveness of their data. Qualitative researchers tend to view reliability as a fit between what they record as data and what actually occurs in the setting under study, rather than the literal consistency across different observations. As the preceding discussion indicates, two researchers studying a single setting may come up with different data and produce different findings. Both studies can be reliable. One would only question the reliability of one or both studies if they yielded contradictory or incompatible results.

8. *How does qualitative differ from quantitative?*   There are many authors who have elaborated the different assumptions, techniques, and strategies of qualitative as opposed to quantitative research. Most writing about the qualitative approach defines it in contrast to quantitative (Bruyn, 1966; Rist, 1977). Although a certain amount of comparison is unavoidable, we have attempted in this book to concentrate on describing what qualitative research is and how to do it rather than presenting what it is not. We refer you to others for examination of the differences (see Campbell, 1978; Eisner, 1980).

While we have not been comprehensive in discussing the qualitative/quantitative distinction, Figure 1–1 provides a chart summarizing the characteristics of both approaches. This chart also serves as a useful summary of the points we have raised in this chapter, many of which we elaborate in the pages that follow.

FIGURE 1-1

CHARACTERISTICS OF QUALITATIVE AND QUANTITATIVE RESEARCH

Qualitative

Phrases Associated with the Approach

-ethnographic
-field work
-soft data
-symbolic interaction
-inner perspective
-naturalistic
-ethnomethodological
-descriptive

-participant observation
-phenomenological
-Chicago school
-documentary
-life history
-case study
-ecological

Key Concepts Associated with the Approach

-meaning
-common-sense
understanding
-bracketing
-definition of situation
-everyday life

-understanding
-process
-negotiated order
-for all practical purposes
-social construction

Quantitative

Phrases Associated with the Approach

-experimental
-hard data
-outer perspective
-empirical

-positivist
-social facts
-statistical

Key Concepts Associated with the Approach

-variable
-operationalize
-reliability
-hypothesis

-validity
-statistically significant
-replication

(continued)

Qualitative

Names Associated with the Approach

Max Weber
Charles Horton Cooley
Harold Garfinkel
Margaret Mead
Anselm Strauss
Eleanor Leacock
Howard S. Becker
Raymond Rist
Estelle Fuchs

Herbert Blumer
W. I. Thomas
Everett Hughes
Erving Goffman
Harry Wolcott
Rosalie Wax
George Herbert Mead
Barney Glaser
Hugh Mehan

Theoretical Affiliation

–symbolic interaction
–ethnomethodology
–phenomenology

–culture
–idealism

Academic Affiliation

–sociology
–history

–anthropology

Goals

–develop sensitizing
  concepts
–describe multiple realities

–grounded theory
–develop understanding

Quantitative

Names Associated with the Approach

Emile Durkheim
Lee Cronbach
L. Guttman
Gene Glass
Robert Travers
Robert Bales

Fred Kerlinger
Edward Thorndike
Fred McDonald
David Krathwohl
Donald Campbell
Peter Rossi

Theoretical Affiliation

–structural functionalism
–realism, positism
–behavioralism

–logical empiricism
–systems theory

Academic Affiliation

–psychology
–economics

–sociology
–political science

Goals

–theory testing
–establish the facts
–statistical description

–show relationships
  between variables
–prediction

Qualitative	Quantitative
Design	**Design**
–evolving, flexible, general	–structured, predetermined, formal, specific
–design is a hunch as to how you might proceed	–design is a detailed plan of operation
Written Research Proposals	**Written Research Proposals**
–brief	–extensive
–speculative	–detailed and specific in focus
–suggests areas research may be relevant to	–detailed and specific in procedures
–often written after some data has been collected	–through review of substantive literature
–not extensive in substantive literature review	–written prior to data collection
–general statement of approach	–hypotheses stated
Data	**Data**
–descriptive	–quantitative
–personal documents	–quantifiable coding
–field notes	–counts, measures
–photographs	–operationalized variables
–people's own words	–statistical
–official documents and other artifacts	
Sample	**Sample**
–small	–large
–nonrepresentative	–stratified
–theoretical sampling	–control groups
	–precise
	–random selection
	–control for extraneous variables
Techniques or Methods	**Techniques or Methods**
–observation	–experiments
–reviewing various documents and artifacts	–survey research
–participant observation	–structured interviewing
–open-ended interviewing	–quasi experiments
	–structured observation
	–data sets

(continued)

Qualitative

Relationship with Subjects

-empathy
-emphasis on trust
-equalitarian
-intense contact
-subject as friend

Instruments and Tools

-tape recorder
-transcriber
(the researcher is often the only instrument)

Data Analysis

-ongoing
-models, themes, concepts
-inductive
-analytical induction
-constant comparative method

Problems in Using the Approach

-time consuming
-data reduction difficult
-reliability
-procedures not standardized
-difficult studying large populations

Quantitative

Relationship with Subjects

-circumscribed
-short-term
-stay detached
-distant
-subject-researcher

Instruments and Tools

-inventories
-questionnaires
-indexes
-computers
-scales
-test scores

Data Analysis

-deductive
-occurs at conclusion of data collection
-statistical

Problems in Using the Approach

-controlling other variables
-reification
-obtrusiveness
-validity

ETHICS

Like the words *sex* and *snakes, ethics* is emotionally charged, surrounded with hidden meaning. Nothing is more indicting to a professional than to be charged with unethical practices. While the word conjures up images of a supreme authority, ethics in research are the principles of right and wrong that a particular group accepts. Most academic specialities and professions have codes of ethics that set forth these rules. Some codes are thoughtful and help sensitize members to dilemmas and moral issues they must face; others are narrowly conceived and do more to protect the professional group from attack than to set forth a moral position.

Two issues dominate recent guidelines of ethics in research with human subjects: informed consent and the protection of subjects from harm. These guidelines attempt to insure that:

1. Subjects enter research projects voluntarily, understanding the nature of the study and the dangers and obligations that are involved.
2. Subjects are not exposed to risks that are greater than the gains they might derive.

These guidelines are usually implemented through the use of forms that contain the researcher's description of the study, what will be done with the findings, and other pertinent information. The subject's signature on this form is taken as evidence of informed consent. Committees on human subjects now exist in most institutions to review proposals, checking that the proposed research insures proper informed consent, and safety for the participants.

These bureaucratic responses to the concern for exploitation and harm of subjects were precipitated by public exposés of research projects which endangered their human subjects in extraordinarily blatant ways. It was discovered, for example, that upon admission at Willowbrook State School the mentally retarded patients were injected with hepatitus virus as part of a study on vaccines. In another part of the country headlines revealed that, unknown to them, a group of men known to have syphilis were not treated for their condition. Still other experimental subjects were lied to while they participated in and watched what they thought was the electric shocking of other human beings who were actually actors working for the project. It is clear that such abuse must be stopped. It is not clear, however, what the relationship is between the present regulations and what qualitative researchers do (Duster, Matza, and Wellman, 1979; Thorne, 1980; Wax, 1980).

The past few years have generated discussion on a possible code of ethics for qualitative researchers (Cassell, 1978; Cassell and Wax, 1980). Many qualitative researchers have come to the conclusion that the relationship between researcher and subject is so different in the qualitative and quantitative approaches, that following established procedures on informed consent and the protection of subjects seems little more than ritual. In the research for which these guidelines were established, subjects have a very circumscribed relationship to the researcher; they fill out questionnaires or participate in specific experiments. The subjects can be told explicitly the content and possible dangers of the study. With qualitative research, on the other hand, the relationship is ongoing; it evolves over time. Doing qualitative research with subjects is more like having a friendship than a contract. The subjects have a say in regulating the relationship and they continuously make decisions about their participation. While the regulations seem to reflect the studies in which the exact design is completed prior to entering the field, in qualitative research no such designs exist. In submitting a research proposal to human subjects committees, for example, only a ''bare bones'' description of what will occur can generally be included.

While regulations about informed consent and protection of human subjects, as they are traditionally formulated, may not fit the qualitative mode of doing research, these ethical issues are of concern. Although qualitative researchers have not developed a specific written code of ethics, conventions have been established regarding ethics in field work.

As we suggest in Chapter 4, different styles and traditions of field work operate on different ethical principles. We make specific suggestions related to ethics in other chapters, but here we want to lay out some general principles that the majority of mainstream fieldworkers abide by in their research. They also apply more specifically to people who are conducting basic research. As we will suggest in Chapter 7, the following ethical principles may be irrelevant to some forms of applied research, particularly to what we call *action research*.

1. The subjects' identities should be protected so that the information you collect does not embarrass or in other ways harm them. Anonymity should extend not only to writing, but also to the verbal reporting of information that you have learned through observation. The researcher should not relate specific information about individuals to others and should be particularly watchful of sharing information with people at the research site who could choose to use the information in political or personal ways.
2. Treat subjects with respect and seek their cooperation in the research. While some advocate covert research, there is general consensus that under most circumstances the subject should be told of your research interests and should give you permission to proceed. Researchers should neither lie to subjects nor record conversations on hidden mechanical devices.
3. In negotiating permission to do a study, you should make it clear to those with whom you negotiate what the terms of the agreement are, and you should abide by that contract. If you agree to do something in return for permission you should follow through and do it. If you agree not to publish what you find you should not. Because researchers take the promises they make seriously, you must be careful as a researcher to be realistic in such negotiations.
4. Tell the truth when you write up and report your findings. Although for ideological reasons you may not like the conclusions you reach, and although others may put pressure on you to show certain results that your data do not reveal, the most important trademark of a researcher should be his or her devotion to reporting what the data reveals. Fabricating data or distorting data is the ultimate sin of a scientist.

While we have stated four ethical principles, as with all rules, there are exceptions and complications so that in many cases the rules seem extraneous or difficult, if
not impossible, to employ. There are times, for example, when people do research in
which the subject's identity is difficult or impossible to hide. Further, the people involved may state their indifference to publication of their names. The rule of anonymity may, in this case, be waived. Some situations pose difficult dilemmas because
they place the researcher in a position where his or her obligations as a researcher conflict with those of being a citizen. You may, for example, see government corruption
and misuse of funds when studying a school. In studies we have done in state institutions for mentally retarded people, we witnessed the physical abuse of the residents.

What is the ethical responsibility of researchers in these cases? Should they turn
their backs in the name of research? In the case of the physical abuse, the solution
may seem obvious at first: researcher or not, you should intervene to stop the beat-
ings. That was our immediate reaction also, but we came to understand that abuse
was a pervasive activity in most such institutions nationally, not only part of this particular setting. Was blowing the whistle on one act a responsible way to address this
problem or was it a way of getting the matter off our chests? Intervention may get you
kicked out. Might not continuing the research, publishing the results, writing reports
exposing national abuse, and providing research for witnesses in court (or being an
expert witness) do more to change the conditions than the single act of intervention?
Was such thinking a cop out, an excuse not to get involved? Such dilemmas are not
easily resolved by a list of rules. While people may make up guidelines for ethical decision-making, the tough ethical decisions ultimately reside with you, with your
values, and with your judgments of right and wrong. As a researcher you have to
know yourself, your values, and your beliefs. You have to know how to define your
responsibility to other human beings and what your responsibility is when you are
put in contact with their suffering. Qualitative research allows for that contact. For
many qualitative researchers ethical questions do not reside narrowly in the realm of
how to behave in the field. Rather, ethics are understood in terms of their life-long
obligations to the people who have touched their lives in the course of living the life
of a qualitative researcher.

WHAT IS TO COME

Having provided you with a general introduction to the foundations of qualitative research, our goal in the rest of the book is to provide guidance on "how to do it." Although people seasoned in the approach will find it useful, reminding them of certain issues and clarifying particular aspects that have been obscure elsewhere, we
write for the novice, the person taking an introductory course in qualitative research
in education.

The design of the rest of the book is shaped by the five characteristics we have
discussed in this chapter. We first consider the issue of research design, emphasizing
the inductive nature of the approach. In Chapter 3, the descriptive nature of what
qualitative researchers collect is central to our discussion. Here we describe various

forms data can take and present some suggestions for its collection. Chapter 4 is concerned with fieldwork relations. The naturalist nature of the research enterprise as well as the dominance of the researcher as the instrument is clear throughout this discussion. Returning to the inductive character of the approach, we deal extensively in chapter 5 with data analysis. The narrative, descriptive nature of qualitative analysis guides the discussion in Chapter 6, on writing and disseminating findings. Because of the applied concerns of educational research, we have devoted a separate chapter, Chapter 7, to the application of qualitative methods to evaluation, social change, and pedagogical work.

ENDNOTES

1. "Field research" carries a mixed meaning in education. Educational researchers trained in psychology have used it to refer to any research, including experimental, that occurs in nonlaboratory settings. Others with training in sociology and anthropology have used it more specifically, and more narrowly, to refer to the kind of research we are describing.
2. It was not until 1957, however, that actual monies appeared.
3. For rich histories of different aspects of qualitative research, see Burnett, 1978; Carey, 1975; Faris, 1967; Matthews, 1977; Wax, 1971.
4. Roy Stryker of the Farm Security Administration's "Photography Unit."
5. Wax notes, in fact, that Robert Park assigned their book to his sociology students at the University of Chicago.
6. They comment, for example, that: "Our specialty has been a comparative study of the working of particular social institutions in a single country, made by observation and analysis, through personal participation or watching the organization at work, the taking of evidence from other persons, the scrutiny of all accessible documents, and the consultation of general literature" (Webb and Webb, 1932).
7. The following discussion is based on Bartlett et al., 1939; Roberts, 1976; and Wax, 1971.
8. Thomas reports, in fact, that he was influenced by the writings of Boas (Baker, 1973).
9. The opposite point of view in what was an ongoing debate was presented by E. T. Kreuger (who had completed his dissertation at Chicago on personal documents) in two issues of the *Journal of Applied Sociology:* The Technique of Securing Life History Documents 9 (1925): 290–298; and The Value of Life History Documents for Social Research 9 (1925): 196–201.
10. They were both done by women in the 1890s. Hanna B. Clark, *The Public Schools of Chicago: A Sociological Study* (1897); and Ira W. Howerth, *The Social Aim of Education* (1898).
11. Faris (1967) lists all the masters and doctoral dissertations in sociology at the University of Chicago completed between 1893 and 1935 and their authors.
12. Whyte's study is an excellent example of participant observation. The term *participant observer* was first used in 1925 by Eduard Lindeman (1925) in his *Social Discovery,* but originally the term described what we would call an informant. To Lindeman, the participant observer, as opposed to what he called the "objective observer" participated in the activities or setting being studied, not in the research project. His description of the participant observer fits "Doc," Whyte's key informant in Cornersville, to a tee.

13. Interestingly, one of the most well-known photographers of these, Lewis Hine, had photographed for the Pittsburgh Survey, and worked for Paul Kellogg again when he was editor of the journal, *Charity and the Commons* (later *The Survey*).

14. In a discussion of documentary expression of the thirties (Stott, 1973), the author suggests that an important dimension of documents, particularly human documents, is their ability to call forth not only an intellectual response, but also an emotional reaction. Documents, Stott suggests, offer a glimpse "of an inner existence, a private self." It is, perhaps, this aspect of the personal documents Chicago sociologists of the twenties and thirties looked to as data that raised such problems for educational researchers, concerned with well-regulated schedules and the seemingly irrefutable number. If quantification was the scientific watchword, these documents were suspect.

15. There was as yet no such thing as an educational anthropologist, George Spindler announced at a conference on education and anthropology in 1954 (Spindler, 1955), though an article was published in the *Harvard Educational Review* that year with the words "educational anthropology" right in the title (Rosensteil, 1954).

16. He did not write the book; it was compiled from his lectures by his students.

TWO

RESEARCH DESIGN

W<small>E HAVE A FRIEND WHO, WHEN ASKED WHERE SHE IS GOING ON</small> vacation, will tell you the direction she is traveling and then conclude with: "I'll see what happens as I go along." Another friend makes detailed plans, with all the stops (including restaurants) and routes set in advance. "Design" is used in research to refer to the researcher's plan of how to proceed. A qualitative educational researcher is more like the loosely-scheduled traveler than the other.

A strategy qualitative researchers employ in a study is to proceed as if they know very little about the people and places they will visit. They attempt to mentally cleanse their preconceptions. To state exactly how to accomplish their work would be presumptuous. Plans evolve as they learn about the setting, subjects, and other sources of data through direct examination. A full account of procedures is best described in retrospect, a narrative of what actually happened, written after the study is completed. Investigators may enter the research with some idea about what they will do, but a detailed set of procedures is not formed prior to data collection. In addition, qualitative researchers avoid going into a study with hypotheses to test or specific questions to answer, believing that finding the questions should be one of the products of data collection rather than assumed *a priori*. The study itself structures the research, not preconceived ideas or any precise research design.

Qualitative researchers have a design; to suggest not would be misleading. How they proceed is based on theoretical assumptions (that meaning and process are crucial in understanding human behavior, that descriptive data is what is important to collect, and that analysis is best done inductively) and on data collection traditions (like participant observation, unstructured interviewing, and document analysis). These provide the parameters, the tools, and the general guide of how to proceed. It is not that qualitative research design is nonexistent; it is rather that design is flexible. Qualitative researchers go off to study carrying the mental tools of their trade, with plans formulated as hunches, only to be modified and remolded as they proceed.

Traditional researchers speak of the design of a study as the product of the planning stage of research. The design is then implemented, the data collected and analyzed, and then the writing is done. While qualitative studies take a similar course, the various stages are not so segmented. Design decisions are made throughout the study—at the end as well as the beginning. Although the most intensive period of data analysis usually occurs in the later stages, data analysis is an ongoing part of the research. Decisions about design and analysis may be made together. In this chapter on design there will be information helpful to understand analysis; similarly, Chapter 5 (Data Analysis) contains useful ideas about design.

This general description of design is the common ground that most qualitative researchers stand on, but not all qualitative researchers embrace design as we have described it. Some are more structured. They may prepare interview schedules and stick to them. Others are even less structured, drifting through data without ever consciously formulating a plan. The particular tradition they are working from affects where they stand; so do research goals and research experience.

This chapter is about design. Our discussion begins with the factors to consider in choosing a topic to study. We then discuss design as it relates to specific types of "case" and "multiple data source" studies. In pursuing the topic of design as it relates to multiple data source studies, we present two designs that have been used to generate grounded theory: analytic induction and the constant comparative method.

CHOOSING A STUDY

Decisions are made throughout any qualitative study. The first are: What should I study? What kind of data should I explore? What specific approach should I take? Do not get bogged down trying to come up with the "right" answer to such questions. While such decisions are important, they are not right or wrong. If you decide on one school over another, your study may turn out differently, but not necessarily better or worse. The exact decisions you make are not always crucial, but it *is* crucial that you make them.

Experienced researchers often have a research agenda. They have thought about how they want to spend their research life—what they would like to study, and what they hope to accomplish. They look for opportunities to carry out that work. Some are so clear about this agenda that they refuse research opportunities because they do not fit into their master plan. For the novice researcher, however, the question of what to study is more perplexing. One's research agenda is developed from a number of sources. Often a person's own biography will be an influence in defining the thrust of his or her work. Particular topics, settings, or people are of interest because they have touched one's life in some important way. Others get started in an area because a professor or someone else they know is doing related research. Sometimes it is even more idiosyncratic: an opportunity arises; you wake up with an idea; you are out doing what you normally do and you come across some material that strikes your fancy. However a topic comes to you, whatever it is, it should be important to you and excite you. Self-discipline can only take you so far in research. Without a touch of passion you may not have enough to sustain the effort to follow the work to the end, or to go beyond doing the ordinary. If someone asks you to undertake a study, be sure it is of sufficient interest to you to maintain your spirit. Of all the thousands of topics and data sources in the world, do not burden yourself with one you find boring.

While the choices are endless, some advice is in order. The first is, be practical. Pick a study that seems reasonable in size and complexity so that it can be completed within the time and resources available. Also take into account your own skill which, at this time, is likely to be untested and underdeveloped. We will have more specific suggestions later about practicality in relation to particular kinds of studies. Qualitative research tends to take a lot of time; it is labor-intensive research. Try to limit the number of hours you clock in and the number of pages of data you review. Try to get a good concentration of information rather than widely scattered pieces.

The location of your data sources can be critical. Before starting a project it may not matter that you have to travel across town to a school, or to another city to look at official documents or interview teachers. But, as you get into your work, travel can become burdensome. It drags the work out, limiting your access and therefore your involvement. Without your data source close by, you cannot spontaneously jump in and out of the field.

The second suggestion is to study something in which you are not directly involved. If you teach at a school, for example, do not choose that school as a study site. In spite of the fact that successful studies have been accomplished by people who were personally involved in the places they study (see, for example, McPherson, 1972; Rothstein,1975), we advise you, the novice, to pick places where you are more or less a stranger. "Why? Don't I have a jump on an outsider studying my own school? I have excellent rapport and I have guaranteed access." This may be true and at times these may be sufficient reasons to ignore our advice, but, especially for a first study, the reasons are compelling. People who are intimately involved in a setting find it difficult to distance themselves both from personal concerns and from their common-sense understandings of what is going on. For them, more often than not, their opinions are more than "definitions of the situation"; they are *the* truth.

Others in the setting in which you are doing your research, if they know you well, are not used to relating to you as a neutral observer. Rather, they see you as a teacher, or as a member of a particular group, as a person who has opinions and interests to represent. They may not feel free to relate to you as a researcher to whom they can speak freely. A teacher, for example, studying his or her own school, might not expect the principal to be straightforward in discussing evaluations of fellow teachers, or decisions that he or she is making about hiring and firing.

Conducting a study with people you know can be confusing and upsetting. Becoming a researcher means more than learning specific skills and procedures. It involves changing your way of thinking about yourself, and your relations with others. It involves feeling comfortable with the role of "researcher." If people you know are your research subjects, the transition from your old self to your researcher self becomes ambiguous.

We are providing advice, but our suggestions are not rigid. You, the novice, might think that you are sufficiently sophisticated, or have a relationship with friends such that you do not have to worry about these issues. So be it. Give it a try; if it works, great; if it does not, we do not promise not to tell you "we told you so."

Another bit of advice: Have preferences, but do not be single-minded in choices. In the beginning you never know what you are going to find. Do not rigidly adhere to prestudy plans. Treat your initial visits as exploratory opportunities to assess what is feasible. If you have a particular interest you may choose subjects or settings where you think these will be manifest, only to find them not there. Be prepared to modify your expectations, change your design, or else you may spend too much time searching for "the right study" when it might not exist.

We have discussed choosing a study as if it does not matter what you choose. Qualitative researchers generally share the belief that you can drop a qualitative researcher off anywhere and he or she will come back with important findings. This position contrasts with the novice's fear only a "great" site will produce worthwhile findings. There may be some truth in the qualitative researcher's optimism, but all sites are not as easy or as interesting to research.

Some topics and settings are difficult to study because those that grant you permission to be there ("gatekeepers") or the subjects themselves are hostile to outsiders. Under those circumstances it can take months to acquire permission and extensive time to get cooperation. As a novice researcher, you may want to avoid such settings. Deciding what to study always involves assessing who is involved, taking into account the feasibility of access. Who, for example, are the gatekeepers of the files (or of the settings and subjects in which you are interested) and what is the likelihood you can get to them? In Chapter 4, in which we cover researcher relationships, we will discuss "getting in" and negotiating initial relationships with sponsors and subjects. We leave the question of access until then.

In addition to considerations of access, a study's potential significance is something to consider. Some research is relevant to issues that are of crucial importance to education or to the society as a whole. In addition, certain topics and sites have been studied over and over again, while others are relatively unexplored. While interests are paramount, you may want to take into account the state of the field in which you work and the salient issues of our time in choosing a research problem.

CASE STUDIES

Thus far we have discussed the first problem: choosing a study. One of the suggestions was to be practical in choosing a topic and a data source that are compatible with your resources and skills. It is by no accident that most researchers choose for their first project a *case study*. A case study is a detailed examination of one setting, or one single subject, or one single depository of documents, or one particular event. Case studies vary in their complexity; both novices and experienced researchers do them, but characteristically they are easier to accomplish than multi-site or multi-subject studies (Scott, 1965). Start with a case study. Have a successful first experience and then move on, if you choose, to the more complex.

The general design of a case study is best represented by a funnel. The start of the study is the wide end: the researchers scout for possible places and people that might be the subject or the source of data, find the location they think they want to study, and then cast a net widely trying to judge the feasibility of the site or data source for their purposes. They look for clues on how they might proceed and what might be feasible to do. They begin to collect data, reviewing and exploring it, and making decisions about where to go with the study. They decide how to distribute their time, who to interview and what to explore in depth. They may throw aside old ideas and plans and develop new ones. They continually modify the design and choose procedures as they learn more about the topic of study. In time, they make specific decisions on what aspect of the setting, subject, or data source they will study. Their work develops a focus. The data collection and research activities narrow to sites, subjects, materials, topics, and themes. From broad exploratory beginnings they move to more directed data collection and analysis. This process is more fully discussed in Chapter 5.

There are many different types of qualitative case studies. Each type has special considerations for determining its feasibility for study as well as the procedures to employ.

Historical Organizational Case Studies. These studies concentrate on a particular organization over time, tracing the organization's development. One might do a study, for example, of a "free school," tracing how it came into being, what its first year was like, what changes occurred over time, what it is like now (if it is still operating), or how it came to close (if it did). You will rely on data sources such as interviews with people who have been associated with the organization, observations of the present school, and existing written records. If your intention is to do this type of study, do some preliminary checking on who is available to interview and what documents have been preserved. Many times historical organizational case studies are not possible, simply because the sources are insufficient for a minimally acceptable piece of work. The determination that sufficient material in your initial inventory of people and documents exists, provides a starting point as well as the design for your data collection.

Observational Case Studies. In these studies the major data-gathering technique is participant observation and the focus of the study is on a particular organization (school, rehabilitation center) or some aspect of the organization. Parts of the organization that become a foci in organizational studies are typically the following:

1. A particular place in the organization (a classroom, the teachers' room, the cafeteria).
2. A specific group of people (members of the high school basketball team, teachers in a particular academic department).
3. Some activity of the school (such as curriculum planning or courtship).

Often studies use a combination of these listed aspects for their focus. In a study of high schools, for example, Cusick (1973) focused on sociability (an activity) among students (a group). While observational case studies often include an historical treatment of the setting, this is supplementary to a concern with the contemporary scene.

The researcher will often choose an organization, such as a school, and then focus on some aspect of it. Picking a focus, be it a place in the school, a particular group, or some other aspect, is always an artificial act, for you break off a piece of the world that is normally integrated. The qualitative researcher tries to take into account the relationship of this piece to the whole, but, out of necessity, narrows the subject matter to make the research manageable. Detaching a piece to study distorts, but the researcher attempts to choose a piece that is a naturally existing unit. (The part that is chosen is one that the participants themselves see as distinct and the observer recognizes as having a distinct identity of its own.)

The researcher has to examine the organization to see what places, groups, or programs offer feasible concentrations. After visiting a school a few times you should be able to determine the choices. A good physical setting to study is one that the same people use in a recurring way. In public schools, of course, you can count on classrooms, an office, and usually a teachers' lounge, but even here you cannot be certain these are feasible to study. Some schools, for example, do not have a teachers' lounge. In other schools, classrooms may not be the physical units that organize pupils and teachers.

Physical units are not the only foci for study, but the issues are similar. Some researchers enter an organization with a very specific idea in mind of what it is they want to study—a new reading program. They arrive at the school only to discover that the teacher who was supposed to implement the program has moved, and the new teacher has dropped the plan. This happens more often than you think. Have preferences, but let the focus evolve from the setting.

When we talk about a *group* in an organization as the foci of study, we are using the word sociologically to refer to a collection of people who interact, who identify with each other, and who share expectations about each others' behavior. People who share characteristics such as age, race, sex, or organizational position may not, however, share "group" membership. Such characteristics may provide the basis of friendship or colloquiality, but the people who share such characteristics do not necessarily form a group. People often enter a setting planning an observational study of, for example, Chicano teachers, only to find out that Chicano teachers in the particular school they have chosen do not spend their time together, and apparently do not hold group identity. Before you make a decision to study a group, you have to know the informal structure of the school.

Individuals who share a particular trait, but do not form groups, can be subjects in a qualitative study, but interviewing is usually a better approach here than participant observation. What they share will emerge more clearly when you individually solicit their perspectives rather than observe their activities. Similarly, sharing the same organizational positions does not necessarily mean that people form a group. All science teachers in a high school have something in common, but in certain schools their contact may be so irregular that they do not form a group. In another school, however, the science department might have regular meetings, eat lunch together, and make a good unit to study.

In choosing a setting or group as the focus of an observational case study, keep in mind that the smaller the number of subjects the more likely you are to change their behavior by your presence. Obviously, hooking up with two students who have a romantic relationship, if such a hook-up were tolerated, would change what went on significantly. A larger number of subjects, on the other hand, usually makes it easier to be unobtrusive. It is keeping track of everyone and managing all the data and relationships present that becomes difficult. For your first study, try to pick a setting or a group that is large enough so that you do not stick out, but small enough so that you are not overwhelmed by the task. This simple rule regarding the size of a setting does not, however, always work. Schools provide some unique and challenging rapport problems that defy the rule. Although there may be twenty-five people in a setting of an elementary school classroom, for example, there is only one adult. Adding the researcher as the second adult may alter the relationships to make it difficult for the observer to be unobtrusive. (For discussions of this concern, see Fine and Glassner, 1979; Smith and Geoffrey, 1968.)

Life History. In this form of case study, the researcher conducts extensive interviews with one person for the purpose of collecting a first-person narrative. When this type of interviewing is done by historians it is referred to as *oral history*. Historians who do this kind of work often interview famous people (presidents and generals) to get the details of history as the people interviewed participated in it. When they interview less famous people (domestics or farmers, for instance), they are more interested in how history appears from the point of view of the "common person." Sociological or psychological first-person life histories collected through case study interviewing are usually directed at using the person as a vehicle to understand basic aspects of human behavior or existing institutions rather than history. Here, the concept of "career" is often used to organize data collection and presentation. Career refers to the various positions, stages, and ways of thinking people pass through in the course of their lives (Hughes, 1934). Sociological life histories often try to construct subjects' careers emphasizing the role of organizations, crucial events, and significant others in shaping subjects' evolving definitions of self and their perspectives on life.

The feasibility of a life history case study is mostly determined by the nature of the potential subject. Is the person articulate and does he or she have a good memory? Has the person lived through the kinds of experiences and participated in the types of organizations or events you want to explore? Does he or she have the time to give? Researchers who do these kinds of case studies usually fall into them. The do not decide on the "type" of subject they want to interview and then go out looking for an example. Rather, they meet a person who strikes them as a good subject and then decide to pursue it. The feasibility and design of such a study is usually determined either on the basis of initial conversations or during the first few interviews. At the onset of a life history study, when the subject and the interviewer do not know each other well, discussion usually covers impersonal matters. Over time, the content becomes more revealing, the researcher probes more closely, and a focus emerges. Life history interviews can involve over one hundred hours of tape-recorded meetings and over 1,000 pages of transcripts. While some life history interviews are directed at capturing the subjects' rendering of their whole lives, from birth to present, others are more limited. They seek data on a particular period in the person's life, like adolescence or elementary school, or on a particular topic, like friendships or courting. (For discussions of the life history method, see Becker, 1970b, Denzin, 1970, chapter 10; and Dollard, 1935. For oral history see McAdoo, 1976; and Shumway and Hartley, 1973.)

There are many other forms of case studies. Some researchers do *community studies*. These are similar to organizational or observational case studies, except the study focuses on a neighborhood or community rather than on a school or other organization. Another form of case study has been termed *situational analysis*. In this type, a particular event (the expulsion of a student from school, for example) is studied from the points of view of all the participants (the student, his or her friends, the parents, the principal, the teacher that initiated the action). Case records may be drawn upon extensively. *Microethnography* is a phrase used in several ways, but most often it refers to case studies done either on very small units of an organization (a part of a classroom) or on a very specific organizational activity (children learning how to draw). While educational anthropologists usually employ this label, ethnomethodologists claim it as well (see Erickson, 1975; Smith and Geoffrey, 1968). Whatever the variety of case study you choose, evaluating how feasible a project is to undertake is often fairly self-evident. You cannot, for example, do a case study or use student records without access.

A few general issues concerning design within the confines of the case study approach need discussion. We referred to one in the first chapter in the discussion of generalizability. People who are in search of a setting or a subject for a case study often feel in a quandary about whether to look for a so-called "typical" situation (one that is similar to most others of the type) or an "unusual" one (clearly an exceptional case). Let us say that you decide to study an urban third-grade class. Should you attempt to find out beforehand what the average size of third-grade classes in American cities is, and the average years of experience third-grade teachers have, and the typical racial and ethnic composition of third-grade classes, choosing your class on the basis of that? Or should you pick a class in which the teacher is trying a new reading program or a new grouping arrangement, or perhaps select the only class in the city that has a child with Down's Syndrome? Should you choose a teacher with a reputation for excellence or one who seems to be having problems?

All the characteristics we have already mentioned that might be associated with the third grade suggest that it is difficult to pick a third-grade class that you could say is typical without being challenged. Even so, some people will try to pick a setting that is not so demonstratively different to forestall the possible charge that it is an oddball case. Researchers who choose to go the "typical case" route are concerned about generalizability as it is traditionally defined. They want to learn something about third-grade classes in general through studying one class. As we have suggested, they are likely to be challenged in making such decisions and therefore either do not make them or leave it up to the reader to come to their own conclusions concerning generalizability. Some researchers lay claim to generalizability on the basis of the similarity of their case study to others reported in the literature.

Purposely choosing the unusual or just falling into a study leaves the question of generalizability up in the air. Where does the setting fit in the spectrum of human events? This question is not answered by the selection itself, but has to be explored as part of the study. The researcher has to determine what it is he or she is studying; that is, of what is this a case? Most qualitative researchers are skeptical of conventionally defined categories anyway, and do not assume that things called by the same name or having the same superficial characteristics are necessarily similar. They feel that the researcher should examine assumptions about what belongs in categories rather than having these assumptions determine the research design. As we said at the start of this chapter, some decisions are not good or bad in themselves; they are just a matter of choice. The "typical" or "unusual" decision is probably one of those kinds of decisions.

We have discussed the general approach researchers take in case-study design, but we have not discussed *internal sampling*. By internal sampling we mean the decisions you make once you have a general idea of what you are studying, with whom to talk, what time of day to observe, and how many documents and what kinds to review. Narrowing the focus of your study will, in many cases, make it possible to examine the entire population of interest; that is, you will talk to everyone in the group, all the people in the setting, or review all the documents present. If you cannot see everything and talk to everybody, you want to make sure that you sample widely enough so that a diversity of types are explored. You want to understand the range of materials and the range of perspectives present. You also make choices, however, on the basis of the quality of the data produced. As we discuss in the next chapter, some subjects are more willing to talk, have a greater experience in the setting, or are especially insightful about what goes on. These people become *key informants* and often you will talk with them, compared to other subjects, a disproportionate amount of time. There are dangers in relying exclusively on a small number of subjects, but you should not approach internal sampling with the idea that you have to spend the same amount of time with everyone. Similarly, with documents and other material, some pieces of data are simply richer and deserve more attention.

In regard to *time sampling,* often the time you visit a place or person will affect the nature of the data you collect. Schools are different at the start of the year than at the end. Similarly, the morning routine in the class can be quite different from the afternoon. Documents collected at one historical time are different from another. What time periods the data represent will depend on the time constraints the researcher faces as well as their research interests. If the focus is a particular class, you may want to sample widely from different times of the day, week, and year. If you decide to study a playground before the school day begins, the sampling concerns differ.

Like most decisions qualitative researchers must make, those relating to choice of informants and allocation of your time are always made in the context of the study. These choices must make sense for your purposes in your particular situation. They logically flow both from the premises of the qualitative approach and from the contingencies of the study as these become apparent in the course of the work. Often the researcher steps back to ask, "If I do it this way, what am I missing? What am I gaining?" The more aware you are about the ramifications of the choices, the better chances you have to choose wisely.

Another design issue involves the amount of time you should set aside for a case study. In many instances you know how much time you have or want to devote to the study and you design the study with those limits in mind. You narrow the study, trying to get a piece that you can manage to complete in the time you have set aside. You may, for example, say that you want to complete data collection in four months and set aside two days a week to devote to the work. As is most often the case, after collecting data for a while you get a sense that you underestimated the time you need. You adjust for the mistake by either increasing the amount of time per week you work on it, extending your time line, or narrowing your focus more.

Some people start studies by devoting a certain amount of time per week to it and leaving the question of how long it will take up in the air. In this approach (and to some extent, in adjusting schedules for studies where the time limit is predetermined), qualitative researchers gauge when they are finished by what they term *data saturation,* the point of data collection where the information you get becomes redundant. Of course, you always learn more by staying in the study, but what happens is that you get to a point of diminishing returns. It is the period where you learn a decreasing amount for the time you spend. The trick is to find that point and bow out. Of course, if you do not have a clearly defined goal you can go on and on, switching your focus and collecting data more or less randomly. One difficulty in case studies is that the subject matter continually changes. When something new happens in the setting that is of interest, the temptation rises to redefine the goals and to continue the study. Be flexible, but to do analysis and to complete the study, you have to define a finishing point. You should realize that most researchers collect too much data. They have more data than they can even analyze. The data for a typical dissertation study usually runs 700 to 1,500 pages of field notes or interview transcripts.

We have provided a general overview to the case study approach. Great diversity exists within the types of case studies we have discussed. One important distinction has to do with whether the researcher is interested in substantive or theoretical conclusions. A more substantively focused study on a classroom, for example, would be one that attempted to understand the dynamics of classroom behavior and the relationship between teacher and pupils. You could also use the classroom, however, to study more basic social processes such as the negotiation of order between the various parties. In the first case, you are using qualitative research to tell you something about schools; in the latter, the classroom provides a place to conduct research to generate theory about human relationships in general. That the research setting is a classroom is of primary importance in the first instance, and relatively unimportant in the second.

Most people think that case studies are only descriptive. Although they tend to be descriptive, there are a variety of goals and forms they can take—the theoretical and abstract, as well as the very concrete. (For examples of case studies, see Erickson, 1976; Florio, 1978; Rist, 1973; Smith and Geoffrey, 1968; and Wolcott, 1973.)

When researchers study two or more subjects, settings, or depositories of data, they are doing *multi-case studies*. Multi-case studies take a variety of forms. Some start as a single case only to have the original work serve as the first in a series of studies or as the pilot for a multi-case study. Other studies are primarily single-case studies but include less intense, less extensive observations at other sites for the purpose of addressing the question of generalizability. Other researchers do *comparative case studies*. Two or more case studies are done and then compared and contrasted (see, for example, Lightfoot, 1978; McIntyre, 1969). Multi-case studies follow most of the suggestions already made. If you are conducting additional data collection to show generalizability or diversity, your concern should be picking additional sites that will illustrate the range of settings or subjects to which your original observation might be applicable. If you are doing a second case study to compare and contrast, you pick a second site on the basis of the extent, presence, or absence of some particular characteristic of the original study. If integration is your focus, for example, you may want to examine an urban, racially-balanced third-grade class if you studied a suburban third grade where the number of minority students was minimal.

After you finish your first case, you will find in multi-case studies that subsequent cases are easier; they take less time than the first. Not only have you improved your technique, but also the first case study will have provided a focus to define the parameters of the others.

MULTI-SITE STUDIES

There are research designs used in qualitative research that call for multiple site and subject studies that are considerably different than the ones we have discussed so far. They employ a different logic than the multi-case study approach because they are oriented more toward developing theory and they usually require many sites or subjects rather than two or three. They require that those who do them have both experience in thinking theoretically as well as some skills in data collection prior to embarking on them. This type of research project is difficult to accomplish for a first undertaking. We provide a brief description of two of these approaches, however, not only to give you some idea if you do want to attempt them, but also to make you familiar with the range of designs that comprise qualitative research. While you may not want to conduct a complete study using these models, many elements of these designs can be incorporated into case studies.

Modified Analytic Induction

Analytic induction is an approach to collecting and analyzing data as well as a way to develop theory and test it. It has had a long and controversial history (Becker, 1963; Denzin, 1978; McCall and Simmons, 1969; Robinson, 1951; Turner, 1953), though the version of the approach we present here differs somewhat from the way early practitioners employed it (Cressey, 1950; Lindesmith, 1947; Znaniecki, 1934). The procedure of analytic induction is employed when some specific problem, question, or issue becomes the focus of research. Data is collected and analyzed to develop a descriptive model that encompasses all cases of the phenomena. It has been used extensively in open-ended interviewing, but it can be used with participant observation and documented analysis as well.

To be concrete, we will illustrate the procedure with a hypothetical study. Jonah Glenn is interested in teacher effectiveness. He thinks that some teachers do a better job at teaching than others and is interested in understanding why (Blase, 1980). That is his general topic and focus. He starts his study with an indepth interview of one teacher whom someone has recommended as particularly "effective." He has a long open-ended tape-recorded discussion with the teacher. He encourages her to talk about her career, her thoughts about teaching and how they have changed over time, and about the question of effectiveness.

During the interview, the teacher describes in detail her disillusionment during her first few weeks teaching when her optimism (concerning what she thought she could accomplish, her plans about how she would conduct herself, and the nature of her relationship with students) confronted "the reality" of her new job. A teacher for twenty years, she describes a variety of issues: the ups and downs of her career, the changing definitions about her role, some of her first teaching experiences, the relationship of her work to her personal life, and what a good teacher is all about for her. In addition, she discusses schools she has taught in and how particular aspects of them contributed to her satisfaction, as well as to her performance in class. She describes her current position and evaluates it in relation to her perceived effectiveness. As a supplement to the interview, Jonah visits the teacher's school and observes her in action.

From that initial interview and observation, Jonah Glenn develops a loose descriptive theory of teacher effectiveness. It consists of a career-stage model in which effectiveness is defined differently at various periods in the teacher's career. The problems faced, and decisions made about how to meet them are included in the theory. It also integrates the teacher's personal life with her professional life to explain effectiveness. Particular aspects of schools and the teacher's relationships with others are also included. The theory consists of propositional statements and a diagram of career and career contingencies as they relate to effectiveness. In addition, his formulation defines effectiveness and explains its dimensions. After Jonah has sketched out his theory, he picks a second teacher to interview. In picking the first few teachers, Jonah used the *snowball sampling technique;* that is, he asked the first person he interviewed to recommend others. He interviewed the second in a similar open-ended manner, withholding the theory he developed on the basis of his first interview.

After the second interview, Jonah rewrites and modifies the theory to fit the new case. He continues choosing and interviewing new people, modifying the theory to fit each new case. After a few interviews, Jonah chooses subjects he hopes will provide examples of *negative cases,* teachers who he thinks will not fit the evolving model. The first few interviews, for example, were all done with teachers born and raised in the city in which they were working. He suspects that mobile teachers have different career patterns and define effectiveness differently. Jonah purposely seeks out mobile teachers to test his theory. He proceeds in this manner, picking new subjects, enlarging the theory, until he no longer comes across any case that does not fit the theory. At the conclusion of the study, he has a theory about effective teachers.

The hypothetical study just presented would probably not go exactly the way we described it. Often you start out with a question and conduct an interview only to learn that the way you have been thinking about the topic does not match the data you are getting. Teachers may not, for example, think in terms of effectiveness. Typically, the first few interviews result in the formulation of the questions or the problem rather than in specific propositional statements. In addition, although the strategy of the design is to conduct interviews until you find no cases that your theory does not fit, this task is too large for most researchers to accomplish in the time they have. Thus some researchers limit their study to tightly defining the population the theory is encompassing. You could decide, for example, to interview teachers in only one school. The theory you develop then would be a theory of teacher effectiveness for the teachers in that school. Similarly, some researchers, prior to the study, decide on the number of subjects they know they will have the time and resources to interview. They develop a theory based on that number, making no claim for the inclusiveness of their work.

Not only is the theory modified during the research process to fit all new facts that arise, but the research question can also be redefined (narrowed) to exclude the cases that defy explanation by it. By choosing what categories to include or exclude, you also control the scope of the work by limiting the theory's scope.

The type of design we are discussing does not allow you to say anything about distribution frequency of the particular types included in your theory. You might find, for example, that to understand teacher effectiveness it is important to think in terms of the teacher effectiveness of beginning teachers, of midcareer teachers, and near-retirement teachers. This research procedure insures that a variety of types of subjects are included, but it does not tell you how many, nor in what proportion the types appear in the population. The method of sampling in analytic induction is *purposeful sampling.* You choose particular subjects to include because they are believed to facilitate the expansion of the developing theory. This is not *random sampling;* that is, sampling to insure that the characteristics of the subjects in your study appear in the same proportion they appear in the total population.

To summarize, this modified version of analytic induction includes:

1. Early in the research you develop a rough definition and explanation of the particular phenomenon.
2. You hold the definition and explanation up to the data as it is collected.
3. You modify the definition and/or explanation as you encounter new cases that do not fit the definition and explanation as formulated.

4. You actively seek cases that you think may not fit into the formulation.
5. You redefine the phenomenon and reformulate the explanation until a universal relationship is established, using each negative case to call for a redefinition or reformulation (Robinson, 1951).

The design does not follow the funnel model we presented earlier. The analysis indeed becomes more encompassing as new cases are presented, although the developing theory usually becomes more refined.

The steps just outlined represent a method of thinking about and working with data. Most qualitative studies borrow parts of the general procedure and employ it more casually. The term *working hypothesis* is sometimes used by participant observers, and some of the procedures of analytic induction are closely aligned to that.

The Constant Comparative Method

As we have suggested, designs of all qualitative studies involve the combination of data collection with analysis. This is clear in the modified version of analytic induction we presented. Analysis and data collection occurred in a pulsating fashion—first the interview, then the analysis and theory development, another interview, and then more analysis, and so on—until the research is completed. In most forms of case studies, the emerging themes guide data collection, but formal analysis and theory development does not occur until after the data collection is near completion. The constant comparative method is a research design for multi-data sources, which is like analytic induction in that the formal analysis begins early in the study and is nearly completed by the end of data collection. As you will see in our discussion, the constant comparative method differs from analytic induction in a number of respects.

We start with a hypothetical and somewhat oversimplified example of how an educational researcher might proceed using this complicated approach. Mary Schriver is about to arrive at an elementary school to begin a rather lengthy study using the constant comparative method. While she has no investment in any specific topic, she is interested in teachers, so she decides (and has received permission) to observe in the teachers' lounge. Her plan is to start there and see what emerges. The first day on the site is awkward, but inspite of all the self-conscious introductions and explanations of what she is doing there, she does have a chance to hear many conversations teachers have with each other. She is struck immediately by how much of the talk that goes on is about other people: teachers talk about students, other teachers, and administrators. The tone of the talk varies from humor to anger, and some of the conversations halt when certain people enter the room. The next day, Ms. Schriver returns to the same room and hears more of the same kinds of conversation. She decides to study this talk and she tentatively terms it "gossip." From then on, Mary concentrates her data-collecting activities on incidents of gossip. She tries to get material on the diversity of kinds and types. Although the teachers' lounge is central to her activities, as she gets to know the teachers she leaves the room with them to collect data in other places, both in and out of school. She learns of special places, less conspicuous than the teachers' lounge, where particular teachers meet and talk together. She listens to those conversations.

She begins to examine how people talk about each other only to discover that "gossip" is only one type of a larger category she has come to call "people talk." As she works, her data suggest to her a number of areas for exploration. They include: the members of the school staff who engage in "people talk"; the content of "people talk," for instance, the persons discussed; the levels of intensity of "people talk"; and the behavior that stems from "people talk." As she collects data on these different issues, she begins to delineate other types of "people talk" besides gossip. She begins to see, for example, that certain types of "people talk" only occur between teachers who define themselves as "close." She terms this "friendship people talk." Other types of "people talk" occur in mixed groups—"mixed group people talk." She notes the wide variety of subjects of "people talk": the central office staff, the principal, teachers in friendship groups, teachers not in groups, students who are high achievers, and students who are low achievers. Some of the "people talk" she notices is "bad news people talk" and other is "good news people talk."

Mary examines the data, coding and reworking it in an attempt to see the connections between who talks and what is talked about, in order to understand the dimensions of "people talk." All through this work she writes about what she discovers and attempts to expand her category by drawing models and writing about it. A theory of "people talk" is developing, but it is limited to the one setting. While she has stayed in one school, Mary has located herself in different places in the school, and has talked with different groups to enlarge the number of incidents observed, and to get at new properties and dimensions of the general category "people talk."

As part of Mary's emerging theory she also begins to see that who talks to whom and what is said in regard to "people talk" relates to ongoing patterns of friendship as well as formal hierarchy in the whole school district. After observing in the original school she goes to another, purposely picking one that has recently opened in the same district. The idea behind her choice is that friendship patterns in this new school may differ, providing a good setting to enlarge the emerging theory of "people talk." Similarly, Mary then chooses an open-space private school, which prides itself in its participatory decision-making structure, as a likely place to collect more incidents of teacher talk to enlarge the theory.

In each of the new sites she chooses, she limits her data collection to incidents related to "people talk," trying to develop new dimensions of the category and working to integrate the new dimensions into the emerging theory, thus enlarging it. Up to this point she has regularly been writing about the data she collects with a mind to working out aspects of the theory of "people talk."

We leave Mary here, but if we continued with her on her research journey we would see her pick new sites to broaden her theory while integrating the new material back into the developing theory. She may go on doing this for as many as forty sites. The decision to stop would be based on her assessing that she has exhausted the dimensions of the categories—the point of "theoretical saturation"—and has developed a theory of "people talk" in schools. (She could go on to enlarge her category and develop a theory of "people talk" in general.)

To recount the steps in the constant comparative method of developing theory:

1. Begin collecting data.
2. Look for key issues, recurrent events, or activities in the data that become categories of focus.
3. Collect data that provide many incidents of the categories of focus with an eye to seeing the diversity of the dimensions under the categories.
4. Write about the categories you are exploring, attempting to describe and account for all the incidents you have in your data while continually searching for new incidents.
5. Work with the data and emerging model to discover basic social processes and relationships.
6. Engage in sampling, coding, and writing as the analysis focuses on the core categories (Glaser, 1978).

As Glaser notes, although you can talk about the constant comparative method as a series of steps, what has just been describe goes on all at once, and the analysis keeps doubling back to more data collection and coding.

The procedure we described is complex and requires an ability to think analytically (categories and their properties are difficult to grasp), but it is an important way of controlling the scope of data collecting and making multiple-site studies theoretically relevant. The constant comparative method, although it may rely on descriptive data to present the theory, transcends the purposes of descriptive case studies. Although those who formulated the constant comparative method (Glaser and Strauss, 1967) suggest their approach is applicable to any kind of data, it is most often used in conjunction with multiple-site, participant observation studies.

ADDITIONAL ISSUES RELATED TO DESIGN

Proposal Writing

Prior to conducting research, people are often asked to write a statement about how they will conduct their study and what the potential contribution of their work will be. Students write them for their professors or for dissertation committees, researchers write them to potential funders. In addition, many researchers write such plans for themselves to help them think through the research problems they may face. As you might guess, those that choose a qualitative research design sometimes have a difficult time describing what they are going to do prior to conducting their research. This often creates problems, especially when those who want to see the proposal are not familiar with the evolving nature of the qualitative design.

This problem can be handled in two ways. First, you can conduct some of the work prior to writing the proposal. After reviewing some data and being in the field for a while, you are in a much better position to discuss what your plans are and what the likely focus of the study will be. You will be able to discuss emerging themes if you write the proposal after doing initial data collection. Of course, you will be sure neither of the outcome of the study at the time of the preliminary observations nor of exactly how to proceed to the rest of the study, but you are in a better position to make an educated guess. In addition, the discussion you engage in can be much more concrete and therefore much more likely to satisfy the curiosity of the proposal readers.

A second alternative is to write a proposal without preliminary observations. Such proposals are necessarily highly speculative; at best they are a rough guess about how you are going to proceed and what the issues to examine might be. This type of proposal is more of an exercise to show those who read it that you are conversant with the qualitative research literature and are imaginative in your thinking about the issues, than an actual, concrete description of what you will do. These proposals can provide an opportunity for you to review the literature, but they are often not very helpful in conceptualizing the study. Those who are reading the proposal, on the other hand, need some indication of your intentions and your familiarity with the issues, if they are to take a chance and allow you to proceed.

Interview Schedules and Observer Guides

We have discussed research design as an evolving process, one in which the questions to be asked and the data to be collected emerge in the process of doing research. There are times, however, when researchers enter the field with an interview schedule or an observational guide. In keeping with the qualitative tradition of attempting to capture the subjects' own words, and letting the analysis emerge, interview schedules and observation guides generally allow for open-ended responses and are flexible enough for the observer to note and collect data on unexpected dimensions of the topic.

Schedules and guides are most commonly used in multi-subject studies and multi-site team research work; that is, in particiant observation studies where a number of researchers are working at different sites. Schedules and guides are used primarily to gather comparable data across sites. If in each site or with each subject similar data is collected you can make some statements concerning the distribution of facts that you gather. While this is important in certain studies, concern with following a schedule rather than with understanding the data can undermine the major strength of the qualitative approach. Qualitative studies that report how many people do this and how many people do that, rather than generating concepts and understanding, are not highly regarded by qualitative researchers. More accurately, they are a poor use of qualitative resources when such data can be collected more easily and cheaply using other methods.

Team Research and the Lone Ranger

The great majority of qualitative research is what is termed *Lone-Ranger research;* that is, the researcher single-handedly faces the empirical world, going off alone to return with the results. More and more qualitative research, however, is undertaken in teams. Some classic qualitative educational research studies, in fact, were accomplished with teams. *Boys in White* (Becker et al., 1961) and *Making the Grade* (Becker et al., 1968), the first a study of medical students, the second a study of university undergraduates, used three and four researchers to collect the data. Unless you become part of a funded study, you are more likely to do a study alone, but you should know that team research can be satisfying and productive. As with every team effort, it is important to be linked to people with whom you feel comfortable— people who work as hard as you, and who share your values and your understanding of the division of labor in decision-making. (For further discussion of team research see Chapter 7.)

CONCLUDING REMARK

Our discussion of design does not provide precise instructions or a formula to plan your work from beginning to end. We have given some suggestions and presented some of the ways qualitative researchers think about design issues. The next chapter, concerned with qualitative data, should further help you incorporate the qualitative way of thinking about research into your research report.

THREE

QUALITATIVE DATA

A PERSON WALKING IN A FIELD SEES A YELLOW BIRD AS IT PLUCKS A red berry from one bush only to go to another bush, drop the first berry, and pick a second. If the observer is an ornithologist studying feeding habits, he or she might be keeping detailed notes—collecting data. If the person is an educational researcher just out for a holiday stroll, the details go unnoticed and are not written down. Similarly, archeologists call data what others consider rubbish. (Ancient garbage dumps are a favorite location for this form of research.) A school principal's memo can be valuable data if you approach it as if it were and if you understand its potential. As a miner picks up a rock, turning it to look for gold, so must a researcher look for the worth of information encountered in the research process. In one sense, then, ordinary events become data when approached from a particular frame of mind—that of a researcher.

Data refer to the rough materials researchers collect from the world they are studying; they are the particulars that form the basis of analysis. Data include materials the people doing the study actively record, such as interview transcripts and participant observation fieldnotes. Data also include what others have created and the researcher finds, such as diaries, photographs, official documents, and newspaper articles.

Data are both the evidence and the clues. Gathered carefully, they serve as the stubborn facts that save the writing you will do from unfounded speculation. Data ground you to the empirical world and, when systematically and rigorously collected, link qualitative research to other forms of science. Data involve the particulars you need to think soundly and deeply about the aspects of life you will explore.

In this chapter, we discuss data and data collection. This topic is intimately tied to our discussion of field relations (see Chapter 4), but our emphasis here is more on the content of data, and the mechanical aspects of gathering it.

Some qualitative studies rely exclusively on one type of data, interview transcripts for example, but most use a variety of data sources. Although we will be discussing different types of data separately, it should be kept in mind that seldom are they found isolated in research. We start with a lengthy discussion of the mainstay of qualitative research—fieldnotes.

FIELDNOTES

After returning from each observation, interview, or other research session, the researcher typically writes out what happened. She or he renders a description of people, objects, places, events, activities, and conversations. In addition, as part of such notes, the researcher will record ideas, strategies, reflections, hunches, as well as note patterns that emerge. These are *fieldnotes:* the written account of what the researcher hears, sees, experiences, and thinks in the course of collecting and reflecting on the data in a qualitative study.

The successful outcome of a participant observation study in particular, but other forms of qualitative research as well, relies on detailed, accurate, and extensive fieldnotes. In participant observation studies all the data are considered to be *fieldnotes;* this term refers collectively to all the data collected in the course of such a study, including the fieldnotes, interview transcripts, official documents, official statistics, pictures, and other materials. We are using the term here in a more narrow sense.

While researchers know that fieldnotes are central to participant observation, some forget that they can be an important supplement to other data-collecting methods. In conducting taped interviews, for example, the meaning and context of the interview can be captured more completely if, as a supplement to each interview, the researcher writes out fieldnotes. The tape-recorder misses the sights, the smells, the impressions, and the extra remarks said before and after the interview. Fieldnotes can provide any study with a personal log that helps the researcher to keep track of the development of the project, to visualize how the research plan has been affected by the data collected, and to remain self-conscious of how he or she has been influenced by the data.

In our discussion of other forms of data (later in this chapter), we will briefly discuss specific aspects of fieldnotes that are unique to these techniques. Here we concentrate on the fieldnotes taken in conjunction with a participant observation study. While we pick the fieldnotes from participant observation to discuss, much of what is said here is directly relevant to fieldnotes written in conjunction with other approaches, such as interviewing.

A set of fieldnotes collected as part of a study of a program that ''mainstreams'' ''disabled'' students in an urban high school[1] is reproduced as Figure 3–1. These notes were taken after the fifth observation at the school. They have been slightly rewritten and edited for the purposes of this book. We include these notes to provide an example of rich data and to illustrate the discussion that follows. We suggest that you read through Figure 3–1 quickly before you go on, and then refer to it as you read. As our discussion indicates, there are many styles of fieldnotes. The notes in Figure 3–1 are offered as an example of one approach.

FIGURE 3-1

EXAMPLE OF FIELDNOTES

March 24, 1980
Joe McCloud
11:00 a.m. to 12:30 p.m.
Westwood High
6th Set of Notes

The Fourth Period
Class in Marge's Room

I arrived at Westwood High at five minutes to eleven, the time Marge told me her fourth period started. I was dressed as usual: sport shirt, chino pants, and a Woolrich parka. The fourth period is the only time during the day when all the students who are in the "neurologically impaired/learning disability" program, better known as "Marge's program," come together. During the other periods, certain students in the program, two or three or four at most, come to her room for help with the work they are getting in other regular high school classes.

It was a warm, fortyish, promise of a spring day. There was a police patrol wagon, the kind that has benches in the back that are used for large busts, parked in the back of the big parking lot that is in front of the school. No one was sitting in it and I never heard its reason for being there. In the circular drive in front of the school was parked a United States Army car. It had insignias on the side and was a khaki color. As I walked from my car, a balding fortyish man in an Army uniform came out of the building and went to the car and sat down. Four boys and a girl also walked out of the school. All were white. They had on old dungarees and colored stenciled t-shirts with spring jackets over them. One of the boys, the tallest of the four, called out, "oink, oink, oink." This was done as he sighted the police vehicle in the back.

O.C.:   This was strange to me in that I didn't think that the kids were into "the police as pigs." Somehow I associated that with another time, the early 1970s. I'm going to have to come to grips with the assumptions I have about high school due to my own experience. Sometimes I feel like Westwood is entirely different from my high school and yet this police car incident reminded me of mine.

Classes were changing when I walked down the halls. As usual there was the boy with girl standing here and there by the lockers. There were three couples that I saw. There was the occasional shout. There were no teachers outside the doors.

O.C.:   The halls generally seem to be relatively unsupervised during class changes.

Two black girls I remember walking down the hall together. They were tall and thin and had their hair elaborately braided with beads all through them. I stopped by the office to tell Mr. Talbot's (the principal) secretary that I was in the building. She gave me a warm smile.

O.C.:   I feel quite comfortable in the school now. Somehow I feel like I belong. As I walk down the halls some teachers say hello. I have been going out of my way to say hello to kids that I pass. Twice I've been in a stare-down with kids passing in the hall. Saying, "How ya' doin'?" seems to disalarm them.

(continued)

I walked into Marge's class and she was standing in front of the room with more people than I had ever seen in the room save for her homeroom which is right after second period. She looked like she was talking to the class or was just about to start. She was dressed as she had been on my other visits—clean, neat, well-dressed but casual. Today she had on a striped blazer, a white blouse and dark slacks. She looked up at me, smiled and said: "Oh, I have a lot more people here now than the last time."

O.C.: This was in reference to my other visits during other periods where there are only a few students. She seems self-conscious about having such a small group of students to be responsible for. Perhaps she compares herself with the regular teachers who have classes of thirty or so.

There were two women in their late twenties sitting in the room. There was only one chair left. Marge said to me something like:"We have two visitors from the central office today. One is a vocational counselor and the other is a physical therapist," but I don't remember if those were the words. I felt embarrassed coming in late. I sat down in the only chair available next to one of the women from the central office. They had on skirts and carried their pocketbooks, much more dressed up than the teachers I've seen. They sat there and observed.

Below is the seating arrangement of the class today:

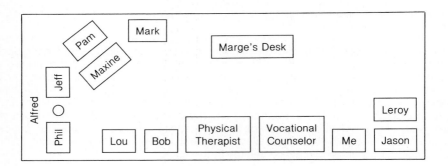

Alfred (Mr. Armstrong, the teacher's aide) walked around but when he stood in one place it was over by Phil and Jeff. Marge walked about near her desk during her talk which she started by saying to the class: "Now remember, tomorrow is a fieldtrip to the Rollway Company. We all meet in the usual place, by the bus, in front of the main entrance at 8:30. Mrs. Sharp wanted me to tell you that the tour of Rollway is not specifically for you. It's not like the trip to G.M. They took you to places where you were likely to be able to get jobs. Here, it's just a general tour that everybody goes on. Many of the jobs that you will see are not for you. Some are just for people with engineering degrees. You'd better wear comfortable shoes because you may be walking for two or three hours." Maxine and Mark said: "Ooh," in protest to the walking.

She paused and said in a demanding voice: "OK, any questions? You are all going to be there. (Pause) I want you to take a blank card and write down some questions so you have things to ask at the plant." She began passing out cards and at this point Jason, who was sitting next to me made a tutting sound of disgust, and said: "We got to do this?" Marge said: "I know this is too easy for you, Jason." This was said in a sarcastic way but not like a strong put down.

O.C.: It was like sarcasm between two people who know each other well. Marge has known many of these kids for a few years. I have to explore the implications of that for her relations with them.

Marge continued: "OK, what are some of the questions you are going to ask?" Jason yelled out: "Insurance," and Marge said: "I was asking Maxine not Jason." This was said matter of factly without anger toward Jason. Maxine said: "Hours—the hours you work, the wages." Somebody else yelled out: "Benefits." Marge wrote these things on the board. She got to Phil who was sitting there next to Jeff. I believe she skipped over Jeff. Mr. Armstrong was standing right next to Phil. She said: "Have you got one?" Phil said: "I can't think of one." She said: "Honestly Phil. Wake up." Then she went to Joe, the white boy. Joe and Jeff are the only white boys I've seen in the program. The two girls are white. He said: "I can't think of any." She got to Jason and asked him if he could think of anything else. He said: "Yeah, you could ask 'em how many of the products they made each year." Marge said: "Yes, you could ask about production. How about Leroy, do you have any ideas Leroy?" He said: "No." Mr. Armstrong was standing over in the corner and saying to Phil in a low voice: "Now you know what kinds of questions you ask when you go for a job?" Phil said: "Training, what kind of training do you have to have?" Marge said: "Oh yes, that's right, training." Jason said out loud but not yelling: "How much schooling you need to get it." Marge kept listing them.

O.C.: Marge was quite animated. If I hadn't seen her like this before I would think she was putting on a show for the people from central office.

Marge continued: "Now you got all these questions down? Have you got them on cards? Can you all ask at least one question when we are out there? Don't ask the same question that the person in front of you asks, but do you all have a question that you could say? Now you know that Mrs. Sharp likes you to ask questions and you'll hear from her after, if you don't ask them. You are all excused through the fifth period tomorrow. If we get back late, I'll excuse you for first period lunch and you can eat lunch during the second period."

I looked around the room noting the dress of some of the students. Maxine had on a black t-shirt that had some iron-on lettering on it. It was a very well-done iron-on and the shirt looked expensive. She had on Levi jeans and Nike jogging sneakers. Mark is about 5'9" or 5'10". He had on a long sleeve jersey with an alligator on the front, very stylish but his pants were wrinkled and he had on old muddy black basketball sneakers with both laces broken, one in two places. Pam had on a lilac-colored velour sweater over a button-down striped shirt. Her hair looked very well-kept and looked like she had had it styled at an expensive hair place. Jeff sat next to her in his wheelchair. He had one foot up without a shoe on it as if it were sprained. Mr. Armstrong (Alfred) had on a white, shiny shirt opened two buttons in the front. He had on light-colored dress pants, the kind without a belt. Phil had on a beige sweater over a white shirt and dark pants and low-cut basketball sneakers. The sneakers were red and were dirty. He had a dirt ring around the collar. He is the least well-dressed of the crowd. Joe had on a regular white old t-shirt and jeans. His long blondish hair was uncombed. He has acne on his face and is over six feet tall. He had on jogging sneakers that were clean and new-looking. He was the only boy who had on jogging sneakers. The rest had basketball sneakers. Jim is probably 5'9" or 5'10". He had on a red pullover. Jason had on a black golf cap and a beige spring jacket over a university t-shirt. He had on dark dress pants and a red university t-shirt with a v-neck. It was faded from being washed. Jason's eyes were noticeably red.

O.C.: Two of the kids told me that Westwood High was a fashion show. I have a difficult time figuring out what's in fashion. Jason used that expression. He seems to me to be the most clothes-conscious.

Marge said: "OK, we are going to have the test now." She went and handed out a sheet of problems. On one side it was a blank check with some instructions about what to put on it. There was also a deposit ticket and a balance sheet of a checkbook with a lot of figures below. They were supposed to put all the figures in the right place, bal-

(continued)

ance the checkbook, and write out a check as well as write out a deposit slip. A great bulk of the period was spent doing that. Marge said: "Get started—remember this is a test." Maxine asked her a question. She said: "Remember this is a test. I can't tell you that." Jason said: "At least can you tell us how to spell a word? How do you spell twenty?" Marge ignored this. She came up to Leroy and said: "Leroy, you are supposed to use a pencil not a pen. If you make a mistake, you can't erase it. Where is the pencil that you have?" He looked towards Jason and Jason gave Leroy back his pencil and then Marge gave Jason a pencil from her desk. She went over to the other side of the room. Bob was using a pen also. She said: "Bob, a pencil not a pen." A few times Jason said: "Miss Katz, Miss Katz," trying to get her to come over and help. He got Mr. Armstrong's attention and asked him some questions about writing out the deposit slip. Armstrong said: "If I answer that question, I'll be answering the test for you."

I leaned over to the person who was the vocational counselor and asked her about her job. She said she had been working for the city for two years but she was also in graduate school at the University. I asked her the reason for the visit. "I heard about this program. I want to explore if L.D. (Learning Disabled) kids are eligible for counseling. I hadn't seen this group so I wanted to come out and take a look, see what kinds of services they were getting and what they might get." I asked about the lady who was with her and she said that she was a physical therapist who was just coming along with her to see if there were any services that physical therapists could give. She was new to the district.

O.C.: I really felt these women were out of place here. Their dress wasn't appropriate and they were like bumps on a log.

During the testing, Marge was walking around the room looking at what they were doing. She said, "You're all so smart. Now all you need is money to put into the bank." Three or four times during the test she used the phrase: "You're all so smart" in praise of them.

At one point, Marge looked around and said, "Where's Mac? Oh, yes, I told him not to come without his mother. Well, that's what you get, he's not here and I guess his mother couldn't come."

Marge came over and talked to the vocational counselor. The vocational counselor asked: "What about mainstreaming the kids?" Marge responded: "Oh, they're in the regular classes with the other kids. This is the only class they are together." The counselor said: "What about gym and Jeff?" Marge said: "They're in the regular gym period. Jeff can use the pool. It's designed so the handicapped can use it." The counselor said: "Do any of the children get any kind of therapy outside of class?" Marge said: "Jeff goes to the C.P. (Cerebral Palsy) clinic once a week." When Marge was talking, she whispered but her voice did carry and I was sure that Jason who was sitting next to me could hear everything that she was saying. The vocational counselor said: "I was watching Bob over there. He has almost a primitive grasp of the pencil." Marge said: "Oh, they all have that. The writing is a real problem not just reading."

Marge said: "Before this class was formed, most of these kids were not labeled L.D. or if they were labeled, they were emotionally disturbed. There was really no place for them. I mean, they would have them in this program or that program but not one that really is what they needed."

At this point, she was raising her voice and I was sure that Jason could hear her say, "Emotionally disturbed."

O.C.: I wonder if the students are as sensitive to these labels as I am. I feel terrible if they are used in front of the students.

The vocational counselor said: "Are there other kids besides those in wheelchairs that could use the therapy?" Marge said: "I don't really know. What kinds of things are you thinking about doing?'' The vocational counselor said: ''Oh, consultation, physical therapy. We can't perform miracles but there are certain things we can do. I remember a C.P. kid's parents say that the first word our child said was car. Now how can she tell him he can't be a mechanic?''

O.C.: This comment came out of nowhere. I couldn't figure out what it was hooked to. I got the feeling that the vocational counselor was nervous. She was young and Marge was being nice but not warm.

At some point during the class, Marge said in a voice that interrupted the class: ''I forgot to hand this out to my homeroom. (Her homeroom is made up of typical students.) Oh, how could I be such a jerk.'' She was holding up a sheet of paper. Jeff asked: ''What's it about?'' Marge said, ''A summer program, it's about visiting colleges. Visiting colleges that you might be interested in.'' Jeff gestured with his hand as if he wasn't interested.

O.C.: This is the second reference that Marge made to colleges today. It really makes you wonder how college oriented secondary school is. I wonder how the kids feel when they hear the word ''college'' said.

Marge started talking to the vocational counselor about some troubles with the way the schools were set up. She said: ''The problem is the stupid credits plus the tests they have to take in order to get a diploma. You are almost forced to put them in academic subjects when that's not what they need. They ought to have some competency-based programs where you can measure them against life skills and have something to give them at the end of the program. They shouldn't be in here four years wasting their time.'' The vocational counselor asked what kind of subjects the students were in. Marge said: ''There'll be a kid who's in here who is in biology. We will have somebody who is in algebra.'' The vocational counselor said, ''Wow, that's something. Do you ever need things like a typewriter?''

O.C.: The vocational person didn't follow up on Marge's concerns.

Marge with a little anger said: ''Well, if we had a typewriter, we could use it. We do have cassettes and we try to make those available.'' The vocational counselor said: ''We are getting some typewriters down in the office. I can't promise that you will be able to use one but they are on order.'' Marge said: ''Now one of the kids does hand in typed stuff. His mother does the typing. He wants to go to college. I don't see it unless he takes her along with him.'' Marge lowered her voice and said, ''He's not realistic. He wants to be a forester.''

Marge continued to talk to the vocational counselor: ''Most of the kids are in C.E.T.A. Now C.E.T.A. is not a career but at least it's a job, something for them to do. The problem is the diplomas. They can go through and take all their credits and then not get a diploma. Only E.M.R.'s (Educable Mentally Retarded) can get adaptive diplomas. My kids, they can take their minimum competency test orally but they're going to have to pass all parts of it, the writing and the reading and math. I don't want to be pessimistic but next year I know that none of my kids will pass it.''

All this time while they were talking, perhaps fifteen or twenty minutes, everyone was very, very hard at work. Mr. Armstrong went from place to place and people were asking him questions. He wouldn't give any information to help solve the problems they had. He would only clarify what the instructions were.

The two women from the downtown office left thanking Marge and saying: ''We'll get back to you.'' Actually, the one woman hardly said a word. After they left the room, Marge said to the class: ''Those two women were from the downtown office. One is a vocational counselor and the other one is a physical therapist. I would have introduced you, but I didn't know one of the lady's names and it was embarrassing. Joe McCloud (pointing to me) is sitting over here. You know he is visiting regularly. He's interested in classes like this. He's from the University.''

(continued)

Marge said: "Do the adding and subtracting the best you can do. If you did this at home, you would have your own calculator and it would be alot easier."

O.C.:   Most of the kids in the class are poor. I can't imagine them having a calculator but I think she was saying that to be encouraging.

Mr. Armstrong came over to Leroy and said: "What do you have this for? This is a test." Leroy looked up with a smile on his face and said, "Well, I wanted to learn how to do it." Apparently Leroy was using a book to work on his test which he wasn't supposed to do. It ended with that.

Jason finished and handed in his test and said: "I got one hundred, this was easy." He asked if he could go to the bathroom and walked out with Marge saying: "Five minutes." A short time later he came back and he had the pencil in his mouth. Marge said, "What are you doing with my pencil in your mouth?" Jason said: "I'm holding it." She said: "Give it to me." He took it out of his mouth and gave it to her and Marge said: "Look at this, you have got your teeth marks in my pencil. Nice way to return it."

O.C.:   The tone of this was mild anger but not confrontational—Marge has a relationship with Jason where she is very direct with him but they are old friends.

Marge collected the papers and Jason said: "Let's see who has got them wrong. I know I ain't got none wrong." As she collected the papers Marge said to Jeff: "Now, you can finish this during the sixth period and some of you can finish this tomorrow."

O.C.:   This gave me the impression that it was a pretend test, not the real thing.

Jason said: "How can they finish it tomorrow if we are leaving at 8:30 on the bus?" Marge said, "Some of the people come in other periods than the fourth period."

The bell rang and everybody began to leave. I can't remember who was wheeling Jeff out or if he was doing it himself but Philip noticed Jeff's leg up and said: "What happened. You sprung you leg?" Meaning you sprained your leg. Marge said: "Sprung your leg, very good Philip. Try sprained." Mark and Laura chuckled.

O.C.:   Marge talks in a joking way because of the tone of her voice. I don't think of it as a putdown. It is more joking. The tone of her voice is not hostile and the kids do seem to like her. She is the same way with the kids who are not in the program. The kids joke back with her.

Everybody left and Mr. Armstrong came over; so did Marge. They sat down next to me and we began to talk. I asked about where Mac was. Marge said: "Mac's a real problem. He just doesn't come. In the other program that he was in, he didn't come. I keep trying to talk to the father but I can't get him. I can't get the mother. I called the other day and Mac was on the phone. I heard his mother say that she couldn't come to the phone because she was too tired. The father works all day and then is a minister at night. They live on Hollow Street." I asked: "What kind of minister is he?" Marge said: "Alfred, maybe you know."

O.C.:   Alfred lives in Mac's neighborhood.

Alfred said: "It's a full-time church and everything. It is just very small." I asked: "Why were the people from the central office here?" Marge said: "Well, she said that she was going to come at 10:30 and then she didn't come until almost 11:45. At 10:30, I could have talked to her. I had some free time. I didn't want to say you can't come in, so I told her to come in and sit down. I don't know if she saw very much. I don't know what she is going to do."

I asked Marge what she felt about the central office and she said: "They don't know I am here. They don't know I exist." I said: "Who do you report to down there?" She said: "Well, not really anybody. Joe Carroll is the person. But Bullard is the one who is in charge of Special Ed. Let me see, Carroll is in charge of some special programs, I guess new programs that they are getting started. I really don't know what Bullard does. For sure, he doesn't make any decisions. I go to see Carroll. He's the supervisor of special programs."

I asked if the people come up and see the program. She said: "Well, Claire Minor who is a teacher on special assignment came once to see if we were alive and well but I haven't seen her since. I called Carroll once because I needed something and he came in, but he didn't initiate coming up. They don't come to see what I am doing. They don't know what I am doing. I don't mind. They must think that I am okay and I can handle my own thing but if there were new teachers, maybe they would come in but for sure, they ought to find out what's going on and what they are doing. I feel that if I had a problem, I could get help but they're really not on top of what I am doing. You will hear people talk. You can't get a decision on anything."

I said: "Can you give me some examples of not getting decisions?" She said, "Well, Jeff, now I have been calling down to that office to try to get a special bus for him so he could go with us to Rollway and I can't get Mike down there. He is going to wind up not going because we don't have the bus."

I asked for any other examples. She said: "At the beginning of the year with the aide. The aide I had, he quit and I called down and told them and Carroll told me that he wasn't going to get an aide this year. They said that I was going to share an aide with the resource teacher across the hall. Now that is kind of impossible because she has the same setup that I do. You can never tell how many kids are going to be in her class or my class so I went crazy. I screamed and yelled. Finally, I went to see Mr. Talbot, the principal. He's really good at screaming and yelling but he didn't seem to get anywhere either. Finally, I mentioned Teachers' Association. I told them that I was going to call T.A. That finished it. They are really afraid of the union. Before you know it, I got a call and they said they were sending up Alfred. That was around October first. This is supposed to be a pilot program. How can they have a pilot program if they don't have an aide for it? Yes, then they called me when I mentioned the union and they said that there was a young man for me."

I asked Marge about how the program began. I said that I hadn't gotten that clear last time. She said: "Let me see, you know Leroy, you see Leroy. Well, he's the lowest functioning guy in the class. He's on five years probation for robbery and some assault, too. I had Leroy at the beginning of last year. Lou Winch tested him and found him to be neurologically impaired. Nobody knew that he had any problems. He just went along and wasn't getting anything. There was a teacher on special assignment and she couldn't believe that he had come up through school functioning at the level he does now. He was labeled emotionally disturbed. He is very very suspicious. Even if you raise your voice, he gets all excited. One time in the library, I mentioned his probation officer and he started yelling at me telling me, "Don't tell this in front of everybody." It's like nobody knows. Everybody knows that he has a parole officer. They put Leroy through the district committee. They said they needed a program for kids like this and they talked to Lou about it and then I volunteered. I also had Mel in the resource room. I was a resource room teacher last year. I hope you meet Mel before you go. He hasn't been coming in." Alfred said: "Yeah, he has got a job in some food store."

Marge said: "Anyway, people started talking about needing a program. Lou Brown at Miron Junior High has more of a self-contained classroom for neurologically impaired and learning disabled kids and we knew some of those kids would be coming here. So there was a need and so it just happened."

I mentioned how hard I thought the kids worked on their test. She said: "Yeah, you give them a task and they will stick to it. Now they don't get it all right. Like Leroy for example, instead of signing his name he signed sweater and pants."

I mentioned that Mark looked fairly sharply dressed and that he had an expensive shirt on. She said: "That's not the way he always looks. The other day he had on a shirt that looked a wreck. I went to his house. It is on East Street. They've moved now. Mark has never been in a regular class, always Special Ed. At Rosetree he was in with Alfred and his program. The Committee on the Handicapped, which was local then, looked at

(continued)

him and they encouraged his mother to develop a lawsuit because there was really no program to meet his needs. His mother didn't have to do very much before they said that there was going to be this program available for him. I mean it wasn't like the committee officially told her to start a lawsuit. It's kind of, they say it on the side. Mary Willow is the person who Alfred used to work with and she's really good.''

Marge started talking about Luca Meta who I have not met. She said: ''Now there is a boy who shouldn't be in here. His father put the old squeeze on Bullard and he wanted a special class for him so here he is. Luca doesn't need living skills. He seems to get something out of the vocational program but then he says that he wants him to be a forester. Well, I don't know about it.''

I told Marge and Alfred that I had been to the Westwood High School play on Saturday night. I asked them about the kids that were in the play in relation to the kids in the special program. I asked generally about friendships in the high school. She said: ''Well the way I think about it is that there's the very top and there's the very bottom. We really don't have a middle. Now that's my impression. Now you noticed there was only one black person in the play. Black kids like to come here because there are lots of other blacks. Some of the other schools don't have as many. But they really don't intermingle the way you would think. Thursday was the fifties day. Everybody was supposed to get dressed up like the fifties. The play was kind of like a fifties play. Very, very few of the blacks would dress up. They don't stay strictly to themselves but at lunchtime you go into the cafeteria, the whites are eating with the whites, the blacks with the blacks. Now the black middle-upper class mix with the white. That's different.''

At one point, Marge told me that she had volunteered to coach the volleyball team. She said, ''I have to get used to talking with kids at a different level. I always talk so slowly here and don't use big words. The volleyball team ought to be good. I play myself and it will give me a chance to practice.''

We continued talking about the very top and the very bottom. Marge said: ''The teachers that I talk to say that in their classes there is a mixture of those who can do the work and those who can't do the work.'' I ask whether it was income or color. Whether they had the kids on welfare from the inner-city and then professional class people. She said: ''Yes, that's pretty much the way it is.''

It's not very clear when this was said, but I remember at one point, she said: ''The L.D. label gets you a better class.'' Meaning that having an L.D. class got you more of the less-troublesome kids.

I don't know what got this started but she started talking about the social background of the kids in the class. She said: ''Pam lives around here right up there so she's from a professional family. Now, Maxine that's different. She lives on the east side. She is one of six kids and her father isn't that rich. As a matter of fact, he's in maintenance, taking charge of cleaning crews. Now, Jeff, he lives on Dogwood. He's middle class.'' I asked about Lou. She said: ''Pour Lou, talk about being neurologically impaired. I don't know what to do about that guy. Now he has a sister who graduated two years ago. He worries me more than anybody. I don't know what is going to become of him. He is so slow. I don't know any job that he could do. His father came in and he looks just like him. What are you going to tell him? What is he going to be able to do? What is he going to do? Wash airplanes? I talked to the vocational counselor. She said that there were jobs in airports washing airplanes. I mean, how is he going to wash an airplane? How about sweeping out the hangars? Maybe he could do that. The mother is something else. His mother thinks that Lou is her punishment. Can you imagine an attitude like that? I was just wondering what could she have done to think that she deserved Lou?

''Now Luca Meta, he is upper class all the way. Leroy, there's your low end of the spectrum. I don't know how many kids they have but they have a lot. His mother just had a kidney removed. Everybody knows he is on parole. Matter of fact, whenever there is any stealing in the school, they look at him. He used to go to gym and everytime he went, something was stolen. Now they don't let him go to gym anymore. His parole officer was down. He won't be here next year.''

By this time it was about 12:00 and I mentioned going and setting up another time. She said: "You could come anytime you want. We're having a Tuesday trip." I said I probably would come the fourth period on Wednesday. She said something about them starting to read ads for apartments.

She said: "By the way, I was talking and maybe you overheard me about what we need is a competency-based program here. I have already finished a competency-based program if they ever took it. It is silly to have kids spend four years sitting here, when it makes no sense in terms of them. They ought to be out working. If they're not going to graduate, what they ought to have is some living skills like what we did with writing the checks. People aren't going to teach them that out in the world so they could do that. Once they had enough skills, living skills, to make it on their own then they ought to go out. There is no sense to this."

At one point, she was talking about Philip's family. She said: "Now that is a nice family. He's a very nice boy, middle-class boy."

Sometime during my visit I asked about the armed services as a possible career. She said: "That is another problem. Most kids can't pass the test to get into the armed services. There was a show on "Sixty Minutes" about how they get kids in by cheating. They can't get a diploma. They can't get in the army. I wish there would be some way to let them cheat with these kids because these kids could really use the diploma. If Phil doesn't get a diploma, he's going to feel very, very bad but I don't see how he can get it. Pam, it will destroy her. It will devastate her if she doesn't graduate. She has a group of friends who are going to get diplomas. She's on the track team."

We left the room. Alfred and Marge walked up the empty hall with me. I asked her how the kids felt about being in this class. She said: "Well, it varies. It really bothers Pam. Like she failed history and she has to go to summer school. The reason she failed it was she wouldn't tell them that she was in this program so she didn't get any extra help and then she failed." Marge walked me to the door. Alfred dropped off at the teachers' room.

On the way to the door she said: "Remember that boy I told you about who's going to be in here? The dentist's son, the Swenson boy? Well, I have been hearing stories about him. I come to find out that he is really E.M.H. (Educable Mentally Handicapped) and a hyperactive kid. I really am going to have my hands full with him. If there is twenty in the program next year, I really am going to need another aide." I said goodbye and walked to my car.

Additions

The night before last I met a woman at a party who teaches at Westwood. She asked me what I was doing at Westwood. I explained. She said she hadn't had that many kids from the program in her class. She did say that she had Luca and he is very good. I remember her saying something like: "He can't read very well but he's intellectually up with the other kids in the class." She said he wrote a report for her that was typed. She said she had Leroy in a class but she didn't see much of him. I said that some time I would set up a meeting to talk to her.

O.C.: This morning I was up talking with Hans about the mainstreaming study. We began talking about Jones Markey School and how perhaps having more than one or two handicapped kids in a class made it easier for the handicapped kids. As we talked I began to realize that maybe a lot of what we are seeing in regard to hostility towards mainstreaming has very little to do with the kids or mainstreaming. Perhaps those schools that are undergoing strain and transition are the ones who are most anti-mainstreaming. Mainstreaming should not be understood as a thing that people are for or against. It should be understood that at different times schools face different problems. At Macri Jr. High one teacher sees the special education class being there as an example that the school is going to close down. The principal may see it as an indication that it is going to remain. Special Ed can alleviate or cause problems in the way it is perceived. It is very important.

A word of encouragement before we go on. Looking at the example of fieldnotes in Figure 3–1, you might be thinking that it is impossible to write so much from one short observation—that your memory, your writing ability, your energy are not enough to meet the challenge. Take heart; do not quit before you give it a try. Some of you will only go out once and never complete a set of notes, but for others, the discipline and skill that taking fieldnotes exercises will be stimulating. Some people actually get hooked on observing and note-taking. Your ability to record notes will increase; the apparently impossible nature of the task will seem quite manageable if you can get through a few sets.

There is at least one important fringe benefit in doing fieldnotes. It can improve the quality of your writing and speed it up as well. Any writer will tell you that a most effective way to learn to write is by writing often. People seldom have the opportunity to write page upon page of concrete description. Even the amount of writing required in most demanding college courses is small compared to what you are asked to do here. The nice thing is that fieldnotes are not like most required writing. It is expected that the fieldnotes will flow, that they will come from the top of your head and represent your particular style. In addition, you are encouraged to write in the first person. No one will scrutinize them for poor sentence construction or spelling; they should simply be thorough and clear. In addition, you will not have the problem of having nothing to write about. What you have seen in the field will become the source of endless sentences and paragraphs. Some people have been liberated from their fear of writing and of the one-half page-per-hour speed limit they operate under by being given the writing opportunity that doing fieldnotes provides.

The Content of Fieldnotes

As our definition suggests, fieldnotes consist of two kinds of materials. The first is descriptive, in which the concern is to capture a word-picture of the setting, people, actions, and conversations as observed. The other is reflective—the part that captures more of the observer's frame of mind, ideas, and concerns. We discuss these two aspects of fieldnotes separately.

The Descriptive Part of Fieldnotes.   The descriptive part of the fieldnotes, by far the longest part, represents the researcher's best effort to objectively record the details of what has occurred in the field. The goal is to capture the slice of life. Aware that all description to some degree represents choices and judgments—decisions about what to put down, the exact use of words—the qualitative researcher in education strives for accuracy under these limitations. Knowing that the setting can never be completely captured, he or she is dedicated to transmitting to paper as much as possible, within the parameters of the project's research goals.

When we say that the researcher attempts to be as descriptive as possible, we mean that what he or she observes should be presented in detail rather than summarized or evaluated. For example, rather than saying, ''The child looked a mess,'' you might choose something like, ''The child, who was seven or eight years old, wore faded muddy dungarees with both knees ripped. His nose was running in a half-inch stream down to his mouth, and his face was streaked clean where he had rubbed it with his wet fingers.'' Rather than saying, ''The class was festive,'' describe what was hanging on the walls and ceilings, what was on the bulletin board, what sounds and movements were there. Whenever you can, quote people rather than summarize what they say.

It is particularly important in working on description not to use abstract words (unless, or course, you are quoting a subject). Do not, for example, say that the teacher was in front of the room ''teaching.'' What was he or she actually doing and saying? Be specific. If the teacher was talking, quote and describe it. You might be interested in when and under what conditions teachers use the word *teaching* to describe their own behavior, but you should avoid using such a term yourself. Generally, replace words like *disciplining, playing, tutoring, practicing, nice person, good student, doing nothing* with detailed renderings of exactly what people are doing, saying, and what they look like. You want to cut into the world you are observing, and abstract words will lead you to gloss over rather than to dissect.

It may be difficult to abandon superficial or overly evaluative description. We have provided questions in the Appendix at the end of this book that may be helpful in bringing you to a deeper level of inquiry. We provide them to sensitize you to some aspects of schools you might study, but not as a set of questions you carry with you and to which you seek answers. The questions serve to increase curiosity and to broaden your range of vision.

As you can see by examining the fieldnotes in Figure 3–1, the descriptive aspects of the fieldnotes encompass the following areas:

1. *Portraits of the subjects.*   This includes their physical appearance, dress, mannerisms, and style of talking and acting. You should look for particular aspects of people that might set them apart from others. Because the set of notes included in Figure 3–1 is the fifth in a study, the descriptions of people are not as extensive as they would be in an earlier set of notes. This is because the people in the setting have been described earlier. After the first full description, only changes are noted in subsequent fieldnotes.

2. *Reconstruction of dialogue.*   The conversations that go on between subjects are recorded as well as what the subjects say to you in private. The notes will contain paraphrases and summaries of conversations, but, as we have suggested before, you should strive to make the subject's own words bountiful. Quote your subjects. You should be particularly concerned with writing down words and phrases that are unique to the setting or have a special use in it. Gestures, accents, and facial expressions should also be noted. Novice researchers are often troubled in not knowing exactly when to put quotation marks around dialogue in the fieldnotes. It is understood that you will not capture exactly, word for word, what the subjects have said. Rather than indicating an exact, literal, word-for-word rendering, quotation marks mean that the conversation is a *close approximation* of what was said. If you think you have

captured the words fairly well, put quotation marks around it. If you are not sure of what the subject has said, before the quotation indicate that you are not sure that it is accurate. Use a phrase such as, ''Joe said something to the effect that'' and then put your transcription. If you are really unsure, note this and then summarize what you believe you remember.

3. *Description of physical setting.*   Pencil drawings of the space and furniture arrangements are useful in notes. Verbal sketches of such things as the blackboard, the contents of bulletin boards, the furniture, and the floors and walls may also be included. You should also try to capture the sense of the building or location where you are observing. What image, for example, does the school you are studying project as you approach it?

4. *Accounts of particular events.*   The notes include a listing of who was involved in the event, in what manner, and the nature of the action.

5. *Depiction of activities.*   For this category you include detailed descriptions of behavior, trying to reproduce the sequence of both behaviors as well as particular acts.

6. *The observer's behavior.*   In qualitative research, the subjects are the people interviewed and found in the research setting, but you should treat yourself as an object of scrutiny as well. Because you are the instrument of data collection, it is very important to take stock of your own behavior, assumptions, and whatever else might affect the data that is gathered and analyzed. Much of the material that is discussed in the section, ''The Reflective Part of Fieldnotes'' is directed at this concern, but the descriptive part of the notes should also contain materials on such things as your dress, actions, and conversations with subjects. Although you attempt to minimize your effect on the setting, always expect some impact. Keeping a careful record of your behavior can help assess untoward influences.

''Rich data'' or ''rich fieldnotes'' are phrases used by experienced fieldworkers to refer to fieldnotes that are well-endowed with good description and dialogue relevant to what occurs at the setting and its meaning for the participants. Rich data is filled with pieces of evidence, with the clues that you begin to put together to make analytical sense out of what you study.

The Reflective Part of Fieldnotes.   In addition to the descriptive material, fieldnotes contain sentences and paragraphs that reflect the observer's more personal account of the course of the inquiry. Here the more subjective side of the researcher's journey is recorded. The emphasis is on speculation, feelings, problems, ideas, hunches, impressions, prejudices. Also included is material in which the researcher lays out plans for future research as well as clarifies and corrects mistakes or misunderstandings in the fieldnotes. The expectation is that you let it all hang out: confess your mistakes, your inadequacies, your prejudices, your likes and dislikes. Speculate about what you think you are learning, what you are going to do next, and what the outcome of the study is going to be. The purpose of reflection here is not therapy. Although some people indicate that fieldwork has therapeutic benefits, the purpose of all this reflection is to improve the notes. Because a researcher is so central to the collection of the data and its analysis, and because neither instruments nor machines nor carefully codified procedures exist, the qualitative researcher must be extremely self-conscious about his or her own relationship to the setting and about the evolution of the design and analysis. In order to do a good study, the researcher must be self-reflective, and keep an accurate record of methods, procedures, and evolving analysis. It is difficult to get the right balance between reflective and descriptive material. Some researchers go overboard on the reflective side to write their autobiographies. It is important to remember that the reflections are a means to a better study, not an end in themselves.

The reflective parts of fieldnotes are designated by a notational convention. The set of notes in Figure 3–1 uses parentheses and the notation of "O.C.," which stands for *observer's comment*. As you can see in our example, observer's comments are scattered throughout the notes. At the end of a set of fieldnotes, the author will also take time to contemplate the day's experience, speculate about what he or she is theorizing, jot down additional information, and plan the next observation. From time to time, not as part of any particular set of notes, the researcher will additionally write "think pieces" about the progress of the research. These longer pieces in addition to or at the end of a set of notes are called *memos* (Glaser and Strauss, 1967). It should be noted that some researchers, particularly those trained in some anthropological traditions of qualitative research, prefer to keep descriptive and reflective parts of the notes completely separate. They keep two sets of notes, entering their personal reflections in a *field diary*.

We have already given you some idea about what the reflective part of fieldnotes includes, but we categorize the materials to elaborate and clarify. Observer's comments, memos, and other such materials contain:

1. *Reflections on analysis.* At this time, speculate about what you are learning, the themes that are emerging, patterns that may be present, connections between pieces of data, adding ideas, and thoughts that pop up. Long reflections that focus on analysis are referred to as *analytic memos* (Glaser and Strauss, 1967). The importance and role of your comments and memos are more thoroughly discussed in Chapter 5. Illustrations of these types of reflections can be found in that chapter as well as in Figure 3–1.

2. *Reflections on method.* Fieldnotes contain material about procedures and strategies employed in the study, and decisions that are made about the study's design. It is also the place to include comments on your rapport with particular subjects along with the joys and problems encountered in the study. Particular problems you are having with a subject, or some other dilemma may be a topic of such reflection. Include your ideas about how to deal with the problem. Assess what you have accomplished and what you have yet to do. Your reflections on method will help you to think through the methodological problems you face and to make decisions about them. When you are finished with your research experience, these methodological discussions will enable you to write an account of what you did.

3. *Reflections on ethical dilemmas and conflicts.*   Because fieldwork involves you in the lives of your subjects, relational concerns between your own values and responsibilities to your subjects as well as to your profession continually arise. We have discussed some of the ethical dilemmas in Chapter 1. Observer's comments and memos not only help you to keep a record of these concerns, but also aid you in working them out.

4. *Reflections on the observer's frame of mind.*   Although they try not to, researchers generally enter studies with certain assumptions about the subjects and the setting they are studying. Some of these preconceptions relate to one's religious beliefs, political ideology, ethical background, position in society, experience in the schools, race, or sex. The list could go on. Like everyone else, qualitative researchers have opinions, beliefs, attitudes, and prejudices, and they try to reveal these by reflecting on their own way of thinking in the notes. Of particular interest are encounters that the researcher has while collecting data that provide breakthroughs to new ways of thinking and revelations of assumptions. Early in the research these can come fast and furiously. What you thought just does not hold up to the empirical world you are studying (Geer, 1964). "Retarded" subjects are not as dumb as you thought, adolescents are not as crazy as you knew they were, schools that you thought you would hate you like, schools that you thought were terrific tarnish, programs that you thought did certain things do not.

The first reflections are usually entered into the notes prior to entering the field. Here, you depict, as fully as possible, assumptions about what is out there, and expectations for the outcome of the study. Put up front, they can be confronted and measured against (compared with) what emerges in the course of the study.

As an observer you should be concerned with your own presumptions. We think your fieldnotes will reveal, however, that these initial thoughts and assumptions become fragile as they smack up against the empirical world you encounter. Qualitative research requires long-term contact with people and places. The evidence that continually amasses can overwhelm groundless assumptions. Reflections on this process both help as well as document it.

5. *Points of clarification.*   In addition to all the heavy pondering we suggest you do, as an observer you also add sentences in the notes that are simply asides or that point out or clarify something that might have been confusing. You correct informational errors that have been recorded at other times. You might note, for example, that you do not know how this happened, but in the previous observation session you confused the names of two teachers. Then you go on to correct that.

Before we move on to other aspects of the fieldnotes, it is important to understand that qualitative researchers are not naive. They know that they can never reach a level of understanding and reflection that would result in pure notes; that is, notes that do not reflect the influence of the observer. Their goal is to purposefully take into account who they are and how they think, what actually went on in the course of the study, where their ideas came from. They are dedicated to putting this on the record in order to accomplish a better study.

All research methods have their strengths and limitations. Some say that the weakness of the qualitative approach is that it relies too heavily on the researcher as the instrument. On the other hand, others say that this is its strength. In no other form of research is the process of doing the study, and the people who are doing it, so consciously considered and studied as part of the project. The reflective part of fieldnotes is one way of attempting to acknowledge and control observer's effect. The reflective part of fieldnotes insists that research, like all human behavior, is a subjective process.

Before we move on from the content of fieldnotes to the process by which fieldnotes are collected, we want to give you some suggestions in regard to the form of the notes and then answer some questions you might have at this point.

The Form of Fieldnotes

The First Page.   While the exact form and content may vary, we suggest that the first page of each set of notes (by set we mean those notes written for a particular observation session) contain a heading with such information as when the observation was done (date and time), who did it, where the observation took place, and the number of this set of notes in the total study. As we will discuss, you should strive to record fieldnotes the same day as the observation, but if that was impossible, the date the observation was recorded should also be given. We also like to give a title to each set of notes. The title is a quick reminder of the session—a handle to grasp what the set is about. The headings help you to keep the notes in order, to keep a record of the conditions under which the notes were taken, and to make retrieval of information easier.

Paragraphs and Margins.   Most methods of analyzing qualitative data require a procedure called *coding*. (See Chapter 5 on Data Analysis.) Coding and other aspects of data analysis are more easily accomplished if the fieldnotes consist of many paragraphs. When writing notes, every time a change occurs—in the topic of a conversation, when a new person enters the setting, or whatever—start a new paragraph. When in doubt, start a new paragraph. Another way notes can prepare you well for analysis is to leave large margins on the left-hand side of the page. This provides room for notations and coding. Some methods of coding require pages in which the lines down one side are numbered. Before you start taking fieldnotes you should read through Chapter 5 to see the analytical options that might affect the form of your notes.

Thinking about these issues, and with an eye to the fieldnotes in Figure 3–1, you might be wondering: How long should a typical set of fieldnotes be? How much detail should I include? How long will the fieldnotes of a total study run?

The many different styles of fieldwork and the different goals of particular studies affect the answers. If you have a more specific focus, your notes may be shorter and there may be fewer of them. Also, as you become more experienced, you will tend to do ongoing analysis in the field and less copious, random note-taking than at first.

Researchers usually take more extensive notes during the first few visits to a new site. It is during this period that the research focus is usually most unclear, and so the observer has not decided what is important in the setting. As a researcher, you cast the net widely, taking copious notes, and often spending many more hours writing than observing. As the focus narrows to particular themes, or you do more directed observations to fill in the picture, you may reverse your earlier practice and spend many more hours observing than writing.

What you observe often affects the quantity of the fieldnotes you take after a particular session. When studying a college class, for example, you would not take notes on the content of the lectures (exactly what is being said in anatomy class, for instance). Rather, you would note the questions asked, the comments students made to each other, the general form of the lecture, key phrases, words the professor used to describe the assignments, and other such materials. Thus an hour lecture may not yield as many pages of notes as an observation of a twenty-minute bull session after class in the student lounge.

In one study we participated in we were interested in what residents and interns learned about how to talk to parents as they went about their training in a pediatric department of a teaching hospital. We would attend long case conferences in which a single patient was discussed, but take only a few pages of notes after such a session. Not only was the discussion too technical to follow in its medical dimensions, but what was of importance to us—the fact that the parents were seldom brought up—could be ascertained without hours of note-taking on tracheotomy, Turner's syndrome, and other such matters.

You would probably take account of the content of an elementary school faculty meeting if you were studying teachers. While you might not be interested in the exact characteristics that differentiate Houghton Mifflin from Open Court basal reading series, you will be interested in who leads the discussion, and what information is presented and in what ways. You may find it very important what it is about the content of these contrasting basal series that attracts different teachers because you may learn important information about this particular group of teachers, and the principal. Additionally, the content of the principal's remarks to the teachers, while perhaps intrinsically interesting, can be important because you learn from it something about the principal and his or her relationship to the school staff.

The Process of Writing Fieldnotes

You have been in the first-grade classroom for close to an hour. There has been a lot going on. Twice, while the children were working, the teacher has come over to you and explained her worries about what would happen to these children next year. She was very explicit about some of the children. The children seem much less conscious of your presence and you believe you are watching them play as they normally do. You have taken a lot in and you know you must leave in order to have time to write out your fieldnotes before your evening plans. You feel tense from concentrating so hard on remembering. Anxiety wells up as you wonder if you are up to the laborious task ahead.

You say your goodbyes, walk out the door, and head for your car. You would rather do other things than take notes. You think of stopping at a friend's or going to a store, but you put those thoughts aside. Sitting in the car, you jot down quickly a topical outline of what you have observed. You include key phrases, important topics, and you list the sequence of events that occurred. You fight the urge to give in to the idea that, "Now that I have an outline of my observation, I could do the complete fieldnotes any time."

You return to your apartment. You sit alone in a quiet room with a typewriter and lots of paper. You resist the temptation to call a friend who is working on a similar study to tell her what happened today. You stay at your typewriter and, working from you outline, you start to reconstruct with words the hour-long observation. You do it chronologically, trying to actually relive the events and the conversations. Thoughts of mistakes or missed opportunities break the line of your reconstruction. These reflections get written down as observer's comments.

You started your writing at one o'clock in the afternoon and by three o'clock you look up, not knowing where the time has gone. You forgot to eat. While it was difficult forcing yourself to sit down and get started, now it is difficult to leave your chair. The sentences run from your fingers in a way they never do when you are working on something else. You have lost your self-consciousness about your writing and the words flow. You are sorry now that you made the date for dinner. You would hate to leave this without finishing, and yet you wish you were done with it so the burden of having to finish would be lifted. You work harder and you finish by five o'clock, leaving just enough time to get ready.

While in the shower you keep going over in your mind what you learned today and how it connects with other things. You remember having left the conversation you had with John, the teacher's aide, out of the notes. As soon as you get out of the shower you return to your typewriter and record the conversation along with some other ideas you had. You get up for the last time resolving that enough is enough. You stick to it with the exception of jotting down a note or two on your napkin over dinner. The next morning you enter those scribblings with the set you completed the day before.

While we do not know how typical this account of writing up a set of fieldnotes is, it rings true to us. It highlights many of the struggles and practices involved in completing the job.

One problem everyone worries about is one's memory. Memories can be disciplined. More important and more immediately helpful in making the most of the ability you presently have, however, are some helpful hints to employ while writing up fieldnotes. The person in our story illustrates some of them:

1. Get right to the task. Do not procrastinate. The more time that passes between observing and recording the notes, the poorer your recall will be and the less likely you will ever get to record them.
2. Do not talk about your observation before you record it. Talking about it diffuses its importance. In addition, it is confusing because you begin to question what you put down on paper and what you said to your colleague.

3. Find a quiet place away from distractions and with adequate equipment to record and get to work.

4. Set aside an adequate amount of time to complete the notes. It takes practice to accurately judge how long completing a set of notes will take. Especially for your first few times out, give yourself *at least* three times as long to write as to observe.

5. Start by jotting down some notes. Sketch out an outline with key phrases and events that happened. Some people draw a diagram of the setting and use it to walk through the day's experience. Like our friend, some people write down notes immediately after leaving the field, and then work from them. Others write fuller outlines when they get to their typewriter.

6. Try to go through the course of the observation session chronologically. While some people do their notes topically, the natural flow of a chronology can be the best organizing outline.

7. Let the conversations and events flow from your mind onto the paper. Some people actually talk through the conversations as they write.

8. If, after you have finished a section of the notes, you realize that you have forgotten something, add it. Similarly, if you finish your set of notes and then remember something that was not included, add it to the end. Don't be concerned about getting everything the first time through. There is always time later to add.

9. Understand that note-taking is laborious and burdensome, but as the Vermont farmer said when talking about winter on a warm day, "It's a sweet suffering. It's like you paid for spring."

We have discussed writing up fieldnotes as though researchers always did them on the typewriter. Some people write out their notes by hand, of course, but in addition, it is common for experienced fieldworkers to speak their notes into a dictaphone or tape recorder. This can be an effective way to record notes quickly, but observers often forget that in order for the material to be coded and analyzed, it has to be transcribed. If you must type your own tapes, the process of getting material down on paper will take more time than typing them out in the first place. Transcribing tapes is laborious, which is a good explanation for the high fees free-lance typists charge per page for this job.

If you do have secretarial services, the recording method can work quite well. Unless the project you are working on is heavily funded, however, you will rarely have such secretarial support. Even if you were lucky enough to have the money to pay someone to transcribe the notes, it is usually very difficult to find an experienced typist who will do the job as you want. Typists are not as accurate in transcribing tapes as the person who took the notes. Researchers often like to read over sets of notes soon after the observation session in which they were taken. Seldom can professional typists keep up the pace of an ongoing study.

As you can see, we advise that you type or write out your own notes. Although time-consuming, the typing and writing of notes has advantages. It can improve your writing, and when you do your own notes you get to know your data better. When you are collecting data in the setting, the knowledge that you must write up notes after you leave forces you to concentrate while gathering evidence. Reliving the experience line-by-line as you write out the notes intensifies concentration further. The note-taking thus encourages the observer to replay the events: seeing and hearing things a second time should improve one's recall. The process helps the observer as well to internalize, to commit to memory, what has been observed. The paper preserves the data, but the researcher's mind stores the thought process used to recall the data. This is like an extra source of data.

The fieldnotes that we provide in Figure 3-1 were written after a formal observation session. It should be noted that fieldnotes are also written after more casual encounters. If you go to a party, for example, and have a conversation with a teacher about what school means to this person, you might go home and write notes on the conversation. Phone conversations that you have with the subjects during the course of the study should go in the notes. Very often the first set of fieldnotes report the initial telephone call you make to inquire about access.

Transcripts from Taped Interviews

Some researchers take extensive fieldnotes after an interview to record their subject's statements on paper. They rely on their recall rather than on a tape recorder. But long interviews are difficult to recapture fully. When a study involves extensive interviewing or when interviewing is the major technique in the study, we recommend using a tape recorder. We shall call the typed interviews *transcripts*. Transcripts are the main "data" of many interview studies.

In Chapter 4 we go into some detail on the process of conducting tape recorded interviews. Here we briefly take up some technical matters and offer some warnings. Some of the hints given in the previous section on participant observation fieldnotes apply to transcripts.

The Form of Transcripts.   In Figure 3-2 we include the first page of an interview conducted with a woman in her twenties in which she is asked to reflect on her years in elementary school. The researcher focused on the significance being a young woman might have had on that experience (Biklen, 1973). This interview is one of more than forty conducted as part of a larger study. The form that transcripts are typed in varies (see Ives, 1974; Wood, 1975). The page we provide here illustrates a typical format.

As with fieldnotes, a heading at the start of each interview helps to organize your data and to retrieve specific segments when you want them. Here, the heading consists of the person interviewed, the time the interview occurred, the place of the interview, and any other information that might help you to remember the content of the interview. In studies where there are multiple subjects and where you conduct more than one interview with the subjects, it is useful to mark the headings indicating which interview this is with the subject. As with fieldnotes, titles can be helpful, especially when you are doing life-history interviewing. Choose titles that summarize the material covered in that interview; for example, "Early Life," "The First Day of School," or "The Year with Mrs. Brown."

FIGURE 3-2

___

INTERVIEW TRANSCRIPT (Excerpt)

Dora Weinstein, Interview #201,
October 17, 1972, 2 P.M.

I first spoke with Dora about the possibility of my interviewing her at a party at a friend's home. When we picked the day to meet, Dora said that she would be in the University library that day because it was a school holiday and she had coursework to do for her Master's Degree. So we planned to meet in my office on the fourth floor of the library at 2 P.M. on October 17th.

She came into my office just a little bit late, apologized for that, hung up her coat and sat down. She was wearing blue jeans, a patterned pink Indian tunic-shirt, and clogs. She commented on how noisy the clogs seemed when she was walking around the library.

I: It's October 17th and I'm interviewing Dora Weinstein. Dora, I can't remember if I told you at Irene's house that anything you tell me will be confidential. When I write up my study your name will be changed or I will refer to you by your code number. So you don't have to worry about anyone else knowing what you say. None of your friends will see this. (Laughter)

D: Thanks—I really appreciate that. Could you remind me about what you're doing? I know you told me at Irene's but I've forgotten—you know, long week.

I: I'm interested in what women remember about life in elementary school, so I'm interviewing forty or fifty women about their experiences.

D: That's right. OK—where do we start?

I: I'd like to start with your age. How old are you?

D: Twenty-eight.

I: Thanks. Could you describe the elementary school you went to?

D: You mean what it looked like and who went there?

I: Yes, exactly.

D: It was in the Bronx; I guess you would call it poor. It was P.S. __. The building has since been condemned. God, it was sixty years old at the time. It was one of these ancient structures with high ceilings and plaster that frequently fell off. The area around there was old Italian, but a lot of the Italian kids went to parochial school, so it was about 50-50 Jewish and Catholic at this school.

I: And where did you live?

D: Oh, about three blocks from the school in an apartment.

I: And your family?

D: I have an older brother. And my parents, too. We lived in this same apartment the whole time I was growing up.

I: What I'd like to do first is go through the grades one by one and I'll ask you what you remember about each one. Okay?

D: Sure, great.

I: Let's start with kindergarten then. Do you have any memories at all? Even if they seem unimportant, not worth mentioning to you, they might be to me.

D: I remember my kindergarten teacher was young and I thought very beautiful. But she wasn't.

I: How do you mean, "she wasn't?"

D: I mean that later on when I saw her she was just very plain. I mean she wasn't physically beautiful, but she was really nice. So I guess she was beautiful to me. I remember she wore brilliant red nailpolish, and I thought her nails were so beautiful. She was very ladylike. Oh—I aspired to be like her. (Laughs)

In typing the transcripts be sure that every time a new person speaks, you start a new line noting clearly on the left who the speaker is. The transcript should, paralleling the interview, be dominated by the subject's remarks. That does not mean that the interviewer's questions and comments are not included. It is necessary to have such material to weigh the respondent's remarks appropriately. When a subject talks for a long stretch of time, break the monologue into frequent paragraphs to facilitate coding. In addition, leave room in the left-hand margin for coding and comments. Interview transcripts can be tedious to read. And, since you may need more than one copy of a transcript (depending on which coding procedure you choose), make sure your typewriter ribbon will enable you to produce dark copy so you can read and reproduce it easily.

Equipment

Tape recorders can create the illusion that research is effortless. Aside from the short fieldnotes describing the setting and subject, the person doing the interview usually does not have to worry about extensive writing after the session. Because of this, the researcher might think that the machine does all the work. As we warned in our discussion on recording fieldnotes, accumulating tapes of interviews without an adequate system to transcribe them can spell the project's failure. Before you gain some practice, it is difficult to estimate how long transcribing takes. It is easy to let recording sessions go on too long, providing you with more dialogue on tape than you can possibly transcribe.

If you choose to record and transcribe interviews, a good rule to follow is "think short." Qualitative interviews are, of course, supposed to be open-ended and flowing. We do not mean that you should force the interview into a short-answer format. Rather, we suggest that you should limit the interview's length. Pick a reasonable number of subjects and spend an amount of time in each interview that make sense in terms of the work involved in transcribing it. You do not want the respondent's discussion to wander all over the field, but to center on a particular area. You should figure that a one-hour interview, when typed, amounts to twenty to forty typewritten pages of data. If you plan to transcribe the tapes yourself, this will mean hundreds of hours of your time. If someone else is typing it, it can mean a great expense to you.

We have a few suggestions about recording equipment (see Ives, 1974; Wood, 1975). Good recording equipment is invaluable. It does not have to be expensive, but it should be easy to operate, in good repair, and capable of making clear tapes. Because many of the expensive tape recorders are designed to capture music, they do more than you need. Since the tonal quality of the tape matters little (unless, for example, you are recording how a teacher uses folk music in his or her classes), an expensive recorder designed to record music is rarely necessary.

The tape recorder must definitely be in good working order. You need to check your equipment both before and during an interview. While intrusive, this equipment check can be handled casually, and is worth it in the long run. We have lost too many interviews because of equipment malfunction that occurred when we took it for granted that the equipment was working. We have been particularly plagued with problems with battery-operated recorders. The frustration of trying to type barely-audible tapes is costly. You can forestall these and other problems by making certain in advance that your equipment is well cleaned and in good condition, or by borrowing or buying a new tape recorder. It is worthwhile paying attention to the quality of the tapes you buy as well.

If you plan to do any transcribing yourself, try to use a transcriber (it is worth buying one if you can scrape up the money). A transcriber does not do the typing for you but it considerably reduces the time it will take. A transcriber is the playback part of a tape recorder with foot pedals to control stopping, rewinding, and starting the machine. Some models have special features to slow down the voice or adjust the number of lines the machine will jump when the pedal is pushed. Though adapters enable some models of regular tape recorders to be run by foot pedals, we have not had much success with them.

If someone is doing the transcript typing for you, you ought to work closely with that person in order to make certain that his or her work is accurate. Capturing the punctuation that gets at the meaning of what you heard is especially difficult, so considerable difference can arise when two typists type the same transcript. The most accurate rendition of what occurred, of course, is on the tape. If you have the money to buy enough tapes, we recommend that you save the tapes so that you can check on the finished transcripts.

Because of the extensive time and expense involved in transcribing interviews, people working without research funding often take short cuts. One short cut is to type transcripts yourself, but leave out a lot of the material that does not address your concerns. While there are some dangers involved in this short cut, the risks are often worth the gains. Another alternative is to transcribe some of the first interviews more or less completely (when we say ''completely'' we mean it would be all right to leave out long discussions of recipes and baseball), and then narrow what you transcribe in later interviews. As the study goes on, you should have a better idea about your focus and be more sensitively selective in what is typed.

THE SUBJECTS' WRITTEN WORDS

The data we have discussed thus far consists of materials that the researchers have a major hand in producing. They write the fieldnotes and conduct the interviews that become the transcripts. While not used as frequently, materials that the subjects write themselves are used as data as well. Such things as autobiographies, personal letters, diaries, memos, minutes from meetings, newsletters, policy documents, proposals, codes of ethics, statements of philosophy, yearbooks, news releases, scrapbooks, letters to the editor, ''Dear Abby'' letters, newspaper articles, personnel files, and student's case records and folders are included. For the most part, the researcher makes use of materials that already exist. They are in the files of organizations, the desk drawers of principals, the attics of buildings, and the archives of historical societies. The major task is to locate and get access to the material.

The quality of this type of material varies. Some provide only some factual details like the dates when meetings occurred. Others serve as sources of rich descriptions of how the people who produced the materials think about their world. Subject-produced data are employed as part of studies where the major thrust is participant observation or interviewing, although at times they are employed exclusively.

We will now review different kinds of subject-written data.

Personal Documents

In most traditions of qualitative research, the phrase *personal documents* is used broadly to refer to any first-person narrative produced by an individual which describes his or her own actions, experiences, and beliefs. The criterion for calling written material personal documents is that it is self-revealing of a person's view of experiences (Allport, 1942). The aim of collecting such materials is to "obtain detailed evidence as to how social situations appear to actors in them and what meanings various factors have for participants" (Angell, 1945, p. 178). Used this way, personal documents include materials collected through interviewing, thus much of the data we discussed as transcripts would be considered personal documents. Here, however, we discuss only materials that the subjects themselves have written.

Personal documents that the subjects write themselves are usually discovered rather than solicited by the researcher. On occasion, researchers do ask people to write for them or get others to help them produce such materials. Clifford Shaw (1966) asked juvenile delinquents with whom he worked to put down on paper their life stories, which he later used for his research. Teachers frequently ask students to write compositions about certain aspects of their lives (for example, ''My Family'' or more commonly, ''What I Did During the Summer''). While raising ethical issues, teachers might be helpful in directing children to write on topics a researcher is studying. Jules Henry reports findings based on 200 school children's written responses to the question: ''What do you like most and what do you like least about your father (and mother).'' Teachers collaborated in this research by asking their students these questions (Henry, 1963). In a study of how teachers' home-school lives interact, teachers were requested to keep journals for a year to give to the researcher—and they did (Hall, 1979). Some researchers have run contests in which they gave prizes for the best essay on a particular topic (Allport, 1942). An advantage of soliciting compositions is that the researcher can have some hand in directing the authors' focus and thereby get a number of people to write on a single event or topic.

We want to discuss briefly some types of personal documents that are unsolicited by the researcher.

Intimate Diaries.   As Allport has stated: "The spontaneous, intimate diary is the personal document par excellence" (Allport, 1942, p. 95). He was referring to the product of a person who keeps a regular, running description and reflective commentary of the events in his or her life. Allport's image of the intimate document reflects his portrait of a young girl or woman writing in detail about various aspects of adolescent life she is experiencing for the first time. While this characterization may be a stereotype, it is also reflective of a type of diary. Adults with families and jobs may have less time to reflect on their lives and record these thoughts. Whatever the source of the diary, educational researchers have not been known to employ them in their own research. Because a diary is usually written under the immediate influence of an experience, it can be particularly effective in capturing peoples' moods and most intimate thoughts. Diaries, of course, are not lying around for the taking. The very intimacy that makes them so valuable also keeps them out of the hands of strangers.

Diaries can surface in the course of interviewing or participant observation. Subjects with whom you have developed relationships may spontaneously mention that they now keep a diary, or have kept one in the past. It may take courage on your part to ask, "How would you feel if I read it?" But the effort may be the only way these kinds of documents will be revealed to you. Whether you see it will depend on your rapport with the subject as well as with the personal value of the diary to the writer. Chances are if the document is mentioned by an informant, the subject is toying with the idea of showing it to you, so you ought to pursue it.

While it may seem like a ridiculous suggestion, one way of locating diaries is to place an ad in a newspaper or publicly announce in other ways your interest in looking at certain kinds of materials and the uses you have in mind for them (Thomas and Znaniecki, 1927).[2] You may be surprised that people will be willing to share their most intimate thoughts with persons who can establish their trustworthiness as well as their pure research interests.

Historians are researchers who depend heavily on diaries and other personal documents. They find these materials in local historical societies and various archives as well as in the boxes of memorabilia that people store in their attics. For educational researchers, teachers' diaries that record in detail first teaching experiences, problems with students, and other such materials are important finds.

There are other materials that are similar to diaries, but much less intimate. There are special-purpose logs like those teachers might keep. Lesson plans with accompanying notes are interesting, especially if they contain personal comments.

Also parents sometimes keep developmental diaries of the growth and progress of their children. Some go as far as to make weekly entries about what the child is doing. This kind of material can be an important source of understanding how parents perceive their children and their expectations for them. Travel logs and other kinds of written records of peoples' activities, although not as intimate or revealing as the diary, can provide some hints about what life is like for the people you are interested in studying.

Personal Letters.   Personal letters between friends and family members provide another source of rich qualitative data. These materials can be especially helpful in revealing relationships between people who correspond. When the letter represents an attempt by the author to share his or her problems and experiences, it can provide insights about the author's experiences. Many people go away to school, or travel to take up jobs in educational institutions. The letters written home describing life and the nature of their experiences offer rich data about the educational system. Much of what has been said about locating diaries applies to letters as well, although letters are a more common form of communication than diaries. The increased use of the phone for communicating may discourage letter-writing, however; now this data source may be useful only to people with historical interests.

Although they should not be classified as personal, letters written to the editors of newspapers about school issues are another possible source of information for the qualitative researcher. Another are the more personal letters written to the likes of Ann Landers and Dear Abby. Perusing such materials can give you some insight, for example, about problems adolescents face. It should be kept in mind, of course, that the published letters are not randomly selected. They represent the choice of the person writing the column or the columnist's staff.

Autobiographies.   Published autobiographies provide a readily available source of data for the discerning qualitative researcher. Virtually thousands of such documents get published and most contain extensive discussions of peoples' educational experiences. There are autobiographies written by school drop-outs, great teachers, world leaders, adolescents, scholars, doctors, check forgers, drug addicts, and ordinary people. Autobiographies range considerably from the intimate and personal (containing materials such as are found in rich diaries) to the superficial and trivial.

With all personal documents it is important to attempt to understand the writer's purpose in producing the documents. The autobiographer's purpose can vary widely. Some reasons to engage in such a task include:

1. Special pleading for one's self or a cause
2. Exhibitionism
3. Desire to give order to one's life
4. Literary delight
5. Securing personal perspective
6. Relief from tension

7. Monetary gain
8. Outside pressures to write it
9. Assisting in therapy
10. Redemption and social reincorporation
11. Scientific interest
12. Public service and example
13. Desire for immortality (Allport, 1942, p. 69).

The motivation will affect the content of the document. An autobiography, rich in detail, written for the purpose of telling the person's own story as he or she experienced it, parallels the role a key informant would play for a researcher. It can be an introduction to the world you want to study. Autobiographies by particular categories of people, ethnic minorities, for example, particularly sections of the work that describe their schooling, can introduce the researcher interested in this issue to the range of educational experiences the particular group encountered.

Novels should not be ruled out as a potential source of qualitative understanding, though they are more troublesome than autobiographies because discerning accurate description from imaginative portrayal is difficult. (See Eisner, 1980, on artistic understanding.) They cannot be taken as the truthful representation of an author's experiences. They can, however, provide insight if not used as data in the strict sense.

Official Documents

Schools and other bureaucratic organizations have reputations for producing a profusion of written communications and files. Most people talk disparagingly about these mounds of paper, and might look askance at us for calling these official documents "data." We are talking about such things as memos, minutes from meetings, newsletters, policy documents, proposals, codes of ethics, dossiers, students' records, statements of philosophy, news releases, and the like. These materials have been viewed by many researchers as extremely subjective, representing the biases of the promoters and, when written for external consumption, presenting an unrealistically glowing picture of how the organization functions. For this reason, many researchers consider them unimportant, excluding them as "data." It is precisely *for* these properties (and others) that qualitative researchers look upon them favorably. Remember, qualitative researchers are not interested in "the truth" as it is conventionally conceived. They do not search for the "true picture" of any school. Their interest in understanding how the school is defined by various people propels them toward official literature. Researchers can get access in these papers to the "official perspective," as well as to the ways various school personnel communicate. Much of what we term *official documents* are readily available to the researcher although some are protected as private or secret. We will briefly discuss some types of official documents, their use, and special problems you may encounter obtaining them.

Internal Documents.   These are memos and other communications that are circulated inside an organization such as a school system. This information tends to follow the hierarchical course, circulating downward from the central office to building teachers and staff. Information flows the opposite way, of course, but it rarely equals the downward tide. Minutes of department meetings and other such gatherings are often passed along horizontally. Internal documents can reveal information about the official chain of command, and internal rules and regulations. They can also provide clues about leadership style and potential insights about what organizational members value. While secret memos exist, secret information is not, by and large, passed along in written form. If a researcher has established good rapport, he or she will have access to most internally produced documents.

External Communication.   External communication refers to materials produced by the school system for public consumption: newsletters, news releases, yearbooks, the notes sent home, the public statements of philosophy, the open house programs. As we suggested earlier, this material is useful in understanding official perspectives on programs, the administrative structure, and other aspects of the school system. It should be kept in mind that, increasingly, school systems hire public relations experts to produce such material so they do not necessary directly flow from the pens of those in charge. Most likely, though, school administrators review and approve the documents. You may be able to put external documents to better use if you know something about who produced them and for what reasons; in other words, the social context. Some external documents are good indicators of school systems' strategies for increasing fiscal support, while in other cases they represent a direct expression of the values of those who administer the schools.

   Usually external documents are easy to get. In fact, they are often produced in such quantities that they far exceed their demand. Very often administrative offices will keep scrapbooks and files to keep these materials as they are issued over the years. Scrapbooks may contain local newspaper coverage of school-related events. Ask to see such holdings for they can save you time.

Student Records and Personnel Files.   In addition to the official documents already discussed, schools keep individual files on every student and in most cases on each employee. The files on students are particularly elaborate and important. They include psychological reports, records of all testing, attendance, anecdotal comments from teachers, information about other schools attended, and profiles of the family. This file follows the child throughout his or her school career.

   Traditional researchers often use such case records to conduct research, but many take the position that they are not very helpful because they do not give accurate information about the child. Qualitative researchers would agree with this wholeheartedly. While they might occasionally want to retrieve a test score or a list of teachers from a file, by and large qualitative researchers approach student records not for what they tell about the child, but rather for what they reveal about the people who keep the records (psychologists, administrators, teachers). In this framework, the information the files contain—the letters, the teacher's comments, the test scores —represent perspectives on the child. They present one side of the picture. They seldom contain unaltered quotations from the students or their parents. Juxtaposing student's records with interviews with the student or the parents can prove to be a revealing combination of data.

PHOTOGRAPHY

Photography is closely aligned with qualitative research and, as we shall explore here, it can be used in many different ways. Photographs provide strikingly descriptive data, are often used to understand the subjective, and its products are frequently analyzed inductively.

Almost from its advent, photography was employed in conjunction with social science research. One of the early photographers who did social photographic documentaries was John Thomson, whose book *Street Life in London,* a portrayal of London's poor, was published in 1877 (Thomson and Smith, 1877). A decade later, in New York City, Jacob Riis's photographic essay on immigrants included portraits of the interiors of dilapidated schools. He educated people about urban conditions (Riis, 1890). Lewis Hine, a sociologist, was one of the first social scientists to use a camera to show the American people poverty in their own country. His photo-documentaries of child labor were influential in passing the first child labor laws and legislation directed toward compulsory education. He said, ''If I could tell the story in words, I wouldn't need to lug a camera'' (Stott, 1973).

While social science and photography have been linked for a long time, it is only recently that photos have captured the attention of a significant number of researchers (Becker, 1978; Wagner, 1979). This interest in photography has been controversial. Some claim that photography is virtually useless as a way of objectively knowing because it distorts that which it claims to illuminate (Sontag, 1977). Others counter with the claim that it represents a significant research breakthrough, since it allows researchers to understand and study aspects of life that cannot be researched through other approaches; they echo Hine's suggestion that images are more telling than words.

While a few argue these extreme positions, most social scientists neither accept nor reject photography outright; they ask, ''What value does it have for me and how can I make use of it in my own work?'' They ask these questions in relation to specific research problems and with particular photographs in mind.

Photographs that might be used in qualitative educational research can be separated into two categories: those that others have taken and those that the researcher has a hand in producing.

Found Photographs

Photographs that fall under this category are available because others have taken them. Many schools and human service agencies have extensive collections of photographs, often going back to the laying of the cornerstone. Yearbooks, class pictures, and amateur photos taken at annual events and outings are usually available for the asking. Students often have their own photo collections, some of which they carry with them in purses or wallets. Newspapers keep photo libraries, although access to this material is often limited. County planning offices keep aerial photographs of all the land that falls within their jurisdiction.

We are, in other words, a photographic society. Cameras are common and they produce millions upon millions of images each year. Often, after photos are taken, they are filed or placed in some archive or collection. One has to inquire about such personal resources as photograph albums and publicity folders as well as those used more technically.

Photos that turn up in a setting under study can provide a good sense of individuals no longer there, or what particular events in that setting were like. As suggested, schools often keep photo collections, yearbooks, and sometimes, albums that offer their own visual history. Photos that staff may have taken of former students or coworkers portray some sense of what these people were like despite your never having met them. While not a substitute for having been there, photos can offer one historical rendering of the setting and its participants. Further, such photos can be incorporated into research reports to communicate this perspective.

While photos provide a general sense of a setting, they can also offer specific factual information that can be used in conjunction with other sources. Pictures taken at retirement parties, for example, can show who attended, and indicate something about seating arrangements, hinting, perhaps, at the informal structure. Aerial photos of a community under study can suggest relationships between population distribution, geographic location, and the educational system.

While photos do give factual information, it is important to understand that photos one finds or are given were taken for a purpose or from a particular point of view. In order to use them more than superficially, one has to know the purpose and the frame of mind of the photographer. In this way, a photo is like all other forms of qualitative data: to use it, one must place it in a proper context and understand what it is capable of telling before extracting information and understanding. Photos can represent the photographer's own view of what was important, or the orders he or she was given from a superior, or the demands of people who are the subjects. While some might contend that this may place them in the realm of the subjective and may detract from their "factual" worth, it does provide another use of photos, one that is much in line with the qualitative perspective; that is, when we study photos, we ascertain clues about what people value and the images they prefer. While photos may not be able to prove anything conclusively, when used in conjunction with other data, they can add to a growing pile of evidence.

Henry W. Brown.

Miss Blanche Lamont with her school at Hecla, Montana, October, 1893. (Courtesy of the Library of Congress)

Photographs serve another function as well. They may present anomalies, images that do not fit the theoretical constructs the researcher is forming. When photographic images are not compatible with a developing analysis, they can push one's analysis and insights further than they might originally have gone. In a recent study we did of photographs taken in the 1920s at a state school for the mentally retarded, we noted how all the pictures presented the students as clean-cut, well-mannered, middle-class youngsters. This image stood in dramatic contrast to what professionals were saying during this period about people with retardation. The time was the height of the eugenics movement when professionals agreed that mentally handicapped people were society's rogues—a terrible danger to everyone's well being. Our attempt to think through the contradiction between the written words and the pictures facilitated a multi-dimensional discussion of these issues.

Miles Brothers.

Public school, Valdez, October, 1902. (Courtesy of the National Archives)

Researchers also use photographs to probe how people define their world: they can reveal what people take for granted, what they assume is unquestionable. Schools and human service agencies, for example, often taken photos to release to the press in conjunction with events they sponsor. They also photograph students and clients for inclusion in the agency's official records. Study may elicit organizational assumptions about students and clients revealed in the photos: What are the clients wearing when they are photographed? In what positions are they posed? When we examined photos taken for fund-raising campaigns by one school whose students are defined as mentally retarded, for example, we found that the students were often cast in the role of children, or clowns, or as helpless. If you have hired an outside evaluator to improve the quality of services, pointing out these specific images can be a strategy to encourage change.

We have just scratched the surface of possible uses of available photographs. Locating and using them takes imagination and care.

Photographer Unknown.

Old-fashioned boy's school, 1905. Does this historical photo capture a typical old-fashioned boy's school classroom scene or is this a posed spoof? Interpreting photographs is complex. (Courtesy of the Library of Congress)

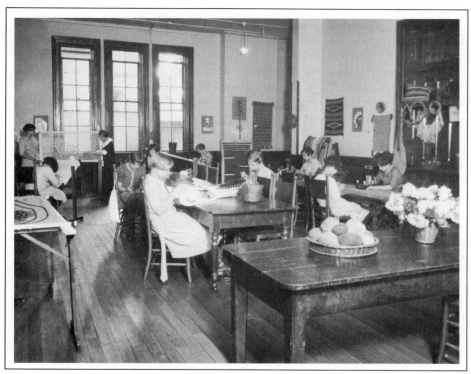

Photographer Unknown.

Craftsmaking at an Institution for the Retarded, 1920s. (Courtesy of Syracuse Developmental Center)

Researcher-Produced Photographs

In the hands of an educational researcher, the camera can produce photos for use in some of the ways already discussed. They can simplify the collection of factual information. Researchers can take aerial photographs, for example, to better grasp population distribution and its relationship to school location. One social scientist we know was asked to help city planners work out plans to redesign a downtown public square. To get a sense of how people use space at given times during the day, a camera with a device that automatically took a picture every ten minutes was placed in a window of a building facing the square. The camera was aimed to include the entire area each time the shutter opened and closed. Such a technique might easily be employed in conjunction with other methods to study the use of playgrounds, college quads, or various indoor spaces.

Perhaps the most common use of the camera is in conjunction with participant observation. In this capacity it is most often used as a means of remembering and studying detail that might be overlooked if a photographic image were not available for reflection. Photographs taken by researchers in the field provide images for later intense inspection about clues to relationships and activities. Insignia and pins indicating organizational affiliations, the appearance of people who attended particular events, seating arrangements, office layout, and contents of book cases can be studied and used as data when the camera is employed as part of the data-collecting technique. Complete photographing of a classroom can facilitate conducting a *cultural inventory*.

A word has to be said about the use of a camera and its effect on rapport. Some controversy exists over the effect of a camera in the hands of the researcher. In our own work we have been reluctant to use cameras because we have thought of them as a hazard for fieldwork. Our feeling is that, in the early stages of research particularly, a camera emphasizes the researcher's role as an outsider or gives the impression that he or she is a spy. It can also intrude in the subject-researcher relationship in another way. Photographers can distance themselves from others by substituting picture-taking for the conversation and interaction that allow the researcher to develop empathy with a subject. The researcher must guard against this. Our rule has been to avoid taking pictures early in the research, before the subjects have had a chance to get to know and trust us. In some cases, it is never the right time to take pictures for it is simply offensive to subjects. A good rule for us has been one that parallels our advice about questioning: Photograph first that in which the people in the setting take most pride (Collier, 1967).

Others do not share the caution we hold about picture-taking. Collier (1967), for example, discusses the camera as an excellent way of establishing rapport. He refers to it as the anthropologists' "can-opener" or "golden key," encouraging its use on the first day. His position is that the camera can provide a researcher with a legitimate purpose and occupation in the setting. After the pictures are taken and developed, they provide a reason to get together for discussion, which produces good data—data on peoples' reactions to the photos. His remarks are mainly directed to its use in cultures very different from the researchers'. We do not think taking pictures on the first day is appropriate in most situations in which educational researchers find themselves, but you should leave yourself open to its potential for establishing rapport. It might, for example, be a useful tool to establish rapport with children.

In the course of fieldwork, you must weigh the costs and benefits of picture-taking, making decisions about how and when to do it. On certain occasions, for example, when others are using cameras, it may be perfectly safe to photograph. At other times, if you have doubts about whether taking pictures is appropriate or not, test out the idea with a trusted informant. We will have more to say about the use of cameras and rapport in the next chapter.

Another way that researchers use cameras as a research tool occurs when the researcher gives the camera to subjects, asking them to take the pictures. While we have not used this technique ourselves, those who have suggest that it can be a way to gain insight on how the subjects see their world. In one project, cameras were strapped to a wheelchair in an apartment complex designed for handicapped individuals. These photos, taken as the person in the wheelchair moved through the complex, were used to sensitize architects about how their designs appeared from the position of those who were using them.

Photos taken by researchers or chosen by researchers and shown to subjects can be used as a stimulant for data gathering. In one study in which the researcher was trying to understand how typical students (nondisabled children) thought of severely disabled children that had been mainstreamed into their classes, the children were interviewed and asked to discuss other students in their classes (Barnes, 1978). Rather than naming the children or describing them, the researcher showed slides to the children and asked them to describe and discuss the students pictured there. In another study in which geographers were trying to understand how various people thought about particular kinds of environments, wilderness pictures of forest areas were projected on a screen and groups of urban dwellers, including inner-city elementary school students, were asked to discuss them.

Photographs as Analysis

Thus far we have discussed photographs as data or as a stimulant for producing data. In the current debates concerning photography's role in social science research, these uses are the least controversial. More the subject of contention is the analytic use of photographs; that is, when the researcher claims that the image stands by itself as an abstract statement, or as an objective rendering of a setting or issue (Goffman, 1979; Trachtenberg, 1979). Many questions on this concern shoot back and forth: Can photos taken by a researcher, or anyone else, capture the inner-life of, say, a school? Can they grasp an essence that is illusive to other approaches? Do the photos that people take oversentimentalize what they are supposed to depict or do they distort by concentrating on the stark or seamy side of life? Do they immortalize what is actually only a moment in an ongoing flow of events? Is the camera like a typewriter (Becker, 1978) that has nothing to say on its own? Is it only an instrument, dependent upon the skill and insightfulness of the one who is holding it? Or is there something about the relationship between the holder, the camera, and the understanding that is transcendent?

These are the questions with which qualitative researchers interested in photography must wrestle. In educational researchers' quest for understanding, photos are not answers, but tools to pursue them. The camera's invention and its extensive use has changed the way we view and experience our world. While we have discussed photography's uses in educational research, it is also important to see photography and the world of picture-takers as important subject matter for study in their own right. We have to understand how society affects and is affected by the photographic enterprise. Only when we do this more fully than we have to date can we explore in-depth photos' analytic worth. Photography can be an educational researcher's tool, but it must be understood as a cultural product and as a producer of culture.

Technique and Equipment[3]

Do you have to be a good photographer to use photography in qualitative research? Yes and no. George Eastman's fortune was made on fulfilling the promise that "you push the button, we'll do the rest." In research, it is not quite that simple, but under certain conditions it might be close.

The question to be answered first is: "What are the pictures supposed to show?" If the goal is to have "inventory" photos of the research setting, very little skill may be required (although it may demand some fancy equipment—to be discussed later). If subtle events of interpersonal behavior must be captured, it might take quite a bit of discipline and practice to learn how to capture them with a camera. The key is to be able to specify ahead of time what the content of the desired photo would be. Anything that can be clearly specified can easily be photographed by anyone. The trick, then, is to know what you are looking for and, especially in exploratory stages of the research, to recognize what you are looking for when it appears.

The special photographic skill that is required when working with data more complex than the inventory is the ability to judge what a scene will look like when converted to a small, flat rectangle. This skill is particularly important when working in black and white media. Amateur snapshots abound in illustrations of how the translation from a real world to a 3 × 5-inch flat one can go wrong. There are the very obvious ones of cut-off heads, missing people, sun in the lens causing blacked-out foreground, or tiny people in a field of unwanted surroundings. It should be possible to overcome these errors simply by knowing what should be in the picture and then making sure it is actually in the view-finder of the camera—and that very little else is.

At a slightly more complex level, one also has to develop a sense of what will "show up" in a photograph. The eye can isolate details in a way a picture cannot. Things that are subtle in color-shading or texture or brightness may not show up, or may be exaggerated. Details that are small may not be resolved and decipherable on film. If they are likely to constitute important data, they should be photographed close up.

A research project certainly should not be one's first experience shooting pictures. None of these skills is difficult to learn, but they must be learned. It would probably be enough, and well worth the time, for you to set up several exercises approximating the sort of pictures that will be wanted in the study. Specify what you want the picture to contain and then find a situation in which to try to shoot it. But do not settle for good pictures—demand of yourself that you get the pictures you set out to get. You cannot rely on accidentally good pictures for good research. The knack will come.

What kind of equipment does it take? The advice must unfortunately be the same as with tape recorders—it should be good. Since serious research is usually undertaken with at least a thought to eventual publication, the photographic data should be as good as possible. Since image quality deteriorates in reproduction, starting from bad negatives can be disasterous.

Thus, miniature pocket cameras should be ruled out. Their film is so small that the 3 × 5 print is virtually the most enlargement they can take and small details could not be salvaged from them. The smallest acceptable format is the full-frame 35 mm camera. Probably larger cameras should be ruled out because of cost—both of the cameras and of the film to put through them.

If demands on the camera will not be great, any good 35 mm camera will do very well. However, it often happens that close-ups are desired, as well as wide-angle shots of spaces which cannot be encompassed with a normal lens. So, if possible, the camera should be of the single-lens reflex type, with interchangeable lenses. A wide-angle lens with a focal length of 24–28 mm should serve "inventory" purposes. A "portrait" lens (about 100 mm focal length) would enable the photographer to fill the frame with one "head-shot" without working disconcertingly close to the subject. The "normal" lens (50 mm) would serve for larger groups or showing more background. An economy might be to have one zoom lens in the wide-angle to portrait range (e.g., 23 mm–85 mm or 35–100), enabling the photographer to choose framing without changing (or carrying) extra lenses. The camera should also have automatic exposure control.

Unless publication can be ruled out for the study, the photography should be in black-and-white. Production costs are so high for color that it is almost never used in journals or professional books.[4] For indoor settings, a fast black-and-white film is the best and necessary choice—Kodak Tri-X, Ilford HP-5, or the like. These films are adequate for most artificially illuminated settings and make it unnecessary to use a flash—definitely an advantage since it is difficult to be unobtrusive if one is setting off a lightning bolt every few seconds.

Of course, photographic equipment is very expensive and these suggestions may sound prohibitive. However, despite the expense, such equipment seems to be available and could perhaps be borrowed. Moreover, it is available to rent, most commonly at university-affiliated stores.

The final impediment to doing qualitative research with photography is the "model release." For publication, it is imperative that each recognizable individual in each picture sign a release which gives permission to publish his or her picture. Parents or guardians must sign one for minors. Steps should be taken to secure releases as soon as the project is underway, since the matter often turns out to be far more time-consuming and difficult than anyone would suppose. In setting up a study and gaining access to a site, you will have obtained permission to visit and photograph, but this is not the same as the model release. Thus, unless releases are also obtained, you will wind up with a store of photographic data you cannot use.

A final note on photographic studies must caution the uninitiated about hazards of the attempt. It is generally more difficult to secure consent to take pictures than to do any other sort of study. In part, this is because a camera is a greater threat to privacy and anonymity. It may also be because cameras are not ordinarily thought of as research tools. But there is also a certain body of negative preconceptions relating to what cameras can do. They can be used to embarrass if not humiliate people—as in

"Candid Camera." The administrators of a setting—principals, teachers, super-visors—understandably do not wish to be humiliated. These feelings are heightened by the almost mystical belief that anyone can be humiliated by a camera, that some-how the camera can generate a negative view of even the most laudible person. Since no human setting is perfect, perhaps they do not trust the photographer to be "fair." And it can hardly put them at ease to know that by far the most well-known type of photographic study is the photojournalistic exposé.

In approaching a setting for permission to photograph, these and other misgiv-ings have to be recognized and handled. With any method of research, subjects need to be assured that the project is undertaken with good and serious intentions; when photography is involved, the assurance is often more difficult to establish.

OFFICIAL STATISTICS AND OTHER QUANTITATIVE DATA

While conducting studies, the qualitative researcher often comes across quantitative data others have compiled. Schools, as we have said, keep and generate tremendous amounts of data. Teachers may choose to keep data for their own purposes. The ad-ministration collects data on racial composition, languages spoken, handicapping conditions, the number of athletic injuries, attendance counts, drop-out rates, achievement scores, the number of acts of violence and suspension, and a host of other numerical computations. At times the qualitative researcher finds it useful to generate his or her own numerical data. What does a qualitative researcher think about and do with such material?

Quantitative data can have conventional uses in qualitative research. It can sug-gest trends in a setting; whether, for example, the number of students served has increased or decreased. It can also provide descriptive information (age, race, sex, socioeconomic status) about the population served by a particular educational pro-gram. These kinds of data may open up avenues to explore and questions to answer. Quantitative data is often included in qualitative writing in the form of descriptive statistics.

Statistical data can also serve as a check on ideas that you develop during research. You might learn through observation, for example, that while male trainees in a job-training program do not speak of training as important in their lives, the women trainees do. You might hold up this "working hypothesis" against official attendance records, assuming that these attendance records empirically indicate seriousness. You would not use attendance records to prove what you have found, but rather to explore the implications of your idea in that particular aspect of the pro-gram. If attendance records were not as high for women as men, you might be forced to explain this.

Looking at actual official statistics and comparing them to what subjects verbally report can be helpful in exploring perceptions. Recently, for example, a researcher who was studying the implementation of a new reading program often heard teachers make reference to how much the reading levels among the pupils had risen since the new program had been incorporated. When the researcher explored this statement, she discovered that reading levels in the school had not gone up; teachers, in fact, had never seen data on reading levels. The enthusiastic support of the teachers for the new program was reflected in their reporting of the data, not in the data itself.

While quantitative data collected by others (evaluators, administrators, other researchers) can be conventionally useful as we have described, qualitative researchers critically dispose themselves to the collection of quantitative data. It is not that the numbers themselves hold no value. Rather, the qualitative researcher tends to turn the compilation process on its head by asking what the numbers tell about the assumptions of the people who use and compile them. Rather than relying upon quantitative data as an avenue to accurately describe reality, qualitative researchers are concerned with how enumeration is used by subjects in constructing reality. They are interested in how statistics reveal subjects' common-sense understandings.

Qualitative researchers are adamant about not taking quantitative data at face value. They see the social processes involved in numerical data collection and the effects of quantification on how people think and act as important subjects for study. This interest in studying the generation of numbers should not be confused with the study by statisticians of how to improve counting and estimation. The qualitative approach to quantitative data focuses on understanding how counting actually takes place, not on how it should take place.

The following describes eight approaches to the quantitative data you may find in a school or human service organization (Bogdan, 1980) to sensitize you to the qualitative perspective:

1. *The concept of "real rates" is a misnomer.* The process of quantification produces rates and measures. They do not appear "naturally" in the world. Rates and counts represent a point of view that subjects take toward people, objects, and events. In addition, because subjects take a numerical attitude toward certain categories of people, objects, or events does not mean there will be a natural concensus concerning how to arrive at rates and counts. Rates of acts of violence in schools, for example, are dependent on how the people who compile the figures at a given time and place define the phenomenon and go about their work. We cannot generate a rate of violent acts until we develop a perspective toward specific actions that deem them quantifiable or important to count. (See NIE, 1978 for an example of how school districts define violence differently.) A social scientist, a policy researcher, or a government official may arbitrarily choose one way to count and develop one set of conventions to arrive at a method of constructing a "real rate," but whatever is derived is the product of the assumptions used, the concepts employed, and the process that evolves. To claim to have the "true measure" is a claim for the supremacy of one definition and one method over the other and should not be confused with "truth" in the absolute sense.

What are the various ways that people define and quantify those things they are required to count? What factors seem to influence the definitions and the ways they proceed? Are there variations from data-gatherer to data-gatherer about how to proceed? How are understandings concerning what to count and how to count developed?

2. *Singling out people, objects, and events to quantify changes their meaning.*   Quantification has the potential to make that which was once taken for granted salient, and make that which was once amorphous concrete. Requirements to keep statistics on racial and ethnic backgrounds, for example, may increase the attention people pay to children's race, changing their ideas about who belongs in what category as well. Statistical data on minority or handicapped children, the number of athletic injuries, acts of violence, or incidence of drug use in schools does more than numerically portray phenomena; it changes how we experience it.

What specific effects does counting have on the meaning of events and people?

3. *Quantifying has a temporal dimension.*   Any attempt to quantify has a history. Any generation or discussion of a measure or count of something is located at a particular historical moment. Numbers, in other words, do not stand alone, but are related to the social and historical contexts that generate them. Changes in reported rates—whether of attendance, drug use, achievement scores, or the number of children with learning disabilities—do not necessarily correspond to actual changes in behavior or to the characteristics of the people being counted. It is premature to make generalizations, but our observations of the counting of handicapped children suggest to us that the greater our concern with a particular phenomena, the more we focus on it and the higher our rates will be. Sarason and Doris (1979), in their discussion of compulsory education and the rise in mental retardation, suggest that rates of mental retardation have to be understood in relation to our changing definition of who should be educated.

4. *Quantification involves many different participants and can only be understood as a multi-level phenomenon.*   How an issue is viewed in Washington and how those at the national level go about measuring may not correspond with how it is thought about at the state or local level. Similarly, superintendents may interpret a directive differently from principals. Of course, the general public may receive data in a manner confounding to those who generated it. As one local newspaper writer put it:

> One child is not necessarily one child the way the State Education Department does it. . . . The way educators count, one child can be a half of a child, a whole child, a child and a quarter, a child and four-tenths or in some cases, one child is actually two children.

What is the original intention of initiating a count? How is the motivation and origin understood at the various levels that it passes through? How do people at the levels that receive data understand the meaning of what they get? How does that result correspond to what collectors understood they were doing?

5. *Both the person and his or her motivation for counting affect the meaning, the process, and the figures generated.* This assumption, while closely tied to the last, is separated to emphasize the important role played by those who initiate counting and the sanctions available to them. When federal funding for an organization, for example, is tied to serving certain categories of people, the tendency rises for these rates to be reached independent of actual changes in who is served and what is done. When the amount of money allocated to a school depends on generating counts, the counts will tend to move toward the levels that are most favorable to the agency seeking the funding. Increasingly, state and local governments are developing elaborate reporting systems because of orders to produce counts. These orders and their results deserve careful study.

Professionals' relationships to rate production are central because they often initiate counts and have a stake in rate production. A study of services to the blind reveals that the definition of legal blindness generally relied upon to produce counts of blind children and which was derived by professionals, results in producing a category of people, the overwhelming majority of who can see (Scott, 1969). The new diagnostic category, "learning disabled," illustrates the importance of studying who initiates counting. Some specialists report that up to 40 percent of all children are learning disabled while some professionals not associated with the specialty claim that "learning disability" is a contrived diagnosis.

What do people who generate counts understand as the consequences of their action? How does having funding attached to achieving certain rates affect counting? How do various professional groups affect counts? How do "lay" counts differ from professional counts?

6. *Counting releases social processes within the setting where the counting takes place in addition to and beyond the activities directly tied to counting.* Counting can shape what people consider important and meaningful, and designate particular activities as expedient. Giving standardized tests at the end of a course of study, for instance, may change the content of the course and the activities that the class engages in during the year. Generating success rates can become the major activity of educational agencies.

How does counting affect the normal activities that people engage in an educational settings? What is the relationship between measuring success and being successful?

7. *People who produce data in educational settings are subject to social processes and structural forces similar to those that touch other work groups.* Studies of factory workers and other work groups have provided useful concepts such as quota restriction, gold bricking, self-aggrandizement, co-optation, and goal displacement to describe the effect of group processes and structural forces on work production.

What concepts clarify the production of official data? Some commonly heard phrases among data collectors include *fudge factor, numbers game, massaging the data,* and *padding.*

What do these terms mean? What underlying social processes and social forces act on those who generate data?

8. *Enumeration and its products have strong affective and ritualistic meaning in our educational system.* Other societies, attempting to explain everyday life, relied on religious systems. We rely on science, the symbol of which is the number. Counting outcomes and producing rates is synonymous with being rational.

What is the symbolic meaning of counting to various people in the educational system? How are numbers used to communicate to the outside world? How are they used internally by administrators? What functions do numbers serve in addition to those we commonly say they do?

We do not advocate the termination of quantitative data collection; our educational system would collapse. Rather, our purpose is to suggest that the pervasive nature of quantification in our educational organizations calls us to study counting and its ramifications from a qualitative perspective, one that moves us from a point of taking it for granted to one of studying it in context. This discussion of the quantitative data a researcher may come across in the course of a study is designed to sensitize you to a qualitative perspective on ''hard data.''

CONCLUDING REMARK

We have described the qualitative approach to data as well as the various forms that qualitative data can take. We have not been exhaustive. Some people make extensive use of video-tape equipment and film to pursue qualitative research; we have not covered their activities. Others inductively analyze themes and images of women and minority groups as presented in the mass media as well as in school textbooks. They have been neglected also. School yearbooks and literary magazines provide another area of data that we only touched upon in our discussion. While these and other types of data also exist, we shall move on, hoping that you have grasped the perspective that data is not only what one collects in the course of a study, but what things look like when approached in a ''research'' frame of mind. Being a good qualitative researcher is, in part, learning this perspective: Specific details are useful clues to understanding your subjects' world. It involves holding objects and events up to the sensitive instrument of your mind to discern their value as data. It means having a grasp on the reason the objects were produced, and how that affects the form as well as the information potential of what you are surveying. It also involves knowing when to discount certain pieces of data as being of dubious value and when to pursue them. The qualitative researcher not only has to know how to work with and collect data, but has to have a good sense of what data is.

ENDNOTES

1. This project is part of a larger study supported by a grant from the National Institute of Education, Grant No. 400-79-0052.
2. Ives (1974) gives the same suggestion for locating subjects for oral histories.
3. This section was written by Andrejs Ozolins.
4. In addition, problems of color balance are very severe and a needless distraction for researchers whose primary concern is the study, not photography.

FIELDWORK RELATIONS

FIELDWORK SOUNDS EARTHY. IT IS THE WAY MOST QUALITATIVE researchers collect data. They go to the subjects and spend time with them in their territory—in their schools, their playgrounds, their hangouts, and their homes. These are the places where subjects do what they normally do, and it is these natural settings that the researcher wants to study. As time is spent with subjects, the relationship becomes less formal. The researcher's goal is to increase the subjects' level of comfort, encouraging them both to talk about what they normally talk about, and eventually to confide in the researcher. Researchers build trust by making it clear that they will not use what they are finding out to demean or otherwise hurt people. (This research style is what is meant by *naturalistic*.)

In one way researchers join the subjects' world, but in another way they remain detached. They unobtrusively keep a written record of what happens as well as collect other forms of descriptive data. They attempt to learn from the subjects, but not necessarily be like the subjects. They may participate in their activities, but on a more limited basis and they do not compete for prestige or status. They learn how the subjects think, but they do not think like subjects. They are empathetic, but also reflective.

Fieldwork refers to being out in the subjects' world, in the way we have described—not as a person who pauses while passing by, but as a person who has come for a visit; not as a person who knows everything, but as a person who has come to learn; not as a person who wants to be like them, but as a person who wants to know what it is like to be them. You work toward winning their acceptance, not as an end, but because it allows you to pursue your research goals (Geertz, 1979, p. 241).

Some will charge us with distortion for romanticizing the relationships qualitative researchers have with their subjects (see Douglas, 1976; Johnson, 1975). It might be said that the relationship captured by fieldwork holds best for participant observation, and, even there, the ideal as we have described it is never reached. Further, it could be charged that in other forms of qualitative research (interviewing and document analysis, for example) the phrase *fieldwork* does not apply. There is truth in these charges, but it is important to understand how the idea of fieldwork relations sets the tone for most qualitative research. To achieve a fieldwork quality is the goal in establishing relations, whether the research method be participant observation, interviewing, or searching documents. In interviews, the researcher often makes repeated visits to his or her subjects, sometimes interviewing them for many hours. Even with less extensive interviewing, the emphasis is on equality and closeness in the relationship rather than on formality. Even when working with case records and archival material, the researcher, where feasible, develops a fieldwork relationship with the keepers of the material. This relationship maximizes access and brings the keepers of the record into the study, too. They can lead you to an understanding of the context in which the materials you are studying were produced. As we discussed in Chapter 3, most qualitative studies involve more than one data-gathering technique. Rarely does one do a qualitative study that does not involve fieldwork.

In this chapter we discuss fieldwork relations. Our focus is on how you, as a researcher, should conduct yourself—from gaining access to leaving the field, and the issues involved in maintaining and establishing rapport.

GAINING ACCESS

The first problem to face in fieldwork relations is getting permission to conduct your study. Some circumvent this problem by doing *covert research,* the collection of data without subjects' knowledge. They might, for example, get jobs at a school or enroll as students without announcing to the school what they are doing. Although some excellent research has been conducted undercover (Cusick, 1973; McPherson, 1972), our advice to the novice is use the *overt approach.* Make your interests known, and seek the cooperation of those you will study. Under most circumstances, if permission is negotiated well, doing research openly provides the advantage of release from the duties of being a regular participant and therefore the freedom to come and go as you wish. It is difficult to conduct research, for example, if you have to be the teacher to thirty-two third graders. The overt role also gives you greater access to the range of people in the setting. The teacher's role may not put you in a good position to interview a principal concerning his or her candid views of, say, corporal punishment or the merits of IQ testing. Lastly, and most important for some, lying is not only awkward, but offensive. A related point is that getting caught in misrepresentation is not only embarrassing, but devastating to rapport.

The position we have just taken in regard to covert research, as well as the style of research we present in our discussion on fieldwork relations, is not embraced by all those who do qualitative research. It is probably the most widely used approach and, although there is no name for it, might be termed *the cooperative style*. Others have critiqued this approach and called for researchers to be more confrontational and deceptive (Douglas, 1976; Garfinkel, 1967). (A small minority have advocated for researchers to become closer to their subjects.) The cooperative style comes more out of anthropology as well as the Chicago School of sociology tradition of conducting fieldwork. (See Geertz, 1979, pp. 225–243, for a discussion of the limitations.) At times even people working in these traditions have used a covert approach, but usually only under circumstances in which the overt approach was not feasible. Ethnomethodologists, on the other hand, often use the confrontational approach believing that by disturbing the everyday world of people they can reveal what we take for granted.

You have decided on the study you would like to do. How do you approach getting permission? There are a number of ways to proceed. Which one you choose depends on who you are, what you want to study, and what you hope to accomplish. But, for purposes of illustration, let's assume you are interested in doing a participant observation study in a local elementary school. No two school systems are organized exactly the same. Most have specific procedures to follow in giving approval to researchers. In negotiating entry, the first step is to find out something about the hierarchy and rules of the particular school system. Ask people, a professor, a friend, or someone else who knows the system for advice on how to proceed. Consult a few people, if they are available. You might even try calling the secretary at the intended school. Do not say that you are calling to ask for permission to do research; limit your set of questions about how you would go about getting permission if you decided on this step. Use your imagination to come up with leads.

In making these preliminary inquiries, you are interested in getting knowledge of not only the formal system, but also the informal system. You are looking for tips, like the name of someone in the system who is particularly receptive and helpful. If you get such advice, and it seems reasonable, call or visit the person to discuss what you are thinking and to hear what the individual has to say.

You may be sent to the school principal; often principals have an important say in these matters, although not ultimate authority. Their influence is felt in a variety of ways. If there are some forms to be filled out for a district committee that approves all research, the principal's support carries a great deal of weight. He or she is often the key *gatekeeper*. The principal usually will not go to bat for you unless he or she knows that the teachers involved are supportive. Meeting and talking with teachers and others you plan to involve in the study may be a necessary step in getting approval. If you know you want to study a particular teacher's class, for example, seeing the teacher and getting an endorsement for your project before you see the principal may be an advantageous route to go. Only in large funded research projects do researchers start at levels higher than the building principal. Permission is almost never granted at the central office level without consulting down the hierarchy.

Even if permission is granted from up-high without first checking with those below, it behooves you to meet those down on the hierarchy to seek their support. Your arrival on the scene with a research permission slip from the central office is likely to ruffle feathers, unless you do the necessary work first to court your potential subjects.

While you may get official permission, you might have your study sabotaged by subjects. Getting permission to conduct the study involves more than getting an official blessing: It involves laying the ground work for good rapport with those with whom you will be spending time, so they will accept you and what you are doing. Helping them to feel that they had a hand in allowing you in will help your research.

Qualitative researchers are in a somewhat unique position when negotiating entry in that many people are not familiar with the approach. For more than a few people, research means controlled experiments or survey research. This perception can provide problems in communicating with gatekeepers, but it also offers some advantages. When people are told, for example, that you plan to spend time on the premises in an unobtrusive way, that you are not going to require people to fill out forms, answer specific questions, or alter their normal routine, the response often is, "then you are not really doing formal research." The researcher is consequently given an opportunity to negotiate entry with a *low profile*. We mean that the people in the school—the teachers, the principal, and the other staff—do not treat what you are doing as research and therefore do not require you to follow official sanctioning procedures. They may just let you proceed or perhaps follow a less complicated entry procedure. You can almost slip into the setting. When seeking research approval, you can facilitate this kind of entry by offering a low-key explanation and not insisting on presenting a researcher role.

Novice researchers are often students conducting their first qualitative project as a requirement for a course. After hearing these students' explanations of their assignments, school personnel often treat the request as they would any request for a student placement. If you mange to get in this way, fine—fine, that is, if what is expected of you is not stifling. You should avoid taking on specific responsibilities like tutoring students or being put in a position where school personnel have a great deal of control over your time and mobility.

Most students are not perceived as threatening. Gatekeepers understand that professors require educational placements; anyway, they feel that is is a good idea for people to learn firsthand what schools are like. In short, they are usually receptive to students. It is a good idea to emphasize that you are a student and seek their sympathetic cooperation.

There are other ways to negotiate a low-profile entry. Some people use friends they have inside the system to slip them in. Low profile is usually expedient, but, for some, it provides ethical dilemmas similar to those involved in doing covert research. They feel that if they do not emphasize that they are doing research, they will misrepresent themselves. We do not feel this way. If you do, you will have to use the more official approach to seek approval.

Going through the formal procedures that some educational systems require can be a long, laborious process. Typically, there will be weeks, if not months, between initiating the request and gaining approval. Many school districts have to have committees review proposals. The teacher's union may have to review it as well. Some districts have application forms. If the district is large, it will have an office in charge of research. The people there will give you suggestions on processing the application and will also help in other ways. At times, approval is a mere formality. We have had staff allow us to start research unofficially before receiving official sanction. Ask if there is any way to speed up the approval process. If you are going through the procedures, try to get an estimate of the time it will take and the likelihood that you will be approved before you start. Because getting permission can take time, it is smart to begin negotiating well in advance of your projected starting date.

While we have been talking about gaining access as if it was something that only occurred at the beginning of your study, throughout many studies permission will have to be sought and cooperation gained as you move out into new territories and meet new people. In explaining yourself at the start of the study and during its course, subjects will have questions, many of which will recur. Below is a list of questions with suggestions about how to respond.

1. *What are you actually going to do?* A general rule to follow in answering all questions is to be honest. Do not lie, but do not be too specific or lengthy in your explanations. Novices are often amazed at how little people want to know. Do not use a lot of educational research jargon. You will scare or turn off people. You might want to start by saying something like: "What I want to do is something called participant observation. It would involve visiting your classroom a few times a week. I want to try to understand what it is like to be a teacher." If you are pushed to be more specific, try to be helpful, but explain that what you will do evolves as you proceed. In your explanation emphasize that you want to learn from them but do not be solicitous to the point of being patronizing.

2. *Will you be disruptive?* This is a common concern of school personnel. They fear that your presence will interfere with their routines and work. It is important to allay these fears. Share with them how it is important in this kind of research to be unobtrusive and noninterfering with what people normally do. Part of being successful is being nondisruptive. Assure them that you will not be making excessive demands and you will attempt to be sensitive to their problems and requirements. Share with them your intention of fitting your schedule around theirs.

3. *What are you going to do with your findings?* Most people are asked this question because they fear negative publicity or the political use of the information the researcher gathers. As we suggested in our discussion on ethics (Chapter 1), you ought to come to a decision about how you intend to use the material, and share that with your subjects. If you have short-term interests, like writing a term paper, mention that fact and tell them who will read it. Tell them that you do not plan to use anyone's name and that you will disguise the location. If you have long-term interests, such as writing a dissertation, mention this possibility, but we suggest you hold off asking permission for that until later when you have established relationships at the site. Think of your early observations as a pilot study. After subjects have the chance to know you better, and after you have assessed the setting's possibilities for the large project, then renegotiate your position.

If you are not sure what you will do with your findings, explain this and assure them you will discuss your plans with them after your work gets underway.

4. *Why us?*   People often want an explanation of why they or their organizations were singled out for study. If you have heard positive comments about them that helped direct your choice, tell your subjects. Say, for example, "I was told that you had a lot of insights about teaching, and that is in part why I came to see you." I'm looking for experienced teachers to talk with; that is why I approached you." "I heard that interesting things are happening here in the area of remedial reading."

Unless you have come to see a particular group whose reputation is exemplary, it is usually important that you communicate to people in the setting that you are not so concerned about the particular people in the study, or the particular organization where you may be collecting data. Rather, your interests center on the general topic of teachers, or education, or whatever specific aspect you are pursuing. You are not a reporter looking into Salem High. You are an educational researcher trying to study Salem High so that you can better understand education.

5. *What will we get out of this?*   Many school personnel expect reciprocity. They figure that if they provide you access, they should get something in return. You should decide what it is you are prepared to give. Some want feedback about what you find, a report, or even a meeting with you after the work has been completed. Some people, of course, want nothing. Try not to promise too much. A meeting or a short general summary of what you find may be in order, but we advise against a lengthy report.

When people find out that the research involves fieldnotes, they sometimes request to see them. Downplay the notes. Do not tell your subjects that you try to remember their every word. Never promise to show your fieldnotes to subjects. Knowing you are going to share the fieldnotes with your subjects restricts what you put into them.

Sometimes school personnel want you to provide services to the school in return for access. You might help out, but be sure that what you agree to do does not overly restrict your research.

Although much of what we have said about gaining access best fits participant observation studies, much of it can be applied to other types of qualitative studies as well. Gaining access to official educational documents often involves procedures we have discussed here. In most interview studies, to request cooperation, each respondent has to be approached individually, but often your subjects will share some organizational affiliation. They may be teachers in a particular school or parents attached to a particular parent's group. When this is the case, you may have to seek permission for the organization as well. You can avoid going through the organization by approaching subjects as individuals (not as members of the organization). While this is often most expedient, at times organizational sanction becomes necessary. Lists of potential subjects with their addresses, for example, may lie in the hands of the administration. Organizational members will at times defer to the administration in deciding whether to participate. Staff of educational organizations are often paternalistic about their students. They are very reluctant to allow researchers to interview them fearing the disapproval from the students or, in the case of youngsters, from their parents. Requesting permission from the school to interview students often results in a complicated set of procedures which include getting the parents' permission, as well as going through the formal research sanctioning channels. Many gatekeepers appreciate avoiding such problems. They prefer that the researcher deal with the student and parents as if they were not members of the particular school. Others become concerned when you go directly to the subjects and their guardians, feeling that it is their responsibility to protect their privacy. As with research design choices, at times there are no right answers or correct approaches.

In some forms of qualitative research the data you seek is at first glance open and available. For example, some historical societies not only allow researchers to look through their materials but provide special personnel and services to help. Even in these situations, some of what we have said about gaining access applies. It is important to understand the structure of the historical society and its personnel before going. In certain historical societies, for example, there are workers who are more helpful than others. There are particular collections of materials that archivists only make available to certain select visitors. Finding out how to become of "the chosen few" is an important part of gaining access. In certain local historical organizations researchers from out-of-town are not welcomed without someone vouching for the sincerity of their interests as well as their character. In this case, gaining access requires a sponsor.

As you can see, negotiating permission is tricky. We offer three bits of advice. *Be persistent.* Often the difference between the person who gets in and the person who strikes out is how long and how diligently he or she is in pursuit. *Be flexible.* If your first idea of how to proceed seems ill-conceived, come up with a different plan or a new approach. *Be creative.* Often gatekeepers appreciate a new idea. One researcher we know, in a manner that fits his personality, brought small gifts (single flowers, buttons) to subjects. Holiday greeting cards are not out of the question, and although they may not get you in, they may keep the door open.

FIRST DAYS IN THE FIELD

You have gotten permission and you are ready to start full speed. The first days in the field can be rough if you do not have a sense of humor and if you are not prepared to make mistakes. Rosalie Wax, a distinguished educational qualitative researcher in the anthropological tradition, has this to say about participant observation in general:

> The person who cannot abide feeling awkward or out of place, who feels crushed whenever he makes a mistake—embarrassing or otherwise—who is psychologically unable to endure being, and being treated like, a fool, not only for a day or week but for months on end, ought to think twice before he decides to become a participant observer (Wax, 1971, p. 370).

We think that this view is more representative of the novice's first days or the researcher's first days at a new site than of the life-long experiences of the qualitative researcher. Becoming a qualitative researcher is like learning to perform any role in a society (teacher, parent, artist, college student). Not only do you have to learn the technical aspects of how to do it, but you have to feel that the role is an authentic one, and that it fits you. During the first times out, novices have not had experiences to draw on and they feel uncomfortable with the label of "researcher." They are not sure that they want to be associated with that title or, in other cases, they do not know if they are worthy of such a high-sounding label. In addition, they do not understand that feeling uncomfortable is part of doing this kind of work. Like any role, that of researcher grows more comfortable with practice. While it may be particularly difficult at first, being a researcher grows on you.

A researcher describing her first observation experience can give you a sense of how disconcerting the first days in the field can be. She had decided to observe a college extension course for engineers:

> I remember walking in there and seeing all those men. I sat down and everyone seemed to be talking at once. I felt so out of place. I panicked. Should I try to remember what everyone was saying, I said to myself? As soon as I started focusing on remembering I got more nervous. I gave that up and decided to just sit quietly and passively to see what happened.

This was not the end of her awkwardness. During the class, the instructor used a word with a double meaning, connoting the lude and sexual. The men in the class smiled with him. The person sitting next to the researcher turned toward her to catch her reaction. As she put it, "I remember half smiling." At the end of the class the instructor introduced the observer and explained her research intentions to the class. After, she got up and said a few words; then the instructor turned, paused, and then said reluctantly, "Well, I'll guess we'll get used to you." And they did, and she got used to them. While never "one of the boys," she developed sufficient rapport to carry out her study which explored the similarities and differences between on-campus and off-campus university offerings.

Another researcher interested in studying the training of para-professionals in a medical laboratory tried to get a parking lot ticket stamped by the secretary at the front desk at the lab. Upon handing in the ticket, the researcher was told by the secretary, "We don't stamp salesmen's tickets." The researcher replied, "I'm not a salesman. I'm a researcher and will be visiting here often." The secretary looked up and said: "We don't stamp researchers' either."

During the first few days in the field you begin to establish rapport, you "learn the ropes," you become comfortable and work at making the subjects feel comfortable with you. It is a time when you are confused—even overwhelmed—with all the new information. There is much to learn. The feeling of incompetence pervades. Subjects' comments, some like the ones we quoted above, weigh heavily; they are taken as signs of rejection or even hostility. It is a time of paranoia.

Here are some suggestions to make your first days in the field less painful.

1. *Do not take what happens in the field personally.*   What you are going through is a typical part of the fieldwork process.
2. *Set up your first visit so someone is there to introduce you.*   One of the people who give you permission can do it or can direct you to someone else. Ask someone to facilitate your entrance.
3. *Don't try to accomplish too much the first few days.*   Ease yourself into the field. Have your first day be a short visit (an hour or less); use it as a time to get a general introduction and overview. There are so many new faces and things to learn; go slow. You will have to take fieldnotes after completing each visit to the field. Taking in too much may mean that you will not have enough time to write it all down.
4. *Remain relatively passive.*   Show interest and enthusiasm for what you are learning, but do not ask a lot of specific questions, especially in areas that may be controversial. Ask general questions that will provide your subjects an opportunity to talk.
5. *Be friendly.*   As you are introduced to people, smile and be polite. Say hello as you pass people in the hall. The first days in the field, subjects will ask about why you are here. Repeat what you told the gatekeepers more or less, but try to use abbreviated explanations. Most of the suggestions on how to behave in the field parallel the norms governing nonoffensive behavior in general. In order to be a good researcher you have to know and practice those skills.

The first few days in the field represent the first stage of fieldwork. The feelings of awkwardness and not belonging that characterize this stage often end with some clear indication of acceptance from the subjects. An invitation to a social event or a request to participate in some activity usually reserved exclusively for participants are indicators. Being told that you were missed on a day you did not show up is another.

THE PARTICIPANT/OBSERVER CONTINUUM

To what degree and how should researchers participate in the activities of the setting? Gold (1958) has discussed the spectrum of possible roles for observers to play. At one extreme is the *complete observer.* Here, the researcher does not participate in activities at the setting. He or she looks at the scene, literally or figuratively, through a one-way mirror. At the other end is complete involvement at the site, with little discernible difference between the behavior of the observer and the subjects. Fieldworkers stay somewhere between these extremes.

Exactly what and how much participation varies during the course of a study. During the first few days of participant observation, for example, the researcher often remains somewhat detached, waiting to be looked over and hopefully accepted. As relationships develop, he or she participates more. At later stages of the research, it may be important once again to hold back from participating. Over-participation can lead to *"going native,"* (Gold, 1958), a phrase used in anthropology to refer to researchers getting so involved and active with subjects that their original intentions get lost. (See Levine, 1980b, for a description of how an attempt to expose the fakery of shamans was subverted this way.)

How much participation is the right amount and how you should participate has to be calculated with the particulars of your study in mind. Many observers of classrooms have situational constraints leading them to partake little in classroom activities; they choose to sit and take it all in (see Rist, 1978; Smith and Geoffrey, 1968). Those who do join activities face the dilemma of choosing how to participate. They ask themselves: "Should I act like a teacher?" "Should I do what the kids are doing?" "How about acting like a teacher's aide?" None of these choices may feel right. There may be pressure, some brought about during negotiating access, for the second adult in the classroom to function as a teacher's helper. As we already suggested, a certain amount of this type of participation can work, but you must be on your guard not to let it dominate your time. In addition, be aware that when acting as a helper, the children will define you in a particular way.

Children present special rapport challenges. Because of our cultural attitudes toward them, adults have a difficult time listening to them seriously. Adults tend to direct conversations with children, a habit the qualitative researcher must break. Some adults use conventionalized jokes to relate to them. Children may look at adults in special ways; they may seek their approval or withdraw. All this has to be taken into account when participating in the setting and understanding what your data mean. An alternative is to participate with the children not as an authority figure (an adult), but as a quasi-friend (see Fine and Glassner, 1979; Mercurio, 1972). It is difficult for an adult to be accepted by a child as an equal, but you can move toward being a tolerated insider in children's society. Observers we have known have had varying degrees of success in doing unobtrusive observations with children. One observer studied kindergarteners and first graders and participated with them, acting as they did, when they worked and played. She felt that by doing what they did (drawing, playing games), refraining from "helping them," the children came to act more naturally in front of her. Another observer we know, studying a "free school," felt that his conversations with the children were always stilted by the fact that he was perceived as an adult, and therefore as an outsider. He went out of his way to enter into the children's world. The children he was interested in were ten to fourteen years old. He went out for sodas with them and did other things they did, but his efforts came to no avail. He even tried to bribe them.

In reporting one success and one failure we do not mean to offer any advice on "how to do it." As with much of our discussion of fieldwork relations, we can inform you of some of the issues and provide some suggestions, but there are many aspects of fieldwork that you have to work out for yourself. Because there has not been extensive writing on the various forms of fieldwork in the various settings that researchers work, there is a great deal of opportunity to publish methodological papers in which you share your experience and advice with others.

Questions concerning how much, with whom, and how you participate tend to work out as the research develops focus. If, for example, your goal becomes understanding a classroom from the students' point of view, you may choose to participate more with them than with the teacher. If you decide to spend a great deal of time with the participants, such as the students, it is important that other participants understand that you are not purposefully slighting them. Share with the teacher your strategy of focusing on the children so he or she does not feel ignored or offended. While participation in the classroom itself may be awkward, studies of classrooms are often enlarged to include interviews or observation sessions with the teacher outside this setting. Participation becomes less problematic.

Balancing participation and observation can be particularly trying in other situations as well. We have found that small groups where group members make a purposeful attempt to be "open" and to "share" are particularly difficult. In sensitivity groups, encounter groups, support groups, and other similar situations the pressure is on for everyone to become a full-fledged member. Fieldworkers feel guilty being on the margin, especially if they share the values of group members. Even in less intense group activities tough and awkward decisions arise. One observer was studying a training course for teachers in which teachers were learning how to teach students "pro-social behavior." As part of the training, the teachers were asked to roleplay a disruptive group of students in a classroom. This occurred early in the observer's research and he was at a loss to know what to do. Should he pass when it came to his turn? How should he act if he chose to participate? How visible should he be? He felt lucky observing the session because the teachers revealed their ways of thinking about disruptive students by performing, but the situation created anxiety for him. When it came to his turn he decided to roleplay, but he chose to play a sullen student rather than a gregarious one. By making this choice, he participated, but uncontroversially.

As the last example suggests, how you participate depends on who you are, your values, and your personality. You can adjust your typical behavior to the research task, but what you feel comfortable doing sets some parameters for how you will behave. People who are very outgoing have to temper their gregariousness, but even when they exhibit this kind of restraint they still may participate more than people who normally are more quiet. The very shy person might have to practice being more assertive in initiating conversations and introducing himself or herself. There is not "the right" personality for fieldwork.

Becoming a researcher means internalizing the research goal while collecting data in the field. As you conduct research you participate with the subjects in various ways. You joke with them and behave sociably in many ways. You may even help them perform their duties. You do these things, but always for the reason of promoting your research goals. You carry with you an imaginary sign that you hang over each subject and on every wall and tree. The sign says, "My primary purpose in being here is to collect data. How does what I am doing relate to that goal?" If what you are doing does not relate to collecting data, you should take that as a warning that you may be slipping out of your research role. This does not mean, however, that you have to spend every minute in the field systematically pursuing leads. Sometimes establishing good rapport requires hanging out and just plain socializing with your subjects. You might even go to a movie or out for a drink. Going to a movie may not produce a great deal of data, but the idea is that the activity may enhance your rapport and put you into a better position to collect better data in the future.

Be Discrete

The hope of "co-operative" fieldworkers is that they will blend into the setting, becoming a more or less "natural" part of the scene. There are a number of things that facilitate this. Appearance is one. People choose to wear clothes to communicate who they are. We do not suggest that you desert your personal style, but that you be aware of what your dress means to subjects. If you are in a place where people dress casually, wear casual clothes also. In a school, the formality of your dress can say something to others about who you are and with whom you identify. Administrators might wear suits or dresses, teachers might be less formal, while students and custodial staff might wear t-shirts and jeans. Beware of the unspoken dress codes and, if they do not make you feel too uncomfortable, dress in a manner that seems appropriate for your status in the situation. Do not imitate the dress pattern of your host unless you feel at ease with it.

If you conduct your research in a systematic and rigorous way, and develop trust, you will soon become privy to certain information and opinions about which even all insiders might not be aware. It is important, however, not to display too much of your knowledge while talking with subjects, since they may feel uncomfortable being in the presence of a "know it all." Do not discuss anything that has been told to you in private by one subject with another. You want to be regarded as a person with discretion. Even if you encounter people whose beliefs and opinions are inaccurate—even silly in light of what you know—do not go out of your way to correct them by displaying that knowledge. One researcher reported that his acceptance by the teachers in the school in which he observed was eased in large part by his reputation as a trustworthy person; while they were not always certain of exactly what he was up to, "at least he didn't gossip" (Smith and Geoffrey, 1968).

The suggestion to refrain from gossiping carries over to talks with people who are not your subjects. Although it is important to discuss with your colleagues or your professor the problems you are facing, and what your study is yielding, avoid being flippant with the information you have. It should not, for example, be the topic of a conversation at a party. Ask yourself, when discussing your experience with others, "What would the people in the setting I am studying think if they heard me talking?" If you think you would be embarrassed, it is a good idea to restrain yourself.

What you say might get back to your subjects and seriously affect your relationships with them. It can fracture trust.

While many teachers find people who observe their classes both nondisruptive and an interesting addition to the class, they have also suggested that it can be a strain to continually feel they are being watched. Feeling like they are in a fish bowl can be difficult enough for teachers, but learning that they are the center of a discussion in a university class simply intensifies their uneasiness. Students doing fieldwork in schools with teachers must continually pay attention to this concern. As one cooperating teacher told a researcher placed with her, "The professors say that they have student teachers observe us to learn, but it really seems like they criticize us. I feel inadequate enough to serve all these different kids, and the last thing I need is more criticism. They are not in here with thirty-one kids all day." (See Sarason et al., 1966, pp. 74–97, for a discussion of this issue.)

The fieldnotes that you keep will likely contain harmless information about what you are learning. Since it will also contain quotations from people, as well as your own personal reflections, it is important to be careful with this material. Be sure you do not misplace your notes where someone in the setting you study may find them. Also, for the sake of anonymity, use fake names for the people about whom you are writing, change the name of the school (if you are studying a school), and adjust other information that might tell a reader where and with whom you have been collecting data.

Although in the overt approach your subjects know your research intentions, after you build rapport, the fact that you are a researcher fades from their minds. You try to encourage them to take you for granted, and not be self-conscious around you. Taking extensive fieldnotes is an intrinsic part of doing qualitative research. We described this in detail in Chapter 3. The procedure we suggest is that the notes be taken after you leave the site at the end of an observation period. We recommend that you try to refrain from writing notes down in front of the subjects. There are times, however, when note-taking is quite appropriate. These are times when the people in the setting are taking notes themselves. While attending classes, high school students often take notes. It would be quite appropriate for you to take notes at this time. Also, when an informant explains some elaborate, detailed information, taking notes in front of them will not be upsetting. When a school principal, for example, describes the organizational chart of the school, it would be perfectly alright to take out a pad and jot down notes.

Subjects are often very curious about what it is that you are writing down. They try to peek. Make sure that anything that you put down on paper is of such a nature that you would not mind your subjects seeing it. Some researchers develop codes to insure privacy.

Try not to walk around with pad and pencil continually in hand, but if you feel you must, jot down a note here and there. One strategy observers sometimes employ during an observation period is to retreat to a private place (like the toilet) and write down some headings or phrases that will help recall. If you do this, make sure you do not carry yourself like a detective and spook your subjects.

Educational Settings in Conflict

It is not uncommon for any organization to have dissension. Debates on policies and procedures often rage in schools. These can pose particular problems for the researcher. People may vie for your allegiance, wanting you to identify with one side or the other. In conducting most forms of research, it is most effective to remain neutral. If you identify with one side, it will be difficult to understand or to have access to the people on the other side. While conflict in a school may cause problems to the researcher, it can provide a unique opportunity for an astute observer to understand the dynamics of confrontation and negotiation. During times of conflicts, people most overtly reveal their perspectives on what is important to them. Therefore, studying a school in conflict can be a particularly productive experience.

Conflicts may also be less intense and not school-wide. Often teachers disagree with each other about how to resolve daily problems. Some researchers in an elementary setting, for example, found that certain teachers disagreed on why pupils had been placed in ''resource rooms.'' A first-grade teacher reported to the researcher that her pupil needed to be in the resource room because he had a ''learning disability.'' The teacher in the resource room, however, felt that the pupil had a ''behavioral problem,'' not an academic one. ''He acts up and the teacher sends him to me.'' These two teachers interpreted the child's behavior quite differently, and their contrasting perspective fueled much debate and argument. Following these kinds of controversies, hearing the various sides in the dispute provided important data to the researcher.

Feelings

In our introductory chapters we mentioned the researcher's own feelings and prejudices as possible sources of bias. In our last chapter we discussed how qualitative researchers record their feelings as a method of controlling bias. Here, we approach the topic of feelings in a different light—for its positive impact on research. Feelings are an important vehicle for establishing rapport and for gauging subjects' perspectives. Feelings are not something to repress. Rather, if treated correctly, they can be an important aid in doing qualitative research.

We now recount two research experiences that illustrate the use of feelings to generate understanding. The first time an observer visited a cafeteria of a junior high school where she was conducting research, she became overwhelmed with a feeling that things were out of control—''chaos'' is how she described it: the deafening noise, the smell of steamed foods and garbage cans, the pushing and yelling. She felt most immediately after arriving that if she did not leave, she would scream. Teachers in the study described similar feelings when they first went to the cafeteria. In fact, one teacher came up to the observer amidst the chaos and said: ''How's your head? This is some zoo.'' Later, when the observer was in the teachers' room, someone mentioned the cafeteria. The observer indicated that being there for one period had almost ''wiped her out.'' Teachers began discussing how it was for them the first few weeks on cafeteria duty. But they assured her. ''You'll get used to it. Some of us actually enjoy it now.'' Sharing her feelings with the teachers enabled her to get in touch with theirs.

In a teaching hospital on the intensive care unit for infants, interns had a very difficult time finding arteries to place needles in their tiny patients. (Many of them were premature infants, some weighing as little as a pound.) This meant they had to stick the infant time and time again until they got blood. The first few times he

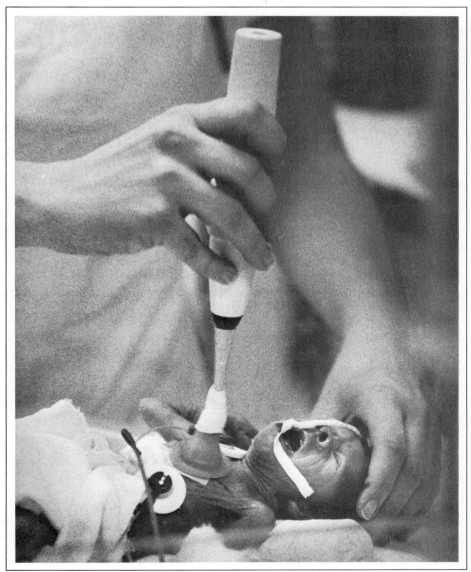

Andrejs Ozolins.

Cardiac arrest on a neonatal unit. Medical instrument is fashioned from an electric toothbrush.

watched this process, the observer had trouble controlling his feelings of compassion for the babies as they cried, twisted, and turned from their apparent pain. After a while, however, the observer found it less difficult to watch these procedures. Interns seldom showed any emotion except exasperation at not being able to accomplish their tasks. Parents, however, reacted to the children's treatment by becoming noticeably upset. The observer shared his feelings with the interns, and they were able to talk about how difficult this process had been for them at first and how they had developed techniques to control it. One technique was to insist to themselves that what they were doing was helpful to the baby. They further discussed how the infants they were treating tended to lose their personhood in their eyes and that how losing feeling was upsetting to them. Their patients were becoming objects to treat. But they felt they could not afford to cringe at needle procedures. They also realized how parents felt about their babies' pain and had explanations to give them to ease these feelings: the undeveloped nerves were not like adults' and the infants would not remember.

As these two accounts suggest, the researcher's feelings can be an important indicator of subjects' feelings and, therefore, be a source for reflecting. They also can help formulate questions to get at subjects' experiences. In this sense, the observer's emotional reactions are a source for research hunches. If carefully sorted out, selectively presented, and appropriately expressed, they can also be a wonderful avenue for building rapport. (Of course, if your feelings are counter to your subjects', if shown, they might create hostility.) Becoming part of a group, after all, means that you can share insiders' reactions (see Everhart, 1977).

Many people in schools say that outsiders cannot really understand what it is like to be a teacher, that they can never know "what it's really like." This refrain refers, in part, to the inability of the outsider to know the frustration, the anger, the joy, and the feelings of accomplishment teachers experience. We do not want to suggest that you, the researcher, can come to feel all these things in the way that the teacher or any other group of subjects does, but you can experience some of them, and develop empathy. Being there on a bad day when tension fills the air, or on the last day of school when people say their goodbyes, you can share part of the emotional world of the teacher and you can feel closer to them and they to you.

How Long Should an Observation Session Be?

As we suggested, for the first few days limit the sessions to an hour or less. As your confidence and knowledge of the setting increase, so can the hours you spend at any one time. With the exception we cite below, you should not stay in the field for periods longer than your memory or the time you have available to take notes after the session allows. Fieldwork is often more fun than doing the notes, so there is a tendency to stay in the field longer than you should. Fieldwork takes discipline. Practice restraint—remember the sign.

Sometimes, after being in the field a few times, people feel that they have not had enough time with the subjects to have established sufficient rapport. They may decide to spend a longer period, a whole day for example, even though they know they cannot possibly record the data that would result. Here, they are willing to sacrifice detailed notes for the rapport gained. This is reasonable.

INTERVIEWING

Most of us have conducted interviews. The process is so familiar we do it without thinking. An interview is a purposeful conversation, usually between two people (but sometimes involving more) that is directed by one in order to get information. In the hands of the qualitative researcher, the interview takes on a shape of its own.

In qualitative research, interviews may be used in two ways. Either they may be the dominant strategy for data collection, or they may be employed in conjunction with participant observation, document analysis, or other techniques. In all of these situations the interview is used to gather descriptive data in the subject's own words so that the researcher can develop insights on how subjects interpret some piece of the world.

In participant observation-like studies, the researcher usually knows the subjects beforehand, so the interview is often like a conversation between friends. Here the interview cannot easily be separated from other research activities. When the subject has a spare moment, for example, the researcher might say, ''Have you got a few minutes? I haven't had a chance to talk to you alone.'' Sometimes an interview has no introduction; the researcher just makes the situation an interview. Particularly toward the end of a study, however, when specific information is sought, the participant observer sets up specific times to meet with the subjects for the purpose of a more formal interview. This is true of qualitative studies involving archival and document research as well.

In studies that rely predominantly on interviewing, the subject is usually a stranger. (It is common in studies that involve long-term interviewing with one or very few subjects, however, for the researcher to be acquainted with the subject before the research begins.) A good part of the work involves building a relationship, getting to know each other, and putting the subject at ease.

Most interviews begin with small talk. Topics can range from baseball to cooking. The purpose this chit-chat serves is to develop accord: You search for common ground, for a topic that you have in common, for a place to begin building a relationship. In situations where the subject knows you, you usually get right down to business, but in situations where you and the subject are strangers, the ''ice has to be broken.'' This may take some time; in long-term interview projects it may take a whole interview session. Early in the interview you try to briefly inform the subject of your purpose, and make assurances (if they are necessary) that what is said in the interview will be treated confidentially. Many subjects feel self-conscious at first, speaking self-effacingly that they have nothing important to say. In these cases, the interviewer must be reassuring and supportive. Less often, the potential subject will be challenging, questioning your methods and the soundness of the study. In those cases, you must stand your ground without being defensive.

Qualitative interviews vary in the degree to which they are structured. Some interviews, although relatively open-ended, are focused around particular topics or may be guided by some general questions (Merton and Kendell, 1946). Even when an interview guide is employed, qualitative interviews offer the interviewer considerable latitude to pursue a range of topics and offer the subject a chance to shape the content of the interview. When the interviewer controls the content too rigidly, when the subject cannot tell his or her story personally, in his or her words, the interview falls out of the qualitative range of interviewing.

At the other end of the structured/unstructured continuum is the very open-ended interview. The researcher, in this case, encourages the subjects to talk in the area of interest, and then probes more deeply, picking up on the topics and issues that the respondent initiates. The subject plays a stronger role in defining the content of the interview and the direction of the study in this type of interview.

Some people debate which approach is more effective, the structured or the unstructured. With semi-structured interviews you are confident of getting comparable data across *subjects,* but you lose the opportunity to understand how the subjects themselves structure the topic at hand. While such debates may enliven the research community, from our perspective you do not have to take sides. You choose a particular type to employ depending on your research goal. Furthermore, different types of interviews can be employed at different stages of the same study. At the beginning of the project, for example, it might be important to use the more free-flowing, exploratory interview because your purpose at that point is to get a general understanding of a range of perspectives on a topic. After the investigatory work has been done, you may want to structure interviews more in order to get comparable data across a larger sample or to focus on particular topics that emerged during the preliminary interviews. (For another discussion of structure and types of interviews, see the section on analytic induction in Chapter 2.)

Good interviews are ones in which the subjects are at ease and talk freely about their points of view. Good interviews produce rich data filled with words that reveal the respondent's perspectives. Transcripts are filled with details and examples. A good interviewer communicates personal interest and attention to the subject by being attentive, nodding one's head, and using appropriate facial expressions to communicate. The interviewer may ask for clarification when the respondent mentions something that seems unfamiliar, using phrases such as, "What do you mean?" "I'm not sure I am following you." "Could you explain that?" The interviewer also probes the respondent to be specific, asking for examples of points that are made. When asking respondents about the past, for example, the interviewer suggests that the subject think back to that time and try to relive it. He or she may ask for the respondent to quote what was said at particular times. People being interviewed have a tendency to offer a quick run-through of events. Informants can be taught to respond to meet the interviewer's interest in the particulars, the details. They need encouragement to elaborate.

Certainly a key strategy for the qualitative interviewer in the field is to avoid as much as possible questions that can be answered by "yes" or "no." Particulars and details will come from probing questions that require an exploration. "Were you a good student in elementary school?" can be answered in one word if the respondent so chooses, but "Tell me about what you were like as a student in elementary school," urges description. As a corollary, interviewers need not fear silence. Silences can enable subjects to get their thoughts together and to direct some of the conversation. It is a poor habit for interviewers to interrupt subjects and change the direction of the conversation.

Not all people are equally articulate or perceptive, but it is important for the qualitative researcher not to give up on an interviewee too early. Some respondents need a chance to warm up to you. Information in the qualitative interview project is cumulative, each interview building and connecting on the other. It is what you learn from the total study that counts. While you might not learn as much from some interviews as from others, and while you cannot get the same intensity from everyone with whom you speak, even the bad interview contributes something.

There are no rules we can give that you can constantly apply across all interview situations, but a few general statements can be made. Most important is the need to listen carefully. Listen to what the people say. Treat every word as having the potential of unlocking the mystery of the subject's way of viewing the world. If at first you do not understand what the respondent is getting at, ask for clarification. Question, not to challenge, but to make clear. If you cannot understand, assume that you are at fault. Assume the problem is not that the subject does not make sense, but that you have not been able to comprehend. Return and listen and think some more. It requires flexibility. Try different techniques, including jokes or sometimes gentle challenges. Sometimes you might ask them to elaborate with stories, sometimes you might share your experiences with them.

Photographs and memorabilia can serve as stimuli for conversation. When doing interviews in people's homes, or in the classroom, ask people about objects and pictures hanging on the walls or displayed. In a study of parents' thoughts about their child's development, a researcher purposely asked parents if they had any pictures of the child. The interviews were conducted at the home and most parents were delighted to get out the family photograph album. The pictures then served as a protocol to structure the conversation. Request pictures, ask about trophies displayed, and inquire about other objects you see about.

To be flexible means to respond to the immediate situation, to the informant that is sitting before you, not to some predetermined set of procedures or stereotype of what these types of people are like. In his dissertation research with Chicago school teachers, Howard Becker reported how he used different approaches with different teachers. He felt that with the young new teachers he could be more direct about their political feelings. With the older teachers, on the other hand, he had to be more circuitous (Becker, 1951).

If you ask people to share part of themselves with you, it is important that you not be evaluative or else they will feel demeaned. Even if a teacher's racist comments about his or her students upsets you, for example, you must control your reaction by reminding yourself that the purpose of the research is to learn people's perspectives, not to instruct your subject. While you may feel value conflicts with the views you hear, you want to encourage your respondent to say what he or she feels. You are not there to change views, but to learn what the subjects' views are, and why they are that way.[1] Often subjects hold stereotypic views, for example, of what university people are like. Many feel that all university types are "super liberals" or "radicals," and therefore may be reluctant to talk if their views are conservative. It is important to create an atmosphere where they can feel comfortable expressing themselves. Subjects may often begin to open up with a phrase like, "You people up at the University don't think this way, but you haven't had the experiences that I've had . . . ," "You may think that what I am saying is alot of bunk, but . . . ," "There's a big difference between what you read in those books and what you learn first hand. . . ."

In most interview situations, you can counteract subjects' potentially stereotypical views of you, but this is not always the case. Since formal interviews involve a one-to-one relationship, your race, sex, age, and other characteristics may influence the rapport you establish (Wax, 1979). The specific effect your personal characteristics have on subjects will vary among subjects and settings. Some men talk freely to researchers who are women, while others will not open up. It is important to be sensitive about effects personal characteristics might have on an interview. Rarely, however, should these be so pronounced to disqualify you from participation (though a woman studying a men's locker room, or a minority group member studying the Klu Klux Klan might cause difficulties).

Group interviews can be useful to bring the researcher into the world of the subjects. In this situation, a number of people are brought together and encouraged to talk about the subject of interest. You might bring teachers together, or parents, or principals to talk about their work or about those who work with their children. Usually this is a good way of getting insights about what to pursue in individual interviews. When reflecting together on some topic, subjects can often stimulate each other to talk about topics that you can explore later. Group interviews can also be a cue to the language teachers or principles or aides might share. Problems with group interviews include starting them and controlling the person who insists on dominating the session. An additional problem arises when the group interviews are tape recorded. Unless the cassettes are transcribed very soon after the session, the interview will be difficult to reconstruct. Recognizing who is speaking, and the likelihood that several people will speak at once contribute to making transcription difficult.

Using a tape recorder during interviews raises some special considerations for fieldwork relations. We discussed tape recorders in Chapter 3, but here we focus on their implications for the researcher-subject relationship. If you choose to use a tape recorder, ask respondents if they mind. The point in the encounter where you ask permission can be touchy. Either out of shyness or out of the fear of being turned down, many people have a difficult time raising the issue. Never record without permission. Force yourself to ask. Some subjects simply will not care if the interview is recorded. Others will ask what you intend to do with the tapes. They want assurance that private information they share with you will not be revealed to others at their expense. In addition, some people think that once their words are recorded on tape, the tapes could come back to haunt them (or get them in trouble if, for example, they revealed something illegal they did). They need reassurance. Some subjects simply will say "no," and you must accept their wishes. For short interviews that are part of a participant observation study, you have to take fieldnotes after the session. In long interviews you may jot down notes to supplement your memory. Sometimes people will change their minds as they begin talking. Provide the opportunity for people who originally refuse to change their minds.

What place should the tape recorder have in the relationship between subject and researcher? Edward Ives (1974), an oral historian and recorder of folklore, suggests that when interviewing, the tape recorder should be thought of as a third party that cannot see. When subjects gesture or show size with their hands, these nonverbal cues have to be translated into verbal language so that the tape recorder can play them back for typing.

The interviewer tries not to feed respondents responses or make them feel uncomfortable with their own thoughts. During an interview focusing on sexual development in elementary school, an informant stated that she thought she had started developing secondary sex characteristics in the third grade. Later she said, "It must have been at the end of the fourth," to which the researcher replied, "That sounds a little more like it." This statement signified to the informant that the interviewer distrusted her, and later she stated that she was having trouble remembering things because she had been confused by the researcher's "doubting." The interviewer's thoughtless remark, which measured the respondent against some imaginary guideline of "normal development," had caused the interviewee to feel distrusted.

Good interviewers need to display patience. You often do not know why respondents reply as they do, and you must wait to find out the full explanation. Interviewers have to be detectives, fitting bits and pieces of conversation, personal histories, and experiences together in order to develop an understanding of the subject's perspective.

PHOTOGRAPHY AND FIELDWORK RELATIONS[2]

The camera in the hands of a qualitative researcher can be used in an uncomplicated manner to take inventories of objects in a setting. The bulletin board, the contents of a book case, the writing on the blackboard, and the arrangement of furniture can be recorded on film for later study and analysis.

Inventory photos can be taken at any convenient time and can certainly be postponed to give interviewing and observing a chance to be carefully conducted. During that time, the researcher can keep notes on what inventory he or she wants to have photographed, or what categories of detail may be too numerous or ambiguous to record verbally and will need to be visually available later. The pictures can be taken quickly whenever the opportunity arises, and it takes no technical expertise.

If the intention is to get more than an inventory of photographic record, things are rather difficult. All the interpersonal issues related to observation and interviewing re-emerge in the special variation relating to photography. The presence of an observer changes the setting to be observed; the presence of a photographer also changes it, but in different, often more dramatic ways. These effects can never be eliminated, but they can be accounted for in the design of the study. Basically, there are three ways to do this. The effect of the presence of a camera can be: (1) compensated for, (2) exploited, or (3) minimized.

1. If pictures are taken (say, in a classroom) where people are conscious of the camera, we can use our knowledge of how people change their behavior in the presence of cameras to filter our interpretation. For example, if we found photos showing a lot of giggling and preening during a history lesson, we would know that those behaviors are probably not a product of the aspects of the setting that relate to teaching history. We would thus compensate our assessment of the scene to take account of the fact that a photographer was there.

2. Some researchers choose to exploit the effect cameras have on people. The subject of a study, for example, might be the way people react to cameras in settings where cameras are not usually present, or the way people interact with each other when all are aware of being photographed. At other times researchers might use the impact of a camera as the social "can-opener," to develop rapport with their subjects. In this case, it should be noted that the primary agenda is not photographic—the same result could be achieved by doing magic tricks or dressing as an elephant. However, the photos obtained in this way can provide information about how subjects behave, interact, and present themselves in a certain kind of situation.

The effect of the presence of a camera can also be exploited to elicit information about the "best" that subjects have or wish to show. Here, "best" does not mean any absolute judgment, but what the subjects value and consider worthy to photograph, such as their "best" clothes and grooming, possessions, postures, etc. The clearest examples of this can be seen in formal portraits, group photographs, snapshots with tropies, prize fish and game, and so on. For the purposes of some studies, it might be desirable to arrange to photograph certain "best" performances, such as classroom decorations, special activities, costumes, lessons, etc.

3. In both of the previous approaches to photography, the one thing the pictures cannot provide is a sense of what is typical and ordinary in a setting. If the study is concerned with typical occurrences, a way must be found to minimize the distortion of routines by the photographer. The photographing researcher must become, as much as possible, invisible. There are two ways to go about this: by familiarity and by distraction.

People can become accustomed and indifferent to anything in their environment, and a photographer is no exception. By being "always" present and familiar, the photographer eventually ceases to be a special stimulus. One friend remembers being in a classroom long enough that, when a new child entered and asked who he was, she was curtly told, "Oh, he's just the photographer," and no further attention was paid to his activities. This indifferent familiarity can set in amazingly quickly. In some settings, such as groups of active young children, the photographer can cease to be a novelty in as little as fifteen minutes and slip into oblivion by a half an hour. In other settings, it may take two or three days of returning for hour-long sessions before people cease responding to the camera and begin to be "themselves." This "extinction time" must be reckoned with in designing any study focused on typical events, and enough time allowed for it. It should be evident that the photography site-visits have to be scheduled not so far apart that the process of becoming familiar and ignored has to be begun from scratch each time.

The second way for the photographing researcher to become invisible is by distraction. If there are sufficiently engaging activities going on in the setting, subjects will have little attention for the camera. However, usually it is important to make arrangements and come to an understanding that the regular activities should proceed. Often when a photographer arrives on the scene, people wonder what they "should do." As long as this uncertainty is unresolved, they may be reluctant to proceed as usual. If someone is clearly "in charge," such as a teacher in a classroom, the researcher should arrange that, at the time of his or her introduction to the setting, the purpose of the visit be defined as nonintrusive ("He just wants to see what we do every day" or "We won't pay any attention to her."). In less structured settings, it is best if an insider can be found to perform the introductions and "decontaminate" the researcher by explaining that the subjects are not "supposed to do" anything special. In the rare event that no one is available to present and define the nature of the photographic visit, the researcher should be sure to answer the questions many subjects will have even if they do not verbalize them ("Who are you?" "What are you doing?" and, most important for the study, "What do you want me to do?") As the photographer proceeds to work, the subjects will gradually do the same.

Most of these remarks relate to studies that involve groups of people in defined settings. Some of the suggestions would not be useful in studies focusing on individuals and/or where the subjects move about through various activities and places. It would be virtually impossible for a photographer to become "invisible" if he or she was the only other person in the room besides the subject. It would also be impossible, or very difficult, to remain invisible if the subject or subjects passed through other settings where other people were not cognizant of the purpose and nature of the photography. In general, these situations indicate the limits of the photographic researchers' ability to work invisibly. It would not be too difficult for an observer to accompany a subject through an entire day's activity from breakfast to supper, including shopping, visiting, as well as periods of solitude. But to do so with a camera, photographing every episode would quickly become grotesque and anything but unobtrusive. The point is that, as with any method of research (or anything else), there are limits beyond which it is unproductive or silly to press. This is not to say a qualitative researcher would never want to photograph a subject shopping for groceries or riding a bus, but that the intensity and unobtrusiveness of photography (that is, the method's thoroughness and validity) is diminished in certain setting. In designing a study, these limits should be recogized and compensated for.

There is, however, a way to make photographic study of individual subjects minimally disruptive. It is also a very useful technique with groups that do not have their own (distracting) activities to pursue. It is to introduce a second researcher whose role is to interact with the subject or subjects so as to focus them on "being themselves" while the photographer-researcher takes pictures. The second researcher can—and should—be more than merely a "stooge." His or her activities should be designed as part of the qualitative research project to elicit and enhance the type of information under study.

While this suggestion of collaboration arises from the discussion of difficulties with purely photographic research designs, it can be recommended on much more fundamental grounds. Basically, the problem is this: A photographer is not a good observer; moreover, a photographer is a poor interacter. It may seem paradoxical to say that the photographer doesn't observe well—afterall, is not a photograph the best possible observation of the scene? In fact, it is a human observer who can be sensitive to and recall (within limits, of course) the entirety of a scene. A photographer works very differently. The two operations basic to photography are framing (deciding what to include in the picture and from what perspective) and timing (deciding when to trip the shutter). It is not that the one research method is better than the other, but that they are very different ways to gather data. A good photographer can isolate and freeze relationships or behaviors in a way that cannot be recreated verbally; but a human observer can give a sense of the entire fabric of events that cannot be conveyed photographically. Thus, a collaboration may be the ideal way to do some studies.

It should be needless to say these are very general guidelines; there are times when all of them should be and have been disregarded. There have been studies of individual subjects done entirely through photography, with little verbal elaboration. Their scientific status has been questioned, but it has also been defended. There have also been studies in which researchers have alternated between periods of interviewing and observing and periods of photographing. Some have observed while photographing as well. Thus, the considerations discussed here are offered as something to think about in planning a study involving photography, not as rules of how it should or should not be done.

LEAVING THE FIELD

The first days in the field you feel awkward and unwanted. As time progresses you begin to feel more comfortable, a part of the scene. Then comes the point when you have accomplished what you set out to do and you have to leave. Leaving can be difficult (Maines, Shaffir, and Turowetz, 1980). Usually you become interested in and fond of the people you came to study. You may feel as if you are deserting them, especially if they were working under adverse conditions and serving devalued populations. The feeling hangs on that if you leave you will miss something important—some new piece of data that will lead to a new insight. While there are many reasons one can use to argue against leaving the field, there comes a time when procrastination must end.

Rather than abruptly ending this phase of their research, many people ease out of the field by coming less frequently and then eventually stopping altogether. This transition is probably psychologically helpful to both researchers and subjects. Often, researchers stop data collection only to find later that more fieldwork is needed, thus requiring them to return to the field. To prepare for this contingency, it is important when stopping fieldwork to leave the door open for such returns. Depending on the bargain you negotiated with the gatekeeper there may be some obligations to keep, such as delivering a report or discussing your experience with organizational members before you say goodbye.

Many fieldworkers report that they keep ties with the people with whom they were involved, returning to the research sites periodically to keep up with subjects' activities and situations. Sometimes subjects become life-long friends. Qualitative researchers have reported that they enter and leave a site periodically, studying the same people and places longitudinally.

Remember the sign: ''I am here to collect data. How does what I am doing relate to that goal?'' If you have internalized the researcher's role, you must abide by that sign. There comes a point where you have enough data to accomplish what you have set out to do, and the explanation of why you remain is hollow. This is the time to say goodbye and get on to data analysis and writing.

ENDNOTES

1. You may be doing action research for social change on a topic like racism in American education, but to do this you must understand sources of particular views. We discuss these issues in Ethics in Chapter 1, and in Chapter 7 on Applied Research.
2. This section was written by Andrejs Ozolins.

FIVE

DATA ANALYSIS

Data ANALYSIS IS THE PROCESS OF SYSTEMATICALLY SEARCHING and arranging the interview transcripts, fieldnotes, and other materials that you accumulate to increase your own understanding of them and to enable you to present what you have discovered to others. Analysis involves working with data, organizing it, breaking it into manageable units, synthesizing it, searching for patterns, discovering what is important and what is to be learned, and deciding what you will tell others. For most, the end products of research are books, papers, presentations, or plans for action. Data analysis moves you from the rambling pages of description to those products.

The analytic task, interpreting and making sense out of the collected materials, appears monumental when one is involved in a first research project. For those who have never undertaken it, analysis looms large, something one can avoid, at first glance, by remaining in the field collecting data when that period should have ended. Anxiety mounts: "I didn't get anything good." "I've wasted my time." "This job is impossible." "My career will end with this pile of unanalyzed fieldnotes on my desk." These fears have crossed the minds of most of us the first time we faced analysis. While analysis is complicated, it is also a process that can be broken down into stages. Confronted as a series of decisions and undertakings rather than as one vast interpretive effort, data analysis takes on a more friendly cast.

Our purpose in this chapter is to help you learn to handle analysis. Some have written about data analysis and we will refer you to them (Becker, 1970a; Cassell, 1978; Lofland, 1971; Schatzman and Strauss, 1973; Spradley, 1980), but in the qualitative research literature, analysis has never received enough attention. The information we provide in this chapter is more rudimentary than sophisticated, more practical than theoretical. We discuss data analysis in order to get you started. We provide some concrete suggestions on how to proceed to make analysis conceptually manageable as well as mechanically feasible.

Before we start we remind you of discussions in previous chapters. There are many different styles of qualitative research and there are a variety of ways of handling and analyzing data. It is useful to think of approaches to analysis falling into two modes. One is an approach where analysis is concurrent with data collection and is more or less completed by the time the data is gathered. This approach is more commonly practiced by experienced fieldworkers. If you know what you are doing it is most efficient and effective. The other mode involves collecting data before doing the analysis. Because reflecting about what you are finding while in the field is part of every qualitative study, researchers only approach this mode, never following it in its pure form.

In our judgment, the beginning researcher should borrow strategies from the analysis-in-the-field mode, but leave the more formal analysis until most of the data is in. Problems of establishing rapport and getting on in the field are complicated and too consuming for beginners to enable them to actively pursue analysis. In addition, new researchers often do not have the theoretical and substantive background to plug into issues and themes when they first arrive on the scene. To do ongoing analysis, one must have an eye for the conceptual and substantive issues that are displayed—something someone new to the field is not as likely to have as an old-timer.

While we recommend holding back attempts at full-fledged, ongoing analysis, some analysis must take place during data collection. Without it, the data collection has no direction; thus the data you collect may not be substantial enough to accomplish analysis later. Though you usually collect more data than you need or can ever use, a focus will keep the task manageable. After you complete a study or two, you can begin analytic procedures earlier, employing them in the field.

ANALYSIS IN THE FIELD

The following are suggestions to help you make analysis an ongoing part of data collection and to leave you in good stead to do the final analysis after you leave the field:

1. *Force yourself to make decisions that narrow the study.* As we said earlier, in most studies data collection is like a funnel. At first, you collect data widely, pursuing different subjects, exploring physical spaces to get a broad understanding of the parameters of the setting, subjects, and issues in which you are interested. After you have developed a research focus, based both on what is feasible to do and what is of interest to you, narrow the scope of data collecting. Do this after three or four visits or some initial interviews. The kinds of decisions one makes are: "I will focus on one third-grade class in this school," "I will explore more deeply women's memories of

puberty," "My major concern will be how the children experience the program," "I will interview women who teach in large schools," or "My major focus will be on communication between teachers and students." Enjoy the initial freedom of exploration, but force yourself to make decisions early. Choices are difficult, for everything is exciting and the world you study seems boundless. You must discipline yourself not to pursue everything and to put some limits on your physical mobility, or else you are likely to wind up with data too diffuse and inappropriate for what you decide to do. The more data you have on a given topic, setting, or subjects, the easier it will be to think deeply about it and the more productive you are likely to be when you attempt the final analysis.

2. *Force yourself to make decisions concerning the type of study you want to accomplish.* In Chapters 1 and 2, we discussed various types of qualitative studies: organizational case studies, observational studies, life-histories, etc. Some accomplished researchers belong to research traditions that favor one of these types over the other and they automatically pursue data directed at producing one of the types. Other experienced researchers are more eclectic, but nevertheless make conscious decisions about what type of study they want to pursue. As a novice, you might not be associated with a particular tradition or may not have the knowledge to collect particular types of data. You should try to make clear in your own mind, for example, whether you want to do a full description of a setting or whether you are interested in generating theory about a particular aspect of it. Are you interested in the minute details of interaction or are you concerned with more general social processes?

While we recommend that you attempt to decide what type of study to pursue, we recognize that it may be difficult to accomplish in advance. For while you can distinguish the different types, you may not feel enough command over your project to do more than merely survive. Try to guide your work with some kind of model, but do not worry if you cannot.

3. *Develop analytic questions.* In our discussion of design, we mentioned that some researchers bring general questions to a study. These are important because they give focus to data collection and help organize it as you proceed. The questions you formulate are closely linked to the type of study you attempt. We suggest that shortly after you enter the field, you assess which questions you brought with you are relevant and which ones should be reformulated to direct your work.

When we began a study of a job-training program for the hard-core unemployed, we brought to the study the question: "What factors in the program effectively bring about changes in the trainees to heighten their employability?" After initial observations it became clear that the people in the program were not necessarily "hard-core unemployed," and that most of what went on in the program was unrelated to preparation for work. The first question was abandoned for: "How does this program continue when what goes on in it is so foreign to its official goals?" (Bogdan, 1971).

Examples of other organizing questions include one that a researcher asked after she started to spend time in a kindergarten class: "What do these children do in school each day?" In a study we did in an intensive care ward for infants in a teaching hospital, we started our fieldwork with no particular focus in mind, but soon organized our work around the question: "What is the nature of communication between parents and medical professionals on the unit?" Later that question was divided into three questions: "Who talks to parents about their children? What do they say? What do parents hear?"

In a study of a program in which instructional technologists encouraged teachers to use media more effectively, the question was: "What happened when media specialists attempted to get teachers to behave differently towards media?" In an interview study of people labeled "retarded," we asked: "How do people labeled retarded come to think about themselves?"

Qualitative researchers often make a distinction between substantive theoretical questions and formal theoretical questions. The questions we just listed are substantive; that is, they are focused on the particular setting or subjects you are studying. To change a substantive question to a formal theoretical question, change the wording; in most cases this can be accomplished by simply omitting phrases or adjectives (Glaser and Strauss, 1967, p. 80). "How does this program continue when what goes on in it is so foreign to its official goals?" becomes "How do programs that engage in activities so foreign to their stated goals continue to operate?" "What is the nature of communication between parents and medical professionals on the unit?" becomes "What is the nature of communication between parents and professionals?" "What happened when media specialists attempted to get teachers to behave differently toward media?" becomes "What happens when outside specialists attempt to change teachers' behavior?"

In research where you observe in a variety of settings, and in studies in which you are employing theoretical sampling, the substantive questions will naturally change to theoretical questions. If you do a great deal of analysis in the field and develop these questions and answers as you move from site to site, you are engaging in what has been called the generation of *formal grounded theory* (Glaser and Strauss, 1967). As we have suggested, this sophisticated analysis while in the field is difficult for the beginner to accomplish. Most beginners will carry out a study within one setting or cohort of subjects. We suggest that you keep your questions at a substantive level for the purposes of guiding your data collection, but speculate in observer's comments and memos about the relation between substantive theory and formal theory. In the formal analysis, after you have completed data collection, you can speculate further. When writing up your findings you might, depending on your audience, attempt to link your substantive findings to formal theoretical issues; that is, reflect on what bearing your findings have on human behavior in general.

In addition to formulating questions, we find it useful to compose statements that capture the project's intent. The statements should be simple and limited to a sentence or two. Pretend an intelligent layperson who knows nothing of your interest or your field of study asks you, "What are you trying to find out in your research?" You should work on being clear enough in your own mind to give a satisfactory answer that neither confuses nor bores the questioner. Work on such a statement; if you can come up with one, you are on your way to clarifying your own purposes—a key to analysis.

4. *Plan data collection sessions in light of what you find in previous observation.* In light of what you find when you periodically review your fieldnotes, plan to pursue specific leads in your next data collection session. Ask yourself, "What is it that I do not yet know?" To answer this question, you will have to think about what it is you know already and what shape your study is taking. Decide if you want to spend more time in one place than another, arrange to see a specific activity, or plan to interview a particular subject with specific questions in mind.

While we suggest that you plan observation sessions to build on previous ones, these plans may fall through. You may go out into the setting only to find that it is impossible to do what you had hoped. While there is no way you can control what your subjects do in the field, the plans can help you focus and strengthen your project regardless of your ability to implement them.

5. *Write many "observer's comments" about ideas you generate.* Fieldnotes are supposed to contain observer's comments. As we discussed in Chapter 3, observer's comments are sections of the fieldnotes in which the researcher records his or her own thoughts and feelings. On first research projects we usually do not spend enough time speculating. Rather than allowing the recording of detailed description to dominate your activities to the exclusion of formulating hunches, record important insights that come to you during data collection before you lose them. Whenever you feel strongly about an event witnessed or a dialogue engaged in, note the images that come to mind. When something occurs that reminds you of incidents in other settings, record these mental connections (this is particularly important in moving substantive theory to formal theory). When words, events, or circumstances recur, mention it in observer's comments and speculate about meanings. If you think you have a breakthrough in understanding something that was previously obscure to you, record it. If you notice that certain subjects have things in common, point it out in observer's comments. The idea is to stimulate critical thinking about what you see and to become more than a recording machine. Figure 5–1 contains examples of observer's comments from the mainstreaming study that were helpful in analysis.

6. *Write memos to yourself about what you are learning.* After you have been in the field five or six times, force yourself to read over your data and write a one- or two-page summary of what you think is emerging. Develop links in that summary between observer's comments. Continue this practice of memo-writing or summarizing regularly. These memos can provide a time to reflect on issues raised in the setting and how they relate to larger theoretical, methodological, and substantive issues.

FIGURE 5-1

EXAMPLES OF OBSERVER'S COMMENTS

Figure 5-1 shows some examples of observer's comments taken from a study of the integration of handicapped children into public school classrooms. If your notes have such paragraphs in abundance, final analysis will be easier.

O.C.:   The principal of Fairview Elementary School refers to having regular (non-special education) teachers coming into this class for autistic children to teach music as "mainstreaming." I have never heard anyone at the University refer to mainstreaming in this way. It is as if the teacher is being mainstreamed into the class.

O.C.:   Ben Shotland often has negative things to say about the district's efforts to mainstream, yet he does so well in his class with the children labeled "handicapped." He is up for tenure and may be feeling that pressure. He seems to be anti-administration, and what he says about mainstreaming may be a manifestation of his general dissatisfaction with the teachers' position in the school or with the administration.

O.C.:   I found it unusual that the teacher said that the child going down the hall in the wheelchair was not handicapped. What she meant was that the child was not receiving any special services and had not had an IEP written up on her. According to the administration, the child isn't handicapped, but according to anyone who would see the child, you would think of her as handicapped. I'll have to pursue the different perceptions of "handicapped." Some kids appear to have nothing wrong with them; yet they are listed on the rolls as having handicaps. I'll have to pursue this further.

O.C.:   This is the third time I've heard from different sources that the scheduling of mainstreamed children is done so that certain teachers do not have handicapped children in their classes. How does this come about? How are they thought of by other teachers? It seems as if the school is divided between pro-mainstreaming and anti-mainstreaming forces.

O.C.:   Mrs. May has little good to say about the workshop she attended to prepare her for taking handicapped children into her class. Her emphasis on "What should I do?" rather than what is the nature of the children's problems seems to be an orientation shared by Mr. Reese, Mrs. Jones, and Sally Bartlett. Lowell Sharp and Minguel seem much more interested in the causes of the problem. It's interesting that those who are concerned with the here and now have never mentioned job mobility. The others are all taking University courses and talk about changing their fields. I wonder if my perceptions are true and if they are, what it all means.

FIGURE 5-2

FIELDNOTE MEMO

A number of themes, ideas, and areas for further investigation have emerged already. I will list them.

1. *Students' use of the class and their label in negotiating a place in the school.* Some kids at some times do not want to be associated with the program because they say they are ashamed to be in special education. Phil and Pam want the door closed when they are in the room, but they talk about negotiating with teachers whose classes they are taking in ways that indicate being associated with the program lets them get certain advantages. It provides them with the opportunity to withdraw from certain activities. Phil's remark during the discussion about the military draft was that if they wanted to draft him he would tell them he was handicapped but he would not tell a girl he wanted to take out. That gets at some of the selective use of "handicapped." Alfred's discussion about how the kids in the program would be thought of as having an inferior brain but now they are thought of as having something particularly wrong with them is related to this. I'll have to look out for material on how kids use the labels and the class and when they choose to identify with it and when not.

2. *Teachers' use of the concept of mainstreaming.* When I first started this study I thought that regular class teachers would or would not want to be involved with disabled children on the basis of their feelings and experiences with "labeled" kids. While this seems to be true in some cases, a lot of the disposition to the program seems unrelated to the particulars about it or the population served. Some teachers feel that the administration is in general not supportive and they approach what they consider "additional" problems with the disposition that "I have enough." When I say "the administration," I mean the central office, those with whom they see as determining the outcome of the contract bargaining. Others concentrate on the principal and feel that he works hard to make things work for them so if he wants them to get involved in a new effort, they will. This needs a lot of working out but it may be fruitful to pursue looking at what one's position is on mainstreaming and how it is talked about as being a manifestation of conflict and competing interests in the school. Also, this reminds me of how particular teachers think of the various special education classes. Marge was telling me that she likes L.D. kids because they aren't trouble-makers like those in the resource room who are emotionally disturbed.

3. *Categories of handicapped kids.* In a very short time I have gotten a lot of stuff on how the teacher perceives the various categories. I just mentioned Marge's comment but teachers who head up the programs have their own way of classifying the kids. Mr. O'Rourke in describing "his kids," said that there were three kids that really didn't belong in the program. Two were there because parents had forced them in (one is "too smart" for the program, the other is "too slow") and the other was there because he knew the kid from last year and there was nothing else for them. Then there are kids who never come. There are twelve kids on the books. If three don't belong and three aren't regular in attendance, that leaves six. Raises questions concerning counting who the program serves. Then there are kids who are referred to as "really having problems." Kids that are going to "make it." Kids that they are "worried about." Kids that "won't be here after the end of the year or after they turn sixteen." "Nice kid" and "off-the-wall" are also terms that I am hearing. I'll have to be more systematic in getting at this and how the regular class teachers classify the students as compared to the special education students. There is some indication that this may be different. Also how the psychologist classifies the kids compared to the teachers should be interesting to look at.

(continued)

4. The relation of the program to the structure and milieu of the school. I have already got a number of items in my notes referring to college and the academic press of the school. Two people have described the school as consisting of two types of kids: very high achievers and very low achievers. I am told that the high achievers are the kids of professional families living in the area immediately around the school, while the low achievers are mainly the inner-city kids, many of whom are on welfare. This is an interesting perception. There must be a lot of students here who don't fit those two categories. I wonder how this perception of who the students are affects what teachers do, if it does affect them. Where do the kids in the L.D. program fit? I am also told and have observed that, while there isn't hostility between blacks and whites, friendship patterns are pretty much along racial lines. White kids eat together in the cafeteria. Black and white kids mix, it seems, when the blacks are of professional backgrounds and the whites are too. The children in the L.D. program are rich and poor, black and white. It is important to explore how racial and economic status patterns in the school at large are reflected in the program for L.D. kids.

The memo shown in Figure 5–2 was written after six observations at a mainstreaming program for "neurologically impaired" and "learning disabled adolescents" located in an urban high school. The form and content of such a memo can vary a great deal and we include this one only to show you an example of one of the many possibilities. Memos often make sense only to the people who are intimately involved in the research, thus parts of this memo may not be clear or may not have the significance it does to the author. As we discussed in Chapter 3, memos also contain material on fieldwork technique and research strategies. This particular one has been edited and rewritten slightly to serve the purposes of this section of this book.

As your research proceeds, your memos may become more analytical. Some may be devoted to just one idea. Others may be more speculative "think pieces" linking your findings to other situations and data. You should not labor over these memos as you might when writing a formal paper. Use a free style, informal language, and let the ideas flow. You will have plenty of time to ponder over what you say when you get to the more formal analysis after you have completed data collection.

7. Try out ideas and themes on subjects. In Chapter 4 on fieldwork relations, we discussed "key informants," subjects who are unusually perceptive and articulate. They can be used as resources in preliminary analysis. During preliminary observations in a study of mainstreaming, for example, you may notice teachers lining up for or against it. You might bring this up to a key informant by saying, "I've noticed that you can group teachers according to their pro and con stance on mainstreaming." See how the idea strikes the teacher. He or she may agree or disagree and explain why the way you are thinking is right or wrong. In the study of residents and interns on the infants' intensive care unit in a teaching hospital, we shared the scheme we developed to account for house staff's unofficial classification scheme of parents of the infants with selected house staff to check it out. They pointed to "types" of parents we had not mentioned as well as to the fact that we had been too categorical in making distinctions between parents and that a continuum better portrayed their thoughts about parents.

While you can use subjects for a resource, it is important not to defer to them completely. They have a stake in seeing things in a particular way which might interfere with their abilities to help clarify and analyze. One perceptive doctor in the teaching hospital study, for example, denied that making judgments about which infants were "nonviable" was problematic. He took the position that the specific nature of the criteria minimized individual judgment. Our fieldnotes were filled with references to the problematic nature of such decisions. His refusal to talk about this area did not mean that it was unimportant to explore; it just meant that he was not a good person to help us figure out that issue.

As we mentioned in our last chapter, it may be unwise to reveal how much you are learning to certain subjects because they may withdraw. Be selective in choosing helpers. While not every one should be asked, and while not all you hear may be helpful, key informants, under the appropriate circumstances, can help advance your analysis, especially to fill in the holes of description.

8. *Begin exploring literature while you are in the field.*   While there is some debate about when someone doing a qualitative study should begin a review of literature (Glaser, 1978), we believe that after you have been in the field for a while, going through the substantive literature in the area you are studying will enhance analysis. What are some of the crucial issues in the literature? What past findings have a bearing on your setting? How does your perspective differ from what you read? How does it agree? What has been neglected in the literature? In addition to reading in the substantive area of your study, just reading widely can help in analysis. We have found that it is very helpful for researchers to read qualitative studies in unrelated fields, for it makes one familiar with how others have worked with their data and it can provide models for one's own work.

The danger in reading literature while you are conducting your study is that you may read and find concepts, ideas, or models that are so compelling they blind you to other ways of looking at your data. Try to avoid jamming your data into pre-formed conceptual schemes. The reading you do should provide you with stimulation rather than be a substitute for thinking. It is perfectly honorable to do research that illustrates others' analytical schemes, but try to distance yourself enough to formulate concepts of your own or to expand the work of others.

9. *Play with metaphors, analogies, and concepts.*   Nearsightedness plagues most research. We get involved collecting data in a particular place and become so captured by the particulars, the details, that we cannot make connections to other settings or to the wide experiential array we carry with us. Ask the question, "What does this remind me of?" about different aspects of the setting. In the study of mainstreaming students with handicaps into public schools, we mentally compared what we were seeing to what we knew of attempts at racial integration to see similarities and differences. In a more adventurous frame of mind, we unburdened ourselves of an historical time frame. In a national study that involved observing people counting the number of handicapped children in particular Head Start programs, we won-

dered how people in Salem in the 1600s might have gone about taking a census of the witch population. Our subjects resorted to empirical indicators, expert judgment, and self-nomination—not very different methods perhaps from those used in Salem. Seen from this perspective, professionals can diagnose children even when symptoms are contrived. The diagnosis becomes reified and the symptoms fall by the wayside whether one is diagnosing witches or emotional disturbance. While this may sound far out, it enlarges the way you think about your research problems.

Another way to expand analytic horizons is to try to raise concrete relations and happenings observed in a particular setting to a higher level of abstraction. We have already mentioned that changing the wording of a statement is one way of doing this. Another way is to make up short phrases to capture the spirit of the generalization you are developing. In observations we did of a training program for the hard-core unemployed, for example, we noticed that the trainees with the most skills, the most talent, and the most potential to obtain jobs received the most attention from the program staff. Playing with that relationship, we developed the phrase the "teacher's-pet principle" to describe the phenomena where the least needy got the most services.

On a pediatric ward in a teaching hospital, we noticed that house staff not only diagnosed the children, but sized up the parents as well. On the basis of their judgments of parents, they decided what to tell them about the condition of their children and how they would involve them in the treatment. We developed the phrase "diagnosis of the third party" to capture the idea that doctors judge others beside their patients. After you come up with such a phrase, you must stipulate under what circumstances and in what other settings it is likely to occur. This process helps you think more deeply about various aspects of your setting and how it compares with other settings. It is through this process that an idea becomes a concept.

MORE ON ANALYSIS IN THE FIELD

There are three general points to make before moving on to the next section, "Analysis after Data Collection." Like some of the ideas and procedures we described under the heading, "Analysis in the Field," these points carry importance for both ongoing and final analyses.

The first point, alluded to earlier, deserves further attention. Do not be afraid to *speculate*. The lack of confidence one usually feels on the first research attempts often makes one too cautious about forming ideas. Worries about getting details and facts straight can hold a researcher down. We do not suggest that the facts and the details are not important, for ideas *must* be grounded in the data, but they are a means to clear thinking and to generating ideas, not *the end*. As C. Wright Mills reminded us, "Facts discipline reason; but reason is the advance guard in any field of learning" (Mills, 1959, p. 205). Barney Glaser, a central figure in the development of qualitative analysis, tells us that good ideas contribute the most to the science of human behavior. "Findings are soon forgotten, but not ideas" (Glaser, 1978, p. 8).

Newcomers to qualitative research often feel guilty when they speculate because they have been taught not to say anything until they are sure it is true. Speculation is, however, productive for this research approach. It helps you take the chances needed to develop ideas. You do not have to prove ideas in order to state them; they must be plausible given what you have observed. Do not put off "thinking" because all of the evidence is not in. Think with what data you have.

The second suggestion we have concerns *venting* (Glaser, 1978). Ideas and understanding will come to you on a regular basis as you go about your research. You are likely to become excited by this creative process. It can be exhilarating. Mulling over ideas creates energy you may want to vent. There are two ways of doing this: talking about the ideas with friends and colleagues or writing memos, observer's comments, and later a text. We do not want to sound antisocial when we suggest that talking things over with others may hinder analysis. We do warn you, however, that talking about your analysis can reduce the energy needed to do the hard work of putting your thinking down on paper. Said once, an idea may no longer compel you to record it; it becomes "something everybody knows," in the public domain. Data analysis must include time when you are alone with your typewriter.

Finally, we suggest that while you review your data during the collection phase of research, mark them up. Jot down ideas in the margins of your fieldnotes. Circle key words and phrases that subjects use. Underline what appear to be particularly important sections. Data should look used—covered with lines and notations, bent edges and coffee stains. We suggest using a pencil so that you can erase confusing notations later on.

ANALYSIS AFTER DATA COLLECTION

You have just finished typing the fieldnotes from your final observation of the study and you open the drawer to put them away. There, facing you, is all the material you have diligently collected. An empty feeling comes over you as you ask, "Now what do I do?"

Many experienced observers know what to do; they take a break. They let the material sit, take a vacation, or do things they have neglected because they were consumed by the data collection, and then come back to it fresh and rested. There is a lot to say for not tackling analysis immediately. You can distance yourself from the details of the fieldwork and get a chance to put relationships between you and subjects in perspective. You will get a new enthusiasm for the data that may have become boring. Also, you get a chance to read and mull over other ideas. However, taking too long a break has drawbacks. It can be a stalling tactic to put off the hard work ahead. It can also cause you to lose touch with the content of your notes. The most serious drawback is that the need to return to the field to collect additional data may arise and if the break has been too long returning can be a problem. Subjects are difficult to locate or have changed positions, or the setting is not the same as when you left it.

Discussions of how long breaks should be and the advantages of putting data aside are esoteric to those who have deadlines to meet, assignments for course requirements, dates on contracts, and appointments to share findings.

Developing Coding Categories

Imagine a large gymnasium in which thousands of toys are spread out on the floor. You are given the task of sorting them into piles according to a scheme that you are to develop. You walk around the gym looking at the toys, picking them up and examining them. There are many ways to form piles. They could be sorted according to size, color, country of origin, date manufactured, manufacturer, material they are made from, the type of play they encourage, the age group they suit, or whether they represent living things or inanimate objects.

Such an activity approaches what a qualitative researcher does to develop a coding system to organize data, though the task for the qualitative researchers is more difficult. The settings are more complex, the materials to be organized are not as easily separated into units, the setting is not void of people, nor are the classification systems as self-evident or clearcut.

As you read through your data, certain words, phrases, patterns of behavior, subjects' ways of thinking, and events repeat and stand out. Developing a coding system involves several steps: You search through your data for regularities and patterns as well as for topics your data cover, and then you write down words and phrases to represent these topics and patterns. These words and phrases are *coding categories.* They are a means of sorting the descriptive data you have collected (the signs under which you would pile the toys) so that the material bearing on a given topic can be physically separated from other data. Some coding categories will come to you while you are collecting data. These should be jotted down for future use. Developing a list of coding categories after the data has been collected and you are ready to mechanically sort it is, as we shall discuss, a crucial step in data analysis.

When we discussed the toys in the gymnasium, we mentioned some schemes that might be used in sorting. The schemes included, for example, the manufacturers and the color. The signs (or the coding categories) for "manufacturers," would say Mattel, Fisher Price, Creative Playthings; and the signs for "colors" would be pink, blue, red, yellow, and multicolored. If you were in the gym and you were told what the purpose of sorting the toys was—let us say, for example, that you were told they wanted piles so they could be sent back to the manufacturer—the task of developing codes would be considerably easier (by manufacturer). Developing coding systems in qualitative research faces similar parameters. Particular research questions and concerns generate certain categories. Certain theoretical approaches and academic disciplines suggest particular coding schemes. It is far beyond the scope of this book to lay out all the coding categories and theoretical approaches that might be used to develop coding systems. What we will do is provide a list of families of codes to suggest some ways coding can be accomplished.

We have made up the families or kinds of codes we will present for the purpose of this discussion. They do not represent universally defined coding conventions. The families overlap. Do not be concerned with which family the individual codes you develop fit under. Our purpose is to help you develop understanding of what codes are and some specific ideas for coding possibilities, not to present an exhaustive scheme from which you can mechanically borrow.

Under each coding family, we will define what we mean by the type, discuss what kinds of data can be sorted by it, discuss when this family of code is most often used, and then provide an example of a unit of data that might be appropriately coded under categories representing the family.

With certain studies you, as a researcher, may have particular concerns and may draw upon one of the types mentioned almost to the exclusion of others. In other studies, categories are mixed. Remember that any unit of data may be coded with more than one coding category from more than one coding family. The coding families presented should provide you with some tools for developing coding categories that will be helpful in sorting out your data.

Setting/Context Codes. This term refers to codes under which the most general information on the setting, topic, or subjects can be sorted. Material that allows you to place your study in a larger context is found under such codes. In most studies one code is sufficient to cover this material. Under such codes much of the descriptive literature (pamphlets, brochures, yearbooks) produced about the setting, subject, or topic can be placed, as well as local newspaper articles and other such media coverage. In addition, general statements that people make describing the subject, the setting, and how the setting fits in the community can be coded here. Also descriptive statistics and other quantitative data that describes the setting can be coded. Particular codes in this family might be labeled: "Descriptions of Elementary Schools"; "Midcity High School." The particular coding label would depend upon your subject.

An example of data that can be coded under such a category is given below. It is a statement made by a principal, describing his school to a researcher on the first day of the project:

> Johnson High is 850 students. Some 90 percent of them go to four-year colleges. The community we serve is mostly upper-middle class professionals. They have had good educations and that's what they want for their own children. We spend more money per pupil than any other high school in this region. We have more merit scholars than any other. As far as football, well that's another story. We've been having a tough time fielding a team. Let me give you a list of our college placements. I'll also give you a brochure describing our philosophy, goals, and programs.

The material given to the researcher would also be coded under the setting/context code.

Definition of the Situation Codes.   Under this type of code your aim is to place units of data that tell you how the subjects define the setting or particular topics. You are interested in their world view and how they see themselves in relation to the setting or your topic. What do they hope to accomplish? How do they define what they do? What is important to them? Do they have a particular orientation that affects how they define participation (religious, political, social class, feminist, right-to-life)? You may be looking at various participants: students, pupils, administrators, as well as parents. You might have a coding category for each type of participant. There may be other distinctions between participants that may be the basis of coding categories. Some "Definition of the Situation" codes in a study of women's perceptions of their own elementary school experiences included "Feminist Awareness," "Image of Present Self," and "Influences on Interpreting Past" (Biklen, 1973).

An example of data that fits in this family is the following statement made by a teacher, which was coded under "teachers' views on their work":

> For me, teaching is my life. I don't separate the two. When I take a shower, I think, "What if I present the material this way, rather than the way I did it last summer?" Sometimes I spend twenty minutes in the shower without realizing it. My husband thinks I'm crazy but he's that way too. We're not big on parties or on vacations; work is really the substance of our lives.

Perspectives Held by Subjects.   This family includes codes oriented toward ways of thinking that all or some subjects share which are not as general as their overall definition of the situation but indicate orientations toward particular aspects of a setting. They include shared rules and norms as well as some general points of view. Often perspectives are captured in particular phrases subjects use. In the study of the intensive care unit of the teaching hospital, the following two phrases were often used. They capture shared understandings and become codes for sorting data.

> "You can never tell" (referred to not being able to predict what will happen to the patient).

> "Be honest but not cruel" (referred to understanding that you should inform parents but not in words that might upset them).

Below is a unit of data taken from that study that was coded under "You can never tell."

> I was with Carol, an intern. She was working on "the Hopkins baby," trying to start an I.V. Joan, a nurse, came in and said to me, "If you want to see what this is all about, come out here." I followed her into the hall and there were three of the nurses standing by the nursing station, standing over a little girl who was toddling around. Next to her was a woman I supposed was her mother. She had on a nice print dress. The little girl was dressed in stretch pants and matching top. Joan said to me in a low voice, "She's doing fine. In for a check-up. She was no bigger than the Hopkins baby when she first came in. We didn't think she would make it. Look at her—see, you can never tell with these kids.

Subjects' Ways of Thinking about People and Objects. This family points to codes that get at the subjects' understandings of each other, of outsiders, and of the objects that make up their world. Teachers, for example, have definitions about the nature of the students they teach. There are types of students in teachers' eyes. In the study of kindergarten, a researcher found that teachers saw children as being either "immature" or "ready for school." In addition, children were categorized according to how they were dressed and the teacher's assessment of the child's home environment. "Teachers View Students" was a coding category in that study. In our study of the intensive care unit for infants in a teaching hospital, we found that professional staff categorized babies according to an elaborate scheme with certain classifications relevant for certain stages in an infant's passage through the unit. Some of the categories referred to were: "feeders and growers," "nonviable," "very sick babies," "good babies," "chronics," "nipplers," and "pit stops." In the same setting, parents were seen as being "good parents," "not-so-good parents," or "trouble-makers." "Patients as seen by professional staff" and "Parents as seen by professional staff" were coding categories in that study. Not only are people subject to classification; in one study of school janitors, different types of trash were made note of and classified.

The following is an excerpt from a study of an urban high school that contains material coded under a "subject's ways of thinking about people and objects" code; in this case, "teachers' definitions of each other."

> Jody began talking about the other teachers in the school. She said, "You know the teachers here are O.K. I can't think of one that I wouldn't want to talk to. Of course there are differences. You've got the type that complains all the time—they think the kids are going to hell—they're doing fine, it's the kids that are lousy. They usually won't do anything to help a kid that's not with it—here there is a group like that. They hang around together—all men. Some jocks—really conservative. Then there are the pluggers—they don't get discouraged and are willing to give it the extra mile. . . ."

Process Codes. "Process" codes refer to coding words and phrases that facilitate categorizing sequences of events, changes over time, passages from one type or kind of status to another. In order to use a process code, the researcher must view a person, group, organization, or activity over time and perceive change occurring in a sequence of at least two parts. Typical process codes point to time periods, stages, phases, passages, steps, careers, and chronology. In addition, key points in a sequence (e.g., turning points, benchmarks, transitions) could be included in the family of process codes (see Roth, 1963).

Process coding schemes are commonly used in ordering life-histories. The coding categories are the periods in the life of the subject that appear to separate important segments. A life-history of a person that emphasizes her education might include coding categories like: (1) early life, (2) moving to New Jersey, (3) the first day of school, (4) Mrs. Nelson, (5) elementary school after Mrs. Nelson, (6) the first weeks of Jr. High, (7) becoming a teenager, and (8) beyond Jr. High School. Notice that the codes suggested here reflect how the subject orders the sequence of her life. The codes do not reflect uniform lengths of time or other researcher-imposed periods. In developing life-history coding systems, the subject's classification scheme usually dictates the codes.

Process coding schemes are also commonly used to organize data in organizational case studies. Here, the change in the organization over time is the focus of interest. Similarly, studies of planned social intervention can be coded by a chronological coding scheme. Chronological coding is the mainstay of history.

While in some studies "process" coding categories dominate, in others they are merely one of a number of approaches used. In the study of a classroom, for example, the following headings suggest coding categories that might be used in addition to codes from other families: "stages in the career of a teacher," "the school year," "the school week," "steps of acceptance into an adolescent peer group," and "the process of dropping out of school."

An example of a unit of data that might be coded under the process heading "stages in the career of a teacher" follows:

> I've been here for five years now. While I don't feel I'm an old-timer like Marge and Sue, I'm not naive either. When I see those teachers coming in, I say to myself, "You'll learn. I did!"

Activity Codes.   Codes that are directed at regularly occurring kinds of behavior are what we are calling "activity codes." These behaviors can be relatively informal and lead to codes, such as a "student smoking," "joking," "showing films," or regularly occurring and a formal part of a setting such as "morning exercises in school," "lunch," "attendance," "student visits to the principal's office," "class trips," and "special education case conference." Units of data that might be coded under such headings are fairly obvious. Below is one such unit taken from a study of a special education program in an elementary school. It concerns a meeting about the placement of a child in a class for "emotionally disturbed" children.

> Although the meeting was supposed to start at 11, no one was in the room when I arrived at 11:05. (*O.C.:*   This is the third such meeting I have attended and the others started ten minutes late with half the participants present.) The first person to arrive was Dr. Brown.

Event Codes.   These kinds of codes are directed at units of data that are related to specific activities that occur in the setting or in the lives of the subjects you are interviewing. Event codes point to particular happenings that occur infrequently, or only once. For example, in a study one of the authors did, which involved interviewing women about their experiences in elementary school, the onset of menstruation was an event mentioned by all the women (Biklen, 1973). The event became a coding category. In the course of participant observation studies events that become coding categories are those that call forth a good deal of attention and discussion by subjects. Events that occurred prior to your research may be frequent topics. In participant observation studies we know the following events became coding categories: "the firing of a teacher," "a teacher strike," "the riot," and "a school pageant."

An example of a unit of data coded under the event code, "the riot," is cited below. It is taken from a conversation with a teacher:

> The day we had the trouble there were more police cars than you've ever seen. Most of the kids didn't know what had happened. Sergeant Brown wasn't messing around. Things had gone too far. The school still hasn't gotten over it.

Strategy Codes.   Strategies refer to the tactics, methods, ways, techniques, maneuvers, ploys, and other conscious ways people accomplish various things. Teachers, for example, employ strategies to control students' behaviors, to teach reading, to get through the year, to get out of hall duty, or to get the classes they want. Students employ them to pass tests, to meet friends, or to negotiate conflicting demands. Principals use them to get rid of teachers, to open new positions, or to reduce absenteeism. The following is a quotation that might be coded under the strategy code "techniques to control class":

> Mrs. Drake walked into the class. No one was in his or her seat. They were all standing about talking, some loudly. Jamie had his radio on. Mrs. Drake said, in a speaking tone of voice but one which indicated she was annoyed, "Let us begin." She waited a second; nothing happened. Then she leaned over to Jason and said something that I couldn't hear. He then said, in a loud singing voice, "Announcement! Announcement! I'm going to make an announcement!" Everyone stopped talking and looked at Jason. He said, "The class has commenced. Cool it." Everyone sat down. Leon said out loud, "Jason, my man, you should be drawing a salary." Mrs. Drake said, with a smile, "Haven't you heard?"

It is important not to impute motives to people's behavior or, if you do, to realize you are. If you perceive behaviors as strategies and tactics, make sure to distinguish between your judgment and theirs.

Relationship and Social Structure Codes.   Regular patterns of behavior among people not officially defined by the organizational chart are what we group under "relationships." Units of data that direct you to cliques, friendships, romances, coalitions, enemies, and mentors/students are what we mean by relationship codes. More formally defined relations, what social scientists refer to as social roles, role sets, and positions, represent another part of this coding family. The total description of relations in a setting refers to "social structure." Coding in this domain leads to developing a description of social structure.

The following unit of data is related to relationships and might be coded under a relationship/social structure code like "student friendships":

> The class came in from home room. A group of four boys—Tim, Harry, Peter, and Brian—stood by the door, half sitting on desk tops, talking. They did the same thing yesterday. Mary and Sue came in together and sat next to each other as did Beth and Allison. (*O.C.:* The boys seem to hang out in groups. Girls, on the other hand, seem to pair off. I'll have to check this out. Some kids have nothing to do with each other, while others are together regularly . . .).

Methods Codes. This coding family isolates material pertinent to research procedures, problems, joys, dilemmas, and the like. For most studies one code, "methods," will suffice. Some researchers, however, turn their research into a study of methodology, focusing, that is, on how to conduct research rather than on a substantive or theoretical topic in the setting (Johnson, 1975). In that case, all coding categories relate to methods. The various chapter headings and sections of this book could be codes in such a study. In fact, this book is a product of our own research experiences, and in preparing it, we have read over data that we and our students have collected. So, in one way, the divisions in this book are a coding system with which we have organized our data. As we have suggested earlier, usually in any given study, more than one coding family is used. People who do methodological studies may use "process codes" to organize their data: the sequence of research activities are the codes (design, choosing a site, establishing rapport, analysis).

Usually observer's comments form the bulk of the units of data that are coded under "methods." The following is an example of an observer's comment from a study of a preschool program that might be coded under "methods":

> (*O.C.:* I feel so odd in this setting with all these three- and four-year-olds. I have no formal responsibilities, which makes me feel awkward. Yesterday, when we went on a trip to the museum, I tried to be like one of the children. I lined up, etc. This didn't work. I felt particularly uncomfortable when my little partner in line refused to hold my hand when I offered it. All the other partners were holding hands.)

Preassigned Coding Systems. As we discuss in chapter 2 on design and evaluation research, researchers are sometimes employed by others to explore particular problems or aspects of a setting or a subject. In that case, the coding categories may be more or less assigned. In a study we conducted of mainstreaming handicapped youngsters, we developed a list of topics (Figure 5–3) about which those doing the research were expected to collect data. These later became the coding categories. Many evaluation research coding schemes are affected by and (at times) are a direct reflection of the agreement between the researcher's sponsors and the people conducting the research. Then the codes derive from the agreement.

The Mechanics of Working with Data

How do you physically handle your data after you have collected it? Remember, by "data" we mean the pages of descriptive materials collected in the process of doing fieldwork (interview transcripts, fieldnotes, newspaper articles, official data, subjects' written memoranda, etc.). Your own memos, think pieces, observer's comments, and the insights you have gained and recorded should be handled in the same manner as the actual data. By the mechanical handling of data, we mean the actual methods of physically sorting the material into piles, folders, or on cards, in order to facilitate access to your notes. You organize them so as to be able to read and retrieve data as you figure out what there is to learn and what you will write. Techniques of mechanically working with data are invaluable because they give direction to your post-fieldwork efforts, thus making manageable a potentially confusing time. Having a scheme is crucial; the particular scheme you choose is not.

FIGURE 5–3

OBSERVATION GUIDE FOR MAINSTREAMING CASE STUDIES*

Below are the general areas you should collect data in with some specific topics listed under each general area. We are interested in information in the area only if (and in ways that) they relate to mainstreaming and children with handicapping conditions. For example, if the school has a reputation for being innovative in general, we are interested because it might tell us about the disposition of staff toward change.

Description of the School (to provide a few pages, context statement)

- Physical
- Historical
- Student population
- Neighborhood
- Teachers
- Special distinctions
- Reputation
- Well-known graduates or people affiliated with school
- Location

The Class or Program

- Location in School
- Its history (how and when it got started with children who are handicapped) e.g., placement procedure, how child is assigned, teacher involvement, parent choice
- Physical description of class
  use of space (e.g., learning centers, separate cubicles, etc.)
  adaptation of class space and equipment for handicapped child
  things on walls
  seating arrangements/location of teacher desk
  condition
- Organization—including authority (decision-making), dispersion of resource people, etc.
- Grade
- Inservice program and opportunities

The Teacher and/or Other Personnel

- Style
- Physical description
- History as teacher
- Perspective on what he or she is doing, especially how he or she tries to integrate disabled children
- Perspective on mainstreaming, handicapped children, the administration, parents, etc. What affects successful mainstreaming?
- How he or she came to see things as he or she does
- Typical day

(continued)

*This figure was compiled by Robert Bogdan and Ellen Barnes. Funds for this research were provided through a grant from the National Institute of Education, NIE No. 400-79-0052.

- Relationship to typical and handicapped children
- Additional personnel in classroom (aides, student teachers)
- Resource personnel relating to classroom (their role, perspective)
- Use of "special" teachers—art, music, gym—how relate, perspective, importance to mainstreaming program
- Relation to other regular teacher peers (how viewed, team, support)
- Whom teacher perceives as supportive

Children Defined as Handicapped

- How what they do is the same or different from what typical kids do
- Peer relations—what are they (sociometrics); how teachers affect
- Typical day
- Physical description
- Clinical description (severity of disability, independence)
- School and family history
- How they are treated and thought about by others in the class
- Physical location—where seated, etc. in relation to teacher, other kids
- Words others use to describe them
- How teacher defines child's progress (same/different from others) balance of social vs. academic goals
- I.E.P. (see Curriculum)
- Amount and nature of contact with teacher (compare with typical)

Typical Children

- Physical description
- Academic description
- Dress
- Background
- How they get along with each other and the teacher

Curriculum

- Content (materials used, any adaptive equipment, individualized?)
- Process (whole group, small groups, individualized, one-to-one, integrated or handicapped served separately)
- Amount of time spent with disabled vs. typical
- Individual Education Plan (is there one, who wrote it, is it implemented, is it appropriate)

Parents

- Nature and amount of teacher contact with parents
- Parents asked about placement of child in mainstreamed program?
- Parent input into classroom and child's program
- Parent participation in IEP of disabled child
- Parent perspective on mainstreaming and success of program

Principal and Other Supportive and Administrative Personnel

- Their part in and relationship to the program (including initiation, placement of child, parent contact, etc.)
- Their definition of the class and the program including if and why it is a success
- Description of things done or not done in support of the class or program (including materials, personnel resources, positive public relations, development of inservice opportunities)

We will describe three ways to mechanically sort the material. They have much in common and what one you choose depends on how detailed your analysis is, your personal fancy, resources available to you (secretarial help, money, time), the amount of data you have, as well as your goals. There are other ways to handle analysis besides these three. Some researchers do little in the way of mechanically working with their data. They "eye ball" it, which means they look over the data and write from it from memory. This technique can be effective if there is a small amount of data and if you have limited goals, but even then we do not recommend this approach to you. It is difficult, if not impossible, to think deeply about your data unless you have the data sorted and in front of you.

We assume you have followed the suggestions in our discussion of fieldnotes, so your notes and transcripts have a wide margin and the text is broken into many paragraphs.

The first step in all three methods involves a relatively simple task—going through all the pages and numbering them sequentially. The data is usually numbered in chronological order according to when it was collected, but if you have different types of data (from interviews, fieldnotes, official documents), you may want to number them in a such a way as to keep similar kinds of material together. It does not make much difference. Your purpose is to facilitate locating data you may want. The important thing is not to have more than one page with the same number.

After the data is numerically ordered on paper, take long undisturbed periods and read over your data at least two times. We recommend undisturbed time because if your concentration is continually broken by other tasks, you are not as likely to get a sense of the totality of your data. While you are reading you should begin developing a preliminary list of coding categories. Keep a pad of paper beside you and as possible codes come to you jot them down. You should also write down notes to yourself which might include lists of ideas and diagrams that sketch out relationships you notice.

In developing codes, look out for words and phrases that subjects use that are unfamiliar to you or are used in ways to which you are unaccustomed. This special vocabulary may signify aspects of the setting important to explore. If the phrases will not make coding categories in themselves, take specific words and try to fit them together under some generic code. (For a good discussion of one way to do this, see Spradley, 1980.)

After generating preliminary coding categories, assign them numbers and then read through your data once again, assigning the coding category numbers to units of data as you do so. By "units of data" we mean pieces of your fieldnotes, transcripts, or documents that fall under the particular topic represented by the coding category. Units of data are usually paragraphs in the fieldnotes and interview transcripts, but sometimes they can be sentences or a sequence of paragraphs. Your first attempt to assign the coding categories to the data, is really a test to discover the workability of the categories you have created. The coding categories can be modified, new categories can be developed, and old ones discarded during this test. It is important to realize that you are not attempting to come up with *the* right coding system, or even *the* best. What is right or best differs according to your aims. You might look at the data again after you complete more research projects and code it differently.

Try to develop a coding system with a limited number of codes, say thirty to fifty. The codes should encompass topics for which you have most substantiation as well as topics you want to explore. Play with different coding possibilities. After you have drawn up a new list, test them again. Speculate about what the new scheme suggests for writing possibilities. You might even try to outline a paper with the coding categories as topics or sections and see if they work for you. You may experience indecision at this point. The data you have might be thin around your interests. Reformulate in light of what you have; you may come up with a list of codes that is extremely long. Try to cut that down. If you have over fifty categories, they probably overlap. While it is difficult to throw away data or categories, analysis is a process of data reduction. Decisions to limit codes are imperative. And at some point—preferably about now in the analytic process—your codes should become fixed, at least for this research project.

After you have developed your coding categories, make a list and assign each one a number. Some people put the list in alphabetical order or group-related categories before numbering. This can be helpful because it facilitates memorizing the coding system. (See Figure 5–4, the coding system used in a study of a training program for the hard-core unemployed.)

Now go through all the data and mark each unit (paragraph, sentence, etc.) with the appropriate coding category number. This involves scrutinizing sentences carefully and judging what codes the material pertains to. It involves making decisions concerning when one unit of data ends and another begins. Often units of data will overlap and particular units of data will fit in more than one category. Thus many, if not most, units of data will have more than one coding number next to them. When you assign numbers, be sure to indicate by pen or pencil exactly what sentences are encompassed by the code. We have included an example of coded fieldnotes (Figure 5–5) that indicates one method of doing this.

We usually mark the original copy of notes with the coding categories, reproduce it on a copier, and then put the original away to serve as the unadulterated master copy. After this point, the three approaches to sorting data differ.

The Cut-Up-and-Put-in-Folders Approach.   One approach to handling the data after this point is to take a scissors and cut up the notes so that the units of data can be placed in manila folders which have each been labeled with one code. If you use this approach you need to do some more work before you start cutting. Go through all the notes, placing a number next to each coded unit of data which corresponds to the number of the page it is on. It is less confusing if you circle that number or in some way mark it so you do not confuse the coding numbers with the page numbers. The page numbers enable you to refer back to the master copy if confusion arises concerning the original context. If your data consists of interview transcripts, another method is to assign each interview a number and use it instead of page numbers for referral. Using numbers other than code numbers helps avoid confusion (like 101, 102, 103, 104).

FIGURE 5-4

CODES USED IN A STUDY OF A "HARD-CORE UNEMPLOYED" TRAINING PROGRAM

1. Trainees attendance
2. The training center (physical aspects, reputation, other programs)
3. Companies participating in the program
4. Staff definition of their involvement
5. Trainees as seen by the staff
6. Trainees as seen by company personnel managers
7. Jobs as seen by trainees
8. Trainees perspectives on training, work
9. Trainees views of staff
10. Trainees views of other trainees and of self
11. Recruitment of trainees (how and why they are in the program)
12. Trainees backgrounds
13. "Holdovers"
14. Trip to factories
15. The program's success (measuring success, how success is seen by various people)
16. Method (getting in, etc.)
17. "Hard core"
18. Joking
19. Follow up
20. Relationships between trainees
21. "lying"
22. "drop outs"
23. Counseling
24. Referral meetings
25. Boredom
26. "Killing time"
27. Poverty programs
28. "On the job training"
29. History of the program
30. Trainees troubles
31. Hustling
32. "The cost of working"
33. Children
34. Neighborhood living conditions
35. Big businesses involvement
36. "Counseling"
37. State employment service
38. Time (trainees definition of)
39. Rapping
40. Money
41. The director
42. The stolen television
43. The Chamber of Commerce
44. Training activities

FIGURE 5-5

TRANSCRIPT OF INTERVIEW WITH TWENTY-SEVEN-YEAR-OLD
WOMAN ON HER PERCEPTIONS OF ELEMENTARY SCHOOL*

#101, p. 2

(101)
6
35
15

I remember being very conscious of how I looked. I had more clothes than anyone else.

S: Why?

K: My aunt was a fashion designer. I had ten dresses to every dress of every other girl.

S: How did that make you feel?

(101)
6
10

K: Um, well at that time I was at the center of attention. I had all this prestige and status. I remember at that time I was always singled out to take the bow for the whole chorus because I had fresh flowers in my hair. You know, it was a whole set of stuff like that. I would untie the sashes of my dresses and the teachers would spend time tying my sashes back up and patting me on the head.

S: You mean, you would untie them to get attention?

K: Uh-huh.

S: What grade was that in?

K: Fourth grade, I think.

S: Let's move on—what do you remember about fifth grade?

(101)
4

K: OK. I remember always leading the people developing the bulletin boards. School work was—I loved doing it; I loved to read, though I think I spent more time reading outside of school, stuff that was not required for school than anything else. I remember doing covers for endless reports.

S: More than the contents?

(101)
4

K: Yes, right. Although I always did a very good job. But it was not particularly exciting as I recall. I don't remember being really stimulated. I got . . . I remember being very excited about getting A's but in terms of the work I did to get there, I don't have any recollection of it really.

(101)
9
41

In the sixth grade you had to take sewing in home economics and I hated it. It took me like a year to make one thing.

S: Why did you hate it?

K: All I can remember is that the teacher used to say, "It's not the machine, it's the operator. It's not the machine, it's the operator." And I kept thinking, "It's the fucking machine." I didn't think "fucking" at that time; I didn't even know the word. But the same sort of sense. I couldn't believe I was so inept that I couldn't make the bobbin do what it was supposed to do and I never could. I felt like it was something I was supposed to be doing and I didn't like it.

Code Translations

6 = Attention/Praise	4 = Schoolwork
35 = Clothes	9 = Sex Role Awareness/Expectations
15 = Looks	41 = Methodological Issues

See S. Biklen, "Lessons of Consequences: Women's Perceptions of their Elementary School Experiences; a Retrospective Study," unpublished Ed.D. dissertation, University of Massachusetts, 1973.

Because some of the data units will be coded for more than one category, more than one copy of the notes will be needed. Do this after you put on the page or interview numbers. Look through the data and see how many units you have that are multicoded. If you have many with, say, three codes, and a few with four codes, you might want to make three and four copies of only the pages that have multiple-coded units. This saves the expense of making several complete copies.

All that is left to do is to label manila folders with the coding numbers and the corresponding words and phrases, and to find a box or some other type of container to hold the folders. Then you go to it, cutting and filing. The mention of a box or other method to hold the folders may seem rather mundane, but many of the folders will contain many slips of paper that fall to the bottom making the folders awkward to handle and hard to keep upright. Sometimes straightening out little matters like these can save you energy that might be better used on the more complex issues of analysis.

With all the units of data in the respective folders, you might want to regroup them according to some scheme. Then you take folders out and carefully pour over each one's content. (We discuss this further in the next chapter.) Which one you go over first are of little importance. You might want to take one that you think you know a good deal about or about which you have some ideas. You might, on the other hand, want to look at the fattest folder. As you work with a particular folder and see what patterns and themes appear in it, you can sort that data into piles and work with it. If there is a great deal of data in a file, you may want to develop coding subcategories for it. While you do this, you pencil out different ways of putting things together, drawing up lists and diagrams. When you think you understand the contents of a folder, you might want to briefly write about it. There will be connections between the folders and you will want to note these, so put off formal writing until you examine and play with a number of folders. People who use this approach to handle data sometimes use a large piece of thumbtack board and arrange data from each folder on the board as they work with it. You do need a large space when you start poring through the folders.

The File Card System.   To handle data with this method, the paper on which you type your original fieldnotes and transcripts has to have each line on the page numbered consecutively, starting at the top with line 1. Paper numbered in this fashion can easily be produced by numbering a stencil and running it through a mimeograph machine. You also need a stack of note cards with the code number and corresponding phrase and word written on the top. You then go through the data recording on the cards on what page in the data and on what lines on that page units of data relevant to the category can be found. It may be helpful not only to give the page number and the line, but to make a note next to the card entry as well that tells you something about the unit. You might mark it "memo," or "observer's comment," or "quotation." If you think that the unit is particularly valuable, your entry might look like "p. 89 l.7-14, terrific quote" (see Cassell, 1978a).

This method has a number of advantages. It does not require the expense of making multiple copies, and it does not involve the mess of cutting and bulky files. Some disadvantages include: difficulty skimming the data arises because you have to find each piece of data to look at, rather than having it right there in front of you; and retrieving data becomes laborious and when you pull pages of the notes that contain units of data for a particular code, you have to put them back in order to make it accessible in case it is crossed-coded. We advise this approach when you have a small amount of data and a small number of coding categories.

Information Retrieval Cards.   Information retrieval cards (like Indecks or McBee, two brand names) provide a third way of mechanically organizing data. Each card contains a large space in which you type units of data. You must go through your notes, unit by unit of data, and type them onto the cards. (Although if you plan on using this system ahead of time, you can type your fieldnotes with the right margins on plain paper to enable you to paste the units on the cards.) As you will notice, each card has the same numbered holes around the rim. After each unit of data is typed on the card, take a scissors and cut off all those holes except those that correspond to the numbers of the coding categories to which the unit of data pertains. After all the data has been transferred to the cards and they have been cut, they are placed in the box that came with them. The box is the same dimensions as the face of the card. Thus holes with the same numbers line up perfectly.

These card systems include a long, needle-like instrument to pull cards out of the box. You line up the cards and pass the needle through the hole that corresponds to the category you want and then gently shake and pull with the needle. The cards you do not want will fall off. You can then take the cards off the needle and study them. After you are through with that category you can put them back and then pull another. It does not matter what order your cards are placed in because order is determined by the holes on the rim, not position in the box. The neatness of the system is its main feature. Its expense is its major problem. The cost in time or expense if services are bought to transfer the data onto the cards can be substantial.

A CONCLUDING REMARK

We have ended our discussion of data analysis rather abruptly. The actual process happens differently. Analysis continues into the writing stage, which we take up in the next chapter. If you are feeling stuck with piles of coded data, the next chapter will move you farther along toward the final product.

WRITING IT UP
AND DISSEMINATING
THE FINDINGS

WHEN IT COMES TIME TO WRITE UP YOUR RESEARCH, THERE ARE
many different ways to go about it. In fact, sitting before that typewriter, it may seem
as if you are facing *too* many choices. What is most frightening is feeling out of control; that is, you do not know how to choose vocabulary, construct sentences, modulate active and passive voices, or organize your presentation so that the written product reflects your intentions. You can gain control, however, if you can master these techniques, and if you think about the task of writing up your research as a series of discrete decisions rather than as one enormous undertaking that must be accomplished all at once.

Writing from qualitative data is somewhat easier than writing, say, a conceptual piece. The fieldwork and analysis produce piles of coded description which provide a starting point—some words on paper. Not only do you have the descriptive data in front of you, you have a host of observer's comments and analytic memos that may serve as rough drafts of sections of your paper. You have a foundation you can revise and expand as you work toward the production of a report, paper, article, or book.

What you plan to produce with your data will affect what you write and how you organize your writing. If you are doing a dissertation, for example, you need to attend to certain conventions. Articles and research reports usually offer more stylistic freedom, but you always need to have a beginning, a middle, and an end. The beginning tells what you will do in the paper; it lays out the contents. The middle section develops, argues, and presents your point. You discuss your insights; marshalling your data to convince the reader with evidence for what you claim. The conclusion may summarize what you have said, it may draw a few disparate points together, or it may suggest the implications of your findings for more research or practice; it is a tidying up, like dessert or coffee after the meal. (Some helpful hand-books on writing include Baker, 1973 and 1966; Kierzek and Gibson, 1968; Strunk and White, 1972.)

While these are the barebones of what a paper might look like, you may approach your task in a variety of styles and with different ways of organization. While sometimes what you must do is dictated by your assignment (i.e., you are assigned to undertake original research and write it up in the manner of a particular journal), usually within an assignment enough latitude exists for you to have some choices about how to proceed. The more you write, the better you will get, and the easier it will come to you.

While not experts on the written word, we do have experience writing and publishing qualitative research findings in educational journals. In this chapter we get you started on the process of learning how to be a writer of qualitative research for education. We first examine the elements of a good report and offer advice on how to get started. We conclude with a discussion of how to go about getting your work published.

GETTING STARTED

Novice writers are big procrastinators. They find countless reasons not to get started. Even when they finally get themselves seated at their desks, they always seem to find diversions: make the coffee, sharpen the pencil, go to the bathroom, thumb through more literature, sometimes even get up and return to the field. Remember that you are never ''ready'' to write; writing is something you must make a conscious decision to do and then discipline yourself to follow through. People often tell us that we are lucky; they say, ''Writing comes so easy to you.'' Writing comes easy neither to us nor to many others; it is hard work. As one author put it, ''Writing is easy; all you do is sit staring at the blank sheet of paper until drops of blood form on your forehead.'' Some become more proficient at it because they have developed good work patterns, confidence, and skills, but it is never easy. Writing seldom comes naturally. Most people feel very self-conscious before they write: their hands sweat and they experience anxiety.

Where do you start? You have already started. If you have followed our advice—if you narrowed your focus, if you looked for themes, if you made decisions about what type of study you are doing, if you wrote memos and observer's comments, if you have mechanically sorted the data read in the literature, you are on your way. But what about the actual writing: the style, the form, and the content?

A GOOD MANUSCRIPT

A piece of good nonfiction writing has a clear focus. It states a purpose and then fulfills the promise. Coming up with a focus means deciding what you want to tell your reader. You should be able to state it in a sentence or two.

While a good paper has a single focus, there are many types of foci. One kind is a *thesis,* a proposition you put forth and then argue. The thesis can be born out of a comparison of what your research has revealed and what the professional literature says about the subject (e.g., "Researchers have taken the position that . . ." or "Our research has revealed another dimension . . ."). Or, it contrasts what practitioners claim and what your research has revealed (e.g., "The model of . . . presented in the manual takes quite a different form when implemented in the classroom."). The thesis might argue that the unforeseen consequences of a particular change instituted by outsiders is more important than the planned effect. The thesis is a good focus; it is argumentative and can build interest. But people who start arguments are often attacked. In developing a provocative thesis, the case is often overstated; you attack a position that no one would actually take. (This is called setting up a "straw man" [sic].) If you choose something to attack that has already been refuted, your statements sound droning. Academics are particularly critical of the trumped-up thesis. They take the assertion literally rather than as a matter of style. Use the thesis cautiously in writing for them.

A *theme* can also serve as a focus. It lacks the overtly argumentative tone of the thesis, although it shares some of the "big idea" quality. A theme is some concept or theory that emerges from your data: "some signal trend, some *master* conception, or key distinction" (Mills, 1959, p. 216). Themes can be formulated at different levels of abstraction from statements about particular kinds of settings to universal statements about human beings, their behavior, and situations (Spradley, 1980). We presented some potential themes in our discussion of data analysis. The "teacher's pet principle," and "diagnosis of the third party," are potential themes that could serve as the focus for papers. Academic researchers interested in generating theory see the development of "generic themes" (Glazer and Strauss, 1967) as the most laudible goal for researchers. As Lofland puts it, a generic theme (frame) is: "when the structure or process explicated is chosen and brought to a level of abstraction that makes it generally applicable rather than applicable only in a given institutional realm or ideological debate, or other localized concern" (Lofland, 1974, p. 103).

The *topic* provides the third type of focus. Like the theme, the topic is pervasive in your notes, but it is more a unit of a particular aspect of what you were studying than an idea about it. A theme is conceptual; a topic is descriptive. We suggested some topics in our discussion of data analysis; for example, "What is a good teacher?"

For the purposes of presentation, we have made the distinction between *thesis,* *theme,* and *topic,* as examples of foci. These words seldom can be applied definitively to a focus in a given paper. Often the focus will be a hybrid, having elements of all three. We have not stated all possible types. There are other types. The focus of a paper, for example, might be to illustrate the usefulness of concepts or themes that others have developed. If you are involved in evaluation research, very often the focus is the question you agreed to explore when you entered the contract to do the work.

What type of focus is best—the thesis, the theme, the topic, some hybrid, or another type? The writing tradition you work out of may have a preference. Journalists write with an argumentative thesis, as do essayists, while academic writing tends to be more theme-oriented. Practitioners in the professions tend more to the topical focus. No one, though, uses one type to the exclusion of the others.

Making a good decision about what type will work for your material will depend on how familiar you are with the field in which you are working. What is needed? (Of course, your decision may also be determined by what you are asked to do by your professor or contractor.) If we do not have good descriptions of, for example, what a day in the life of a teacher is, a paper with this as a topical theme would be an important contribution to the study of teaching. If, on the other hand, you are working in an area where there is already good description in the literature, a theme or thesis for a focus would make your writing more valuable. Using as a focus a well-known conceptual framework that others have used in studies similar to yours may provide you with a good research experience, but it will not generate much interest. A theoretical theme paper might not be well-received if you agreed to do an evaluation of a program's effectiveness for a particular contractor.

The type of focus you use also depends on your skills. The novice often cuts teeth writing with a topical focus, or a topical focus with the beginnings of a theme. Most experienced writers, and people with broad backgrounds in research and in their substantive fields, tend to write with a thesis or theme, but they choose from the topical realm also.

Most crucial in deciding on what your specific thesis, theme, or topic will be is the data you have collected, analyzed, and coded. You cannot choose a focus in an area in which your data is thin. One simple way of finding a focus is to look over your coding categories and see which have yielded the greatest amount of data. If you have chosen the "folder method" of mechanically sorting the data, look through the folders and pick the fattest ones. If you have a few that are thick, look through them and see if they have some common trust. Also read over the memos you have written to see if you can make connections between codes, or if you have already noted themes.

While you start your writing with a search for a focus, what you first embrace may not work as you proceed with your writing. Your initial selection should be seen as a hypotheses that has to be tested. You have to see if it works. Expect false starts, reformulation, and refinement. Be open to discovery and to flashes of insight that were unobtainable in the field or while doing analysis because you were too close to the data. At times a draft of the paper is needed before you see the light of a workable focus.

The title should reveal your focus. In *The Judged Not the Judges: An Insider's View of Mental Retardation* (Bogdan and Taylor, forthcoming), the authors present the views of a person labeled "retarded" on special education and other aspects of programs for people labeled "mental deficients." "Be Honest but Not Cruel: Professional/Parent Communication on a Neonatal Unit," concerns what professionals tell parents of children who are patients on an extensive care unit for infants. "Be Honest but Not Cruel" is a perspective the staff share on the unit regarding communicating with parents. Although titles are decided after you have finished your writing, the attempt to come up with them before you start can facilitate your search for a focus.

A good manuscript has a coherent structure and a design to carry out the purpose embodied in your focus. As we said earlier, the basic design of nonfiction writing is the beginning or introduction, the middle or core, and the end or conclusion. What we have just said may sound obvious, but it is often forgotten. Too many papers have many beginnings, and resemble a train wreck rather than a line of cars headed by the engine, and with a caboose announcing the passing.

The Introduction

The introduction usually starts by providing the general background needed to understand the importance of the focus. Placing the paper in the context of the literature or some current debate is one strategy; stating the assignment that you are fulfilling is another. Often the introduction concludes with a description of the design of the rest of the paper. The discussion of research methods belongs in the introduction, but its length and specific location vary. In writing in a journalistic mode, you are not likely to include it. In research articles it is imperative that you tell your readers such things as the techniques you used, the time and length of study, the number of settings and subjects, the nature of the data, researcher-subject relations, checks on data, and other information that might help them evaluate the soundness of your procedures and the nature of your subject. Sometimes such information is provided in an appendix. This is especially true in books. Some important contribution to the methods literature can be found in the appendices of such books as *Street-Corner Society* (Whyte, 1955) and *Tally's Corner* (Liebow, 1967).

The Core

The core of the paper makes up the bulk of the manuscript and gets its direction from the focus. You proceed to do what you stated: argue your thesis, present your theme, illuminate your topic. The test of your focus is your ability to carry it through in the middle. You may find you do not have sufficient data to write the middle, a situation that forces you to enlarge or change your focus. You may discover, on the other hand, that you are flooded with data and have too much to write in the length of paper you had planned. Here the focus has to be narrowed.

In writing the middle, the focus keeps you on track. Everything that is included should be directly related to it. Cores have sections; parts that have headings. The test on whether to include each section is your answer to the question: "Does this section relate directly to my focus?"

The nature of the sections, what you include in them and how they relate to each other, grows out of further analysis of your coded data. After you have singled out a few coding categories embodied in your focus, you should begin working with them, reading them over, and looking for patterns, parts, or elements. You can treat them like you treated the whole pile when you originally mechanically sorted the data. The amount of the material will be much less and, therefore, easier to handle. It is the purpose of mechanical sorting to get the data in small enough piles so that you can physically manage it.

In looking through data in a particular coding category, you should look for further divisions (subcategories). For example, one of your coding categories in a participant observation study of a classroom might be "teacher's definition of students." Reading through the material filed under this code, you might notice that the teacher used different phrases to describe the students. The teacher may have had a typology in mind—a classification system of "kinds of students"; "good students," "brats," "poor souls," "drop-outs," "pests," "trouble-makers," might be phrases you notice repeating. You can work on developing the teacher's classification system. Here "teacher's definition of students" is the cover term, "kinds of students" is the subcategory coding system with "good students" etc., being the "subcodes" (Spradley, 1980). These categories can become the major and minor headings for different sections of your paper.[1]

Whatever the specific content of the middle, each section should be structured in a way similar to the entire manuscript. Each should have a beginning, a middle, and an end. The beginning tells you what the section contains and links it to the focus and the parts that come earlier. The middle provides what the introduction promised, and the conclusion summarizes what was in the section, linking it again to the focus and providing a transition to the next section. To keep section content relevant, you ask whether what you are writing relates to what you said you were going to do in the beginning of the section.

Writing up a qualitative study is really like doing a translation (Spradley, 1979). You take what you have heard and seen and put it down on paper so that it makes sense to your readers as it made sense to you. Our image of the translator's task may be simple: He or she takes the words of one language and transposes them rather literally into the words of another. In fact, the process is complicated. Translators must understand nuances of meaning in both languages. Colloquial expressions literally rendered may have different or no equivalent meanings in another tongue. Translation involves understanding the intent and meaning of one linguistic effort (which reflects certain cultural assumptions), and creating an equivalent for it in another language (which reflects other cultural assumptions).

To accomplish translation as a qualitative researcher, you not only explain what you have seen or heard, but you must also convince the reader of the accuracy of your views. Just as the translator's colloquial equivalent for the Chinese expression "it is like a cup of cold water" must re-create that meaning with an appropriate image for the American, so must the qualitative researcher give evidence to support generalizations. The evidence makes the generalizations take hold in the reader's mind. The qualitative researcher, in effect, says to the reader, "Here is what I found and here are the details to support that view." The job involves deciding which evidence to use to illustrate your points; it is a balancing act between the particular and the general. Your writing should clearly illustrate that your abstract ideas (actually summaries of what you saw) are grounded in what you saw (the details that, taken together, add up to the generalization). What is your goal? As one ethnographer has suggested, "A good ethnographic translation shows; a poor one only tells" (Spradley, 1979). Let us look more specifically at what is involved in balancing the particular and the general: the use of quotations, and how many; and how to lead into examples.

A good qualitative paper is well-documented with description taken from the data to illustrate and substantiate the assertions made. There are no formal conventions used to establish truth in a qualitative research paper. Your task is to convince the reader of the plausibility of your presentation. Quoting your subjects and presenting short sections from the fieldnotes and other data helps convince the reader; it also helps your reader get closer to the people you have studied. The quotations not only tell what they said, but how they said it and what they are like.

In the following example, the author of an article on how Italian immigrants experience schooling in Canada mixes quotations from informants with her own description and analysis within the same paragraph:

> For children who have learned to respect school and to take their academic responsibilities seriously, the experience of total immersion in a foreign language environment is nothing short of devastating, "I felt like a piece of wood," says a fifteen-year-old boy. And a thirteen-year-old, from Cantanzaro: "It was as if I was in a corner, sort of hiding, and all the other kids would find me and they couldn't understand that I didn't understand English and couldn't get their messages in my corner." Even the simplest question was torture: "The teacher would ask me my name and I was afraid to say my name because they said it so much different from how I would say my own name, and it was awful." This from a twelve-year-old girl from Molise (Ziegler, 1980, p. 265).

The quotations and the author's interpretations intertwine to form a flowing paragraph which nicely modulates the particular with the general.

Another way to present data is to make a statement (such as "Women who recalled troubled family lives during their childhood had a difficult time remembering details about elementary school"; or "When we asked teachers of mainstreamed classrooms how they first reacted when they learned they were to have a handicapped child in their class, their responses opened up another area of investigation to us"), and illustrate the statement with several examples. Frequently, this way of illustrating abstract material is chosen in more formalized research as in a dissertation. What follows is an example of this style from a dissertation based on interviews with adult women recalling their elementary school experiences. The particular example is from a chapter on teachers:

> Another bit of evidence subjects used to evaluate their teachers was whether the teachers' concern and interest in their job was visible to their students. Teachers were judged as poor if students felt that they did not like children or teaching:
>
> "The teacher I had the following year was a Mrs. Lolly. And she just didn't enjoy kids at all. She was really a mistake for the teaching profession" (#104).

"Second grade was a young woman who was pregnant and I guess she was just not up to teaching at that stage of her life and she had two or three favorites, both boys and maybe one girl, and she and I got along horribly" (#320).

"Fourth grade, Miss Aldan. I don't know what to say about Miss Aldan. Again, she was a woman who was in the role of teaching without caring a lot about it and she made it very boring. She had a monotonic voice and she would go on and on. I did a lot of daydreaming" (#325).

Each of the examples offers a slightly different aspect of the general point to be illustrated (Biklen, 1973). In this case, the data is separated from the generalizations. In the previous example, the particular and the general were alternated.

In the examples we used to illustrate how to intersperse the particular with the general, you can also see how to lead into data. Again, you can intermix analysis and example (as in the discussion of Canadian schooling), or you can set the examples off from the general statements. In either case, you must always indicate for what purpose you are using the data. What follow are a few examples to give you an idea of the variety of ways you can lead into presenting description and quotations.

In the following, the author relies on the "As so and so said" method which she then reinforces with another example:

But in her position as traffic cop she was limited to dealing with that which was observable. As Mrs. Preston said furiously to Lewis when he talked back to her on the playground, "I don't care what you think. Just don't say it and don't look it." Or Mrs. Crane, "I wish Joe wouldn't always insist on the last word. If he would just not argue I could ignore him." As long as the pupil conformed outwardly, as long as he did not defy her directly, the teacher could be in control (McPherson, 1972, p. 84).

You will also notice that after the author presents the example she rounds it out with a concluding interpretation. This concluding sentence can either reinforce the interpretation or offer a slightly new twist.

The following example indicates another method of presenting data—the use of the colon. The colon implies that the material presented next will illustrate the preceding sentence(s):

The observer, too, has had impact on the system. Geoffrey has been reluctant to be as punitive as he sometimes sees himself being. Geoffrey himself admits this in his notes:

When problems arise in class, such as Pete's behavior, the fact that an observer is there seems to affect my behavior to a greater degree than normally. Starting tomorrow, conscious though I may be of what he thinks, I am going to behave as I normally would, or as close to that as I can. (9/11) (Smith and Geoffrey, 1968, p. 61).

In the above example, the participant observer in the class, Louis Smith, records an entry from the teacher's (Geoffrey's) diary as an example of data. With the use of the colon, the transition does not have to be as carefully constructed as it would were one to depend on sentence construction.

Another way to present data is to incorporate it directly into the text, so that it almost becomes part of a story you are telling. In this technique, you incorporate dialogue and description directly into the narrative. To the reader it appears as if you are telling a story; you are much less distanced from the material you are presenting. The following example reflects what the author learned after interviewing children in jail, in this case, ''That kid (who) will end up killing somebody'':

> Bobbie Dijon was always the tallest girl in her class; only a few boys were taller. Some of the children laughed at her in the third and fourth and fifth grade. But by the time she was twelve, she was so strong and so big, nobody ever teased her for they feared that Bobbie would haul off and pound them with her fists, which she was known to do. It was not, her teachers said, that she was a tough girl, or a bad girl. There was a tough part of her, but it was a small part that lived inside her, content not to show itself unless seriously provoked (Cottle, 1977, p. 1).

In this example, the quotations and descriptions gained in the interviews are not isolated and presented separately in the narrative; they flow together with the story line to create an atmosphere of informality of presentation.

Clearly many different ways to incorporate examples from your data can be used. Relying on more than one means will provide variety to your writing. At the same time, to achieve control over your writing, you need to make certain that your style reflects your intent in writing, the audience for whom the piece is intended, and most importantly, what you want to convey.

We said that your paper should be well documented with data taken from your fieldnotes and other materials. That does not mean you should include large sections of it with no discussion nor clear reason for their incorporation. Some novices get so intrigued with the richness of their data that they think what is in it is self-evident and important to the reader as is. The reader is often left cold. Writing and using quotations is hard work. Presenting raw fieldnotes is usually a cop-out from taking that next step of refining your thinking and sharing with the reader the intricacies of what it is you have learned.

There is a place for pure narrative in reporting qualitative research. It is most often used in presenting first-person life-histories. In that case, the whole manuscript may be virtually the subject's own words with the author providing only a short introduction and perhaps the conclusion. But even with first-person life-histories, the material is carefully edited and rearranged prior to publication.

Much of the material in fieldnotes makes good dialogue for plays and short stories. Our discussion of writing has not included this form of presentation. The possibility of using qualitative data in this way is exciting. But your work should be what it is by choice of focus and design and not by default.

In writing up qualitative research you present your point of view, your analysis, your explanation, your rendering of what the data reveals. The discerning reader might be skeptical. Even though you illustrate your discussion with quotations from the data and in other ways present evidence for the plausibility of your analysis, people will have questions: ''Isn't there an alternative explanation for what you have found?'' ''That is your way of presenting it, what about this as an alternative?'' ''Did all the subjects express that point of view all the time?''

It is important that you raise questions that the reader might have and address them in your paper. This is usually done in the core. Present alternative points of view and discuss why the one you chose was more consistent with the data. If there are subjects with a minority point of view that you did not discuss, mention them. You should pretend you are your paper's worst critic—raise all the tough questions and then deal with them one by one. Whatever style you choose, make sure that it permits you to confront alternative explanations for your findings.

Styles of Presentation.   Qualitative researchers are blessed in not having a single, conventionalized mode for presenting findings (Lofland, 1974). Particular schools of qualitative research produce manuscripts with a distinct style—you can identify them by the particular phrases they employ. Diversity, however, reigns. You might want to choose a particular school to associate with, like groups who do ''ethnographies'' or ''constitutive ethnographies'' or ''microethnographies,'' to refer to a few types. Study their style and model your writing after them. This technique is a good one to follow if you are unsure of your abilities to develop your own style. With practice, your own mode of presentation will emerge.

Styles of presentation can be visualized on a continuum. At one end of this continuum you find the more formal or traditional ways of organizing a presentation. These styles may be didactic. At the other end of the continuum you find more informal and nontraditional modes of writing. Articles using these styles may tell a story first and draw conclusions only at the end; they are inductively presented. Let us look at what you would be choosing were you to work toward either end of this continuum.

There are some established formats in which to present information. If you choose one of them your form will require you to cover certain materials and organize them so as to touch certain bases. If, for example, you choose to do a microethnography, you will focus on intimate behaviors in a single setting. In your research efforts you narrow in on more specific aspects of interactions in order to break down the setting further and further. To write out this microethnography, you can take advantage of this organizing factor, this continual breaking down and dissection of events, using it to organize your written presentation. (Some good examples of microethnographies include Florio, 1978; and Smith and Geoffrey, 1968.)

Similarly, in a macroethnography, you lay out the whole realm of a complex situation, making sure to cover all aspects that have relevance to your theme. It is not as if simply choosing a particular format automatically organizes the paper for you, but rather that you can take advantage of the particular requirements of accomplishing one of these modes of qualitative research to order your presentation.

In more traditional forms of presentation, the findings or points of view are usually presented didactically. The author announces near the beginning what the paper, chapter, book, or dissertation will argue, and then proceeds to show the readers by presenting key aspects of the perspective, documenting it with examples from the data. In this style, interestingly enough, the data is discovered inductively, but presented deductively, so the author must make a real effort to show that he or she did not collect data to prove a point of view already held.

A good example of a style that clearly depends on the deductive method of presentation is the illustration of some existing theory. The theoretical perspective may have been chosen after data collection was completed because it seemed to explain what the researcher found (see, for example, McPherson, 1972). There are many examples of qualitative illustration of theory in contemporary qualitative research in education conducted in Great Britain (see, for example, Sharp and Green, 1975). What has been called "labeling theory" is also a popular concept to illustrate (see Rist, 1977).

At the more nontraditional and informal end of the continuum are modes of presentation which might be called *portrait-writing* or *story-telling* (Denny, 1978b). These kinds are more controversial in academic settings, and if you were to attempt one of them for a formal paper at your university, you would probably be well-advised to check this ahead of time with your instructor to see if it is acceptable. Reading this kind of research is almost like reading a story; the writer creates atmosphere. In his book on busing, for example, Cottle portrays the feelings of people involved in both sides of the busing issue in Boston. He helps readers understand conflicting perspectives. In the following example a parent reacts to the news that his son would be bused:

> If Ellen McDonough was upset by the news, her husband Clarence, a tall handsome man with reddish curly hair and a long straight nose, was outraged. "They did it to me," he yelled one evening when I visited their home. "They went and did it to me, those goddam sons of bitches. I told you they would. I told you there'd be no running from 'em. You lead your life perfect as a pane of glass, go to church, work forty hours a week at the same job, year in year out, keep your complaints to yourself, and they still do it to you" (Cottle, 1976a, pp. 111–112).

The author has drawn a portrait in words.

One characteristic of less formal presentations is the presence of the author. The work is not so distanced, and the writer not so hesitant to use "I."[2]

The Conclusion

A paper ends with a conclusion. You can do a number of things in it. Often the focus is incisively restated and your argument reviewed. The implications of what you have presented can be elaborated. Many research reports end with a call for further research. There is nothing that does not *need* further research; it is this belief that makes a researcher's life meaningful. But psychiatrists think that more people should have therapy, and television manufacturers think that people should buy more TV's. The sincerity of your belief does not erase the fact that you are dealing with a cliché.

It is a dangerous cliché because this trite conclusion can substitute for a definitive statement of what you have come to understand and why the work is important. The call for more research is often a tactic used by writers when they have run out of steam, when they do not have enough energy to finish the trip to the end of a uniformly good paper. In the conclusion, the end is in sight; keep at it.

CONCLUDING REMARKS ABOUT WRITING

Hopefully some of our discussion of what makes a "good paper" has given you some suggestions on how to proceed. Breaking the task down into manageable parts is very important. First try to come up with a focus, then begin an outline of the core. Try writing the introduction or a section. Tell yourself that what you are writing is not the final product, but that you are just working on a draft. Force yourself to start, putting your thoughts down on paper. You can always rewrite and change later. Calling something a "draft" can be a device to relieve tension, a way to suspend your over-critical reading of what you have written, a way of putting aside your feelings of inadequacy. Often "drafts" are easily converted into final products by some editing and erasing of words.

First drafts most often suffer from being overwritten: they are too wordy and contain more than the reader could possibly be interested in knowing. Authors have a tendency to think that everything is important, and it may be to them, but it hardly is to the reader. It is most difficult for a writer to throw away something he or she has written. Start a file for sentences, paragraphs, and sections that you have written in the process of producing a paper, but have not used. Read through your manuscript ruthlessly looking for material to put in this file. Try to make your paper short. Although the initial fear of the writer is that there is not enough to say, the concern of the reader is often that it goes on and on. If the paper gets to be over forty pages you probably should have written two papers, or you are on your way to a book. Try to decide roughly how long the paper is going to be and then make a decision about focus and the core, shooting for that limit. Go through your draft looking for words and sentences that can be eliminated without changing the meaning, or through elimination will make meaning clearer.

Try to write in the active rather than passive voice. Say what you want to say once clearly rather than repeating yourself in an effort to redeem yourself for poorly-worded explanations. The dictionary and the thesaurus are important tools. Often the difference between being clear and vague lies in the choice of a word. If you feel that you are not saying what you want, look up the words to see if they can be replaced by something more precise.

Read well-written qualitative research articles and books. This process will enable you to gain a sense of the variety of modes of presentation, as well as provide models of good writing. As we have said, the variety is enormous, ranging from the traditional presentation of research in a more formal mode to more nontraditional examples. Read widely to see how authors present data, how they construct their arguments, how they arrange their sentences, how they organize their format. When we think of contrasting but well-written examples of qualitative research, at the more formal end are titles like *Small Town Teacher* (McPherson, 1972), *The Invisible Children* (Rist, 1978), *Everything in Its Path* (Erikson, 1976). In a somewhat more nontraditional (that is, personal and impressionistic) style are the works of Thomas Cottle, like *Busing, Barred from School, Children in Jail* (Cottle, 1976b, 1976a, 1977), and Robert Coles' series on *Children of Crisis* (see, for example, Coles, 1964, 1977).

Many authors have said that writing helps them to think. That is not, however, the only reason for writing. Most write for a product—a manuscript to share with others. While your first research efforts may be for your professor, there is no reason to stop there. Seek a broader audience. Do not let your status as a novice researcher keep you from thinking about publishing your paper.

PUBLISHING IN JOURNALS

In graduate school, a professor suggested to a student that a paper he had written was publishable. Without seeking any advice, the excited student promptly sent the paper to the first journal that came to mind. There was a wait of approximately five months, and then it finally arrived—an envelope with the journal's address in the upper left corner. Quickly opened, a terse letter informed the young man that the article had been rejected. Enclosed were two short, poorly-typed carbon copies of reactions to the paper.

It took time to recover from this assault on the ego and a longer time to understand who those reactions were from and how naive the student had been in the approach used to seek publication. Since one of the authors of this book was that student, the memories are vivid. Talking to others who have published has led us to believe that this first experience is not unusual. While publishing is something that would-be professionals in academia are encouraged to do, little direct instruction or formal coaching in the more mundane aspects of how to go about it is forthcoming.

This is true for a number of reasons. First, there is the mentality that superior scholarship will naturally find its way into print—that knowing how journals work and how to find a publisher is both unimportant and crassly entrepreneurial. Second, those people who are successful in publishing have short memories. The mechanics of placing a paper become second nature and are therefore not perceived as something to be conscientiously and systematically shared with aspiring students.

Our experience with a manuscript's rejection in one journal and its enthusiastic acceptance by another journal when resubmitted, has led us to appreciate the fact that while the quality of the manuscript is key, one's chances of finding a publisher are greatly enhanced by knowing the ropes. Although you may be reading this book as part of a course, we are sharing this information with you so that you might have a framework within which to approach publishing. Also, we hope you will develop an appreciation for how papers come to be published articles.

To What Journal Do I Send My Article?

In different subfields in education, certain journals are prestigious. When the time comes to think of a journal for possible publication, we think of these journals because we have usually read articles in them for our work. These journals are usually highly competitive, and while they should not be ruled out as places to submit your first work, remember that they are only one possible outlet. Checking journal collections in your library should help expand your awareness of sources of publication.

Sometimes you may write an article with a specific journal in mind. At other times you may complete an article and then search for "the right" journal to publish it. In either case, before you send the article off, you must determine whether what you have written is appropriate for your choice.

A number of issues arise when judging the appropriateness of your article for a particular journal. First, there is style and mode of presentation. Some journals require a standard format (i.e., review of the literature, statement of the problem, methods employed, procedure, presentation of the data, results, and conclusion); others allow considerable variation. Frequently journals requiring standard formats rarely publish qualitative articles, although this is changing. Some journals accept articles written only in a traditional research style (third person, passive voice); while others prefer a more journalistic mode of presentation. Style and format will affect your choice of a potential publication and its acceptance or rejection.

Second, when making your choice you need to ascertain that the journal you are considering publishes articles in the substantive area of your writing. While the editors may accept articles in your general field (e.g., the sociology of education), they may not publish articles on your particular interest (e.g., university teaching). Some journals communicate this directly. The *Journal of Educational Psychology,* for example, announces that it:

> . . . publishes original investigations and theoretical papers dealing with learning and cognition, especially as they relate to problems of instruction, and with the psychological development, relationships, and adjustment of the individual. Preference is given to studies of the more complex types of behavior, especially in or relating to educational settings. Journal articles pertain to all levels of education and to all age groups.

Other journals, particularly those that are more interdisciplinary in nature, like the *Teacher's College Record, Harvard Educational Review,* or the *American Journal of Education* (formerly *School Review*), are less specific because they cover a broad range of issues. In spite of this range, however, you should check to see if the journal or magazine publishes work that is in line with your theoretical and research orientation. Some journals simply do not publish qualitative studies. Others do on occasion; while a few do so exclusively.

The range of issues in educational journals is enormous. Aside from the interdisciplinary ones mentioned, there are journals that are in the "foundations" field, like *Educational Studies,* journals in psychology, school psychology, teacher education, the sociology of education; the list is lengthy. Outside of education, *per se,* are journals concerned with qualitative research, like *Human Organization, Qualitative Sociology,* and *Urban Life,* which frequently publish articles on educational issues. Educational journals like *Phi Delta Kappan,* aimed particularly at practitioners, accept articles in a more popular or journalistic style, and are receptive to the qualitative approach.

Quality is the most difficult aspect of your work to judge. Most authors do have a sense of how their work stacks up to other articles they see. Journals have different standards of quality. Some publish only a small percentage of the articles they receive. Send only those articles that represent your best work to the most competitive journals. The appropriateness of the length of your article is easy to judge. Some journals simply will not publish articles over a certain length, and you waste your time by sending them long theses. Some publish different types of articles in the same issue. These may include substantial articles as well as short research notes or brief statements of opinion. Often the style and format differ for the shorter pieces. Note the different sections of the journal and pick the section for which you are writing when polishing your work. Remember, journals have limited space and the general rule is: The longer the article the less likely it is to get published.

Colleagues are a good source for feedback on your work, particularly people who are critical but supportive. It is important to develop a relationship in which you share your work with others. Of course, the best way to develop this relationship is to provide a similar service for others.

When Do I Know My Article Is Ready for Submission?

Most people simply cannot sit down at the typewriter and construct a coherent, thoughtful, concise article in one draft. An article should be worked and reworked before it is sent to a journal. Let the first draft flow freely. Concentrate on expressing your ideas and getting down the basic content and form. After a first draft is completed, you are often tired and bored by your work; suppress the desire to get it off your mind by sending it off. Let it sit for a few weeks and then return to it, renewed and more detached. Often papers can be reduced in length by as much as one quarter with no loss of content, and with a gain in clarity by carefully editing the drafts. If you want to submit the first draft, give it to a critical but supportive colleague for his or her reaction first. It is through concentrated effort of writing that a person confronts his or her assumptions and examines logical flaws. To write quickly is to shortchange both reader and writer.

Some of the best-known social scientists do as many as ten drafts of an article before they feel it is ready for publication. An accomplished writer does not lament or brood over rewriting; rather it is seen as one stage to a more complete product.

How Do I Send My Manuscript?

When you are ready to have your manuscript typed in the draft you will submit, be sure to check the manuscript's specifications of the journal to which you are going to send it. Many journals will simply refer you to a particular style manual. The American Psychological Association format is a popular one in education and their manual is available at most university bookstores (A.P.A., 1974). Some journals require an abstract of your articles as well. Specific requirements on such things as number of copies, nature of the title page, and so on, vary. Awareness of these details can facilitate the reviewing process.

Include with the copies of the manuscript a short letter saying something like: "Dear Editor (substituting the name of the editor if you know it): Enclosed please find a copy of a manuscript (include the name of the article) that I would appreciate your consideration for publication in (name of the journal). Sincerely, ..." If you think your piece is appropriate for a particular section of the journal, mention that. You might also specifically mention the subject matter, methodology, and theoretical perspective of the article in order to help the editor select a proper reviewer. This is particularly important when sending qualitative articles to journals that do not regularly publish them.

We usually send manuscripts by first-class certified mail. That can be an expensive proposition and we are not sure whether it is necessary. Many journals, upon receiving the manuscript, will send you a postcard. Since time is important to most authors, anything that can be done to avoid the months of delay caused by not knowing whether the manuscript was lost in the mail should be avoided. An alternative to certifying the manuscript is enclosing a self-addressed post card in the envelope.

When Will I Hear from the Journal?

As mentioned, some journals acknowledge your manuscript with a postcard. Often it contains general information about when they will notify you of their decision. It is important to note that the time given usually represents the average time it takes for response. This may provide little help in assessing when they will have completed reviewing your work. You should take the time given on the card as a vague estimate of how long you can expect to wait. You will not hear from some journals until a decision has been made about your article.

Most journals have an initial screening of submitted manuscripts. Someone from the journal staff reads it quickly to see if it contains materials of interest to their readers. This process is usually accomplished within a month of its arrival. If the article does not pass this initial screening, you should receive a letter of rejection relatively quickly. The letters are usually form letters and offer no specific feedback on the decision.

Manuscripts that go through a more complex review generally take between one month and a year to be completed. If you do not hear about your article in four months, it is wise to write or call the editor to inquire about the status of your piece. After four months do not be bashful about pursuing editors. Editors of journals have a responsibility to their readers. If you are keeping an article with the exclusive review rights in one editor's hands, he or she has a responsibility to respond promptly to you.

What Is the Review Process?

In the last section we began discussing the review process. Some of the variations in the time it takes to hear from journals about whether they will publish your article is related to review procedures. Some have editors who are allowed and expected to make unilateral decisions about publishing. In academic publishing this is rare. Most have editorial boards that review the articles. Some meet and make the decisions collectively; others send their recommendations to the editor leaving the final decision to him or her. Many academic and professional journals have strict review procedures that are carefully followed. Typically, such review procedures involve having a standard number of outside readers, most often two or three, respond to the article. They are chosen on the basis of their prominence in the field with the editor attempting to match the article with the experience of the reviewer. These journals, commonly referred to as *refereed journals,* keep the name of the author from the reviewers to maximize the chances that judgments will be made solely on the basis of the merit of the article and not on the basis of personal ties to an author.

Refereed journals often have a standard form that they send to reviewers to fill out. Typically, the forms are multiple choice. Some are asked to rank the article on a scale of one to five in such areas as clarity of presentation, contribution to the field, the degree that the methods employed are appropriate to the problem, and the interest of the article to the readership. In addition, such forms typically ask the reviewer to rank the manuscript by checking a list of such phrases as: (1) definitely publish without revision, (2) definitely publish with minor revisions, (3) rewrite and resubmit, or (4) reject. In addition to completing multiple-choice questions on short-answer forms, referees are also asked to write additional comments on the strengths and weaknesses of the article and how it might be improved. Most often the standardized form that the referees fill in are not returned to the author. They are used exclusively by the editor or the editorial board to reach a decision. The written supplementary comments, on the other hand, are commonly forwarded to the author, especially if the editor thinks that they might be helpful in revisions.

What Kind of Response Should I Expect to Get from My Article?

Our earlier discussion suggests the range of responses that you might get from an editor. First, you can be told that your manuscript has been accepted for publication without revisions. In that case, the acceptance letter may include a tentative date of publication. Because most journals have a backlog of accepted manuscripts, and they are not sure of the content of a specific issue until soon before publication, many letters of acceptance will say something like: ''Your article will be published in the coming year.'' Some letters of acceptance have a form enclosed which you are asked to sign. This form serves as an agreement between you and the journal and gives them exclusive rights to the publication and copyright. Most of these agreements contain a statement giving the author the right to use the article as part of a book he or she may publish in the future. If this is not contained in the letter of agreement you should inquire about it; it is an important right to maintain. The letter of acceptance or the letter of agreement usually states how many copies of the journal or reprints of the article you will receive free of charge when the journal is published. Some journals give nothing, others give a few copies of the journal plus ten or twenty reprints. Some letters of acceptance contain an order form from the publisher for reprints of your article, although this kind of letter may follow closer to publication date. Prices vary considerably and there is no requirement to purchase reprints.

The chance that your response from the editor will be an acceptance with no revisions is highly unlikely. Most positive reviews (that is, acceptance or tentative acceptance pending revisions) require that you do some additional work on the article. The revisions are usually spelled out by the editor in a letter making references to the enclosed reviewers' comments. There are many different types of provisional acceptances.

Some say the article will be definitely published if you make minor style or editorial changes. If the letter says something to that effect, congratulations. This means that the article will not go back to the reviewers; the editor will check the revisions. This kind of a letter of acceptance usually signals publication.

Some requests for revisions are more demanding and the interest in publishing an article is expressed more tentatively. Some suggestions for revisions are so exhaustive that you may feel you have been asked to write a different article. If that is the case, you can expect to have your article go through the review process again and perhaps take as long to get the second response as it did your first. Suggestions for revisions and an indication of interest in publishing can fall anywhere between these two extremes. If you are unsure of what the letter means, write or call the editor for clarification.

If you get a letter that is encouraging and asks you to resubmit, consider this a small victory. Most articles that eventually get published first meet a request for revision. The chances of getting your article accepted are substantially higher when it is rewritten with some guidance from the editor. The most common response that one receives is an out-and-out rejection. Although some of the rejection letters and reviewers' comments can be insulting, it is important that you do not take the rejection as an indication of your inferiority. Most authors get a number of rejections before they get an acceptance. The odds say that you will be rejected. After all, many of the journals have acceptance rates of only 10 percent.

How Do I Increase My Chances of Publication?

The last section closed with a discussion of letters of rejection. It is important not to let the letters of rejection discourage you so that you do not revise and resubmit. The only way to get published is to send your article to journals. Use reviewers' comments in rejection letters to improve your work. Some of the comments will seem quite helpful. If they do, respond to them positively by making actual changes in your article. Some of the criticisms you will receive will not be helpful. They may even reveal that the reviewer was not very knowledgeable about the subject matter. Try not to be defensive. If the criticisms are helpful, rewrite and resubmit; if they are not, look at the article again. If you do not think you can improve it, send it out elsewhere.

Most importantly, do not get discouraged. We have a file thick with letters of rejection. While much of the discussion this far has made the whole selection process sound rational, there are elements of chance to the process. If you happen to have two people review your article that are disposed to your ideas and approach, the likelihood of your getting a favorable response is greatly enhanced. Increase your chances by keeping your work in reviewers' hands.

Do Established Authors Have an Edge on Publishing?

The idea that the "big name in the field" can get anything he or she wants published, anywhere, is false. Occasionally a journal will do a special issue and request particular well-known authors to contribute and thereby modify their referee procedures, but in most journals all authors go through the same procedure in having their work assessed. While the procedures may be the same, however, experienced authors do have advantages. First, if the author is well-known, the editor may do a better job of assigning reviewers to the article. Second, the experienced author has the advantage of writing experience. Your chances of having your work accepted will increase as your writing and your knowledge of publishing in your field increases.

How Long between Having My Article Accepted and Having It Appear in Print?

The time varies widely. You should not expect to see your article in print less than six months from your acceptance notice. Typically, it takes nine to fifteen months to see your manuscript *in vivo*. Reprints may follow immediately after publication or sometimes after a month or so. In some journals the address of the author is given as part of the information that is included in the article. If that is the case, you are likely to receive requests for reprints and letters concerning your work. The number of responses will vary with the nature of the articles and the circulation of the journal.

Should I Send My Article to More than One Journal at a Time?

There is some controversy over this question. One side says no, that you should send your article to one journal and wait for their response. Editors and people who read for journals often take this position. They state that it is unfair for an author to multiple-submit because of the time and effort it takes to review a manuscript. If a given journal is reviewing an article at the same time as another and they both accept it, one has to be turned down, wasting the time and energy of the rejected journal. Authors, on the other hand, often wait months and months to have their articles rejected. This is especially troublesome for articles that are timely.

Some journals have a strict policy on multiple submissions and we would suggest that if you want to submit to such journals you follow their rules. If the journal has no stated policy, it is probably alright to submit to a few journals at a time.

CONCLUDING REMARK

We have presented some general suggestions on how to start your career in publishing. This has only been an introduction—it is neither exhaustive nor detailed. Writers of qualitative research learn more about the process as they go about their own professional work. Possession of a thick skin, an openness to criticism, and self-confidence are good attributes for writers to nurture.

ENDNOTES

1. You can do the kind of analysis that we just discussed from many different types of coding categories. "Kinds of" subcategory coding systems are commonly used, but others, such as "steps in," "ways to," "parts of," "results of," "reasons for," "places where," "uses for," "characteristics of," can be used to work coding categories as well. The subcategories system is a tool that can help you further organize the data because it facilitates thinking through how the sections in the core will look. The middle of your paper, for example, might present the typology and its elements. But do not become obsessed with developing typologies. It's one way to proceed. With a thesis as a focus, your sections might take a different form—a point by point presentation of the aspects of your study that support your thesis.
2. Well-known qualitative researchers in the academic tradition have also suggested that the researcher must talk about his or her role. Rosalie Wax, for example, has said that a writer should tell how she or he has been changed by the research effort (Wax, 1971).

SEVEN

APPLIED QUALITATIVE RESEARCH FOR EDUCATION: EVALUATION, PEDAGOGY, AND ACTION

IT IS HARD TO BELIEVE THAT TEACHING ILLITERATE PEOPLE TO READ and write would cause deportation, but for Paulo Freire, in Brazil during the 1960s, this was the case. Freire felt illiteracy and poverty went hand in hand with self-depreciation. Teaching people to read was to teach them to value their perspective. The process Freire developed to teach literacy heightened consciousness and stimulated an articulate and politicized group where there had been none. The Brazilian dictatorship feared this.

In order to teach reading, Freire and his co-workers had to know their students' understandings of events and actions. Part of the method included group discussion of subjects close to the learners' lives. A teacher would show a group of farmers a picture and they would talk about what it meant to them. The teacher learned what words were central to them and these would become the curriculum for the first lesson. Later, when his program was more developed, Freire knew from his research what themes would emerge, but when he first formulated his method, he needed to continually do research. A particular incident Freire relates reveals the seriousness of this stage of the task. One of Freire's co-workers showed his students a picture of a drunken man stumbling down a city street. The teacher, expecting the picture would provoke a discussion of alcoholism, was surprised by the men's first response: ''The man must have a job,'' they said. ''He must be earning wages if he had money to spend on drink'' (Freire, 1968). The picture did not appear to them as it did to the instructor.

The qualitative perspective in the foregoing example is clear: Freire never assumed he understood how his students thought until he studied them. But he did not study them simply because he was interested in adding to his general store of knowledge; he needed to learn to improve his methods of teaching. This is an example of applied research.

Research is conducted for a variety of purposes and audiences. Scholars have traditionally categorized it into two types: basic and applied. The purpose of basic research is to add to our general knowledge. The audience for this research is the scholarly or scientific communities. As with the Brazilian example, applied research efforts are those which seek findings that can be used directly to make practical decisions about or improvements in programs and practices. Applied research has a variety of audiences (teachers, administrators, officials, parents, students), but what they all have in common is this concern with its immediate practical implications.

The title of this chapter might suggest that we accept the rigid, sometimes antagonistic distinctions commonly made between basic and applied research. This tension between researchers of each type reflect some of the values embodied in the university and scientific communities where basic research carries more prestige and holds higher status because it is seen as more "pure," as less contaminated by the complications of everyday life. Its language is more abstract and less accessible to the average reader.

Both basic and applied research abound in the field of education. Education should ideally be a meld between theory and practice, but in many cases there is hostility where there should be cooperation. Educators face problems when theory and practice are too sharply divided; the contempt many teachers and teacher educators feel toward each other exemplifies this tension. In the university, the education department is often called liberal arts' poor cousin because it is considered an applied rather than a scholarly field. Education professors become defensive. One reaction is for the educational researchers themselves to antagonistically distinguish between applied and basic research, disassociating themselves from their practitioner colleagues.

We prefer to think of these two types of research not as conflicting, but as sometimes complimentary, sometimes intertwined, and not necessarily antagonistic. Some applied research adds to theory, to a pool of knowledge about human beings. Some basic research, like research on learning theory, may be immediately taken by someone and applied to a particular student or class. Sometimes experienced qualitative researchers can serve both applied and basic interests simultaneously; they can assume both stances. The data they collect may be used for both purposes. Of course, this does not mean that the same piece of writing can address both the practitioner and the theorist, but the material written and conceptualized for one purpose can be reworked for the other. In our own case, we have found ourselves returning to practical reports we have written for an evaluation contract, and eyeing them with a more basic-research frame of mind (Bogdan, 1976; Bogdan and Ksander, 1980). Similarly, much of what we have learned through doing basic research has practical applications and we have reformulated that information for those purposes.

When do people undertake applied qualitative research in education? Let us look at some occasions:

A federal agency funds ten school districts around the country to start experimental programs. They hire qualitative researchers to monitor progress and to provide the districts with feedback that might help them modify their activities.

A teacher education training program wants to revamp its curriculum. It employs graduate students to interview and conduct participant observation with people presently in the program to understand how they see the strengths and weaknesses of their education. They will use this data as they develop a new model.

A group of parents worries that a new school redistricting plan will cause the school to be segregated by social class. They go about systematically interviewing other parents, members of the school board, and school principals, as well as pour over official documents and newspaper accounts to make a case for their views.

These examples show the qualitative approach at work. Though the goals are different in each case, in addition to being useful in the here and now, they all focus on change. In the case of the researcher with the experimental programs, the change is a planned, purposeful, initiated innovation. With the teacher-training program, the change is directed at successfully training particular teachers. Change in the case of the activist parents has to do with successfully affecting the political process.

Change is serious because the goal is to improve life for people. Change is complicated because beliefs, life styles and behavior come into conflict. People who try to change education, be it in a particular classroom or for the whole system, seldom understand how people involved in the changes think. Consequently, they are unable to accurately anticipate how the participants will react. Since it is the people in the setting that must live with the change, it is their definitions of the situation that are crucial if change is going to work. These human aspects of the change process are what qualitative research strategies we have discussed in this book study best. Their emphasis on the perspectives that people hold and their concern with process enable the researcher to sort out the complications of change. The qualitative orientation allows for the researcher to simultaneously deal with participants in change, whether in a single classroom or at the many different levels of the educational bureaucracy. The perspective directs us to see behavior in context and does not focus on outcomes to the exclusion of process.

We have organized our discussion in this chapter under three types of applied qualitative research: *evaluation research, pedagogical research,* and *action research.* These distinctions serve our purpose by providing a useful way to organize our discussion, but each category should not be thought of as totally distinct, nor should our discussion be thought of as complete and comprehensive. As we shall see, categories in the real world are seldom as clear and unrelated as they are in books. Three types of applied research we refer to have their own relation to change and are participated in by different people and for different reasons.

In *evaluation research,* the researcher is most often hired by a contractor to describe and assess a particular program of change in order to improve or eliminate it. Evaluation research is the most well-known form of applied research. The product of such research is usually a written report.

In *pedagogical research,* the investigator is often a practitioner (a teacher, an administrator, or educational specialist) or someone close to practice who wants to use the qualitative approach to do what he or she does better. The person wants to be more effective in teaching or in clinical work, and aspects of the qualitative approach are used to reflect on how effective the person is and how he or she might improve. Or the individual uses qualitative research in his or her own teaching; for example, helping students explore their own communities by engaging them in projects where they collect oral histories and descriptions of people doing ordinary things. The recipients of change are the practitioners' immediate clients, students, or supervisees. The persons who engage in this form of research do not necessarily write reports. They translate them immediately into practical changes, they enter them into lesson books, or they reflect on the data to create training programs, workshops, and new curriculum.

In *action research,* persons conducting the research act as citizens attempting to influence the political process through collecting information. The goal is to promote social change that is consistent with the advocate's beliefs. Using the data collected, they develop pamphlets, press conferences, speeches, congressional and legal testimony, TV shows, and exposes to influence change. (See Figure 7-1.)

FIGURE 7-1

APPLIED QUALITATIVE RESEARCH IN EDUCATION

Type	Who Researcher Serves	Purpose	Form of Data Presentation
Evaluation	Contractor	To describe document and/or assess a planned educational change	Written report
Pedagogical	Learner or program	To promote individual change through education	Training program Workshop Curriculum
Action	Social cause	To promote social change in education	Pamphlet, Press conference, Congressional testimony, TV show, Sociodrama, Expose, Report

Some might charge that by including this broad range of activities under the rubric of research, we enlarge our definition so that it loses meaning. We are encompassing more than most researchers would, especially with our inclusion of action and pedagogical research. Clearly these are at variance with traditional research in a number of regards and deserve special consideration. However, our purpose here is not to adorn these activities with the unquestionable title of "research" as much as to speak to the value of pursuing the qualitative perspective in these areas.

Up to this point, our discussion in this book has been based on the assumption that the reader is learning to conduct qualitative research and is undertaking a first study. One's first study is rarely applied. Learning the techniques before the applied is attempted is most effective. We have, therefore, neglected applied and emphasized basic research, but the differences are not all that great. Most of what we have already presented directly applies to or can be modified for applied research. Some particular problems and differences do arise. In this chapter we examine each of the types of applied research, elaborating and discussing these particular concerns.

EVALUATION RESEARCH

Head Start, the nationally funded early childhood education program, was ordered by Congress, in 1972, to increase to at least 10 percent the number of handicapped children served in each program. Head Start program directors around the country received the directive which, among other things, broadly defined what was meant by "handicapped children," and set the fall of 1973 as the date for compliance. The goal of the mandate was to increase the services available to children with disabilities and to promote their inclusion in programs with typical youngsters. The federal agency for the program wrote an RFP (Request for Proposal)[1] to look at the effectiveness of the mandate. They wanted to know if Head Start programs had complied. A company bid on the work and received the contract. They organized the research into two parts which were carried out more or less autonomously. The major thrust of the first part consisted of mailing questionnaires to program directors asking them the number and types of handicapped children they presently had in their programs and how this compared with the composition of the program the year prior to the mandate. On the basis of that data it was reported that the number of handicapped children had doubled since the regulations went into effect and at least 10.1 percent of the children attending Head Start programs now had handicapping conditions.

A second aspect of the research consisted of a series of on-site visits to Head Start programs by teams of observers using a qualitative approach. Using an open-ended design, they went to the projects, observing and talking to parents and staff. The initial observations consisted of data collection around a number of general questions such as, "How was the mandate experienced by Head Start staff and parents?" and "What had changed, if anything, as a result?" The conclusion this group reached was somewhat different. In addition, the reports they submitted to the funding agency also varied considerably. The qualitative teams concluded that the number of handicapped children recruited had not notably increased; rather, there had been a change in how the children were defined. They suggested that the conclusion that Head Start now served 10.1 percent was misleading. The report took the form of a narrative which discussed a number of propositions concerning the mandate's effect. These included an account of the confusion generated by the term "handicap," how staff perceived the mandate in light of their general view of "orders from Washington," programmatic variations in compliance (from "paper compliance" to "active recruitment efforts"), as well as the unanticipated consequences of the mandate (from the labeling of children who previously were not labeled, to a general improvement in individualization in programming for all children).

The funding agency was unhappy with the qualitative report. They wanted to know the facts: "What was the percentage of handicapped youngsters being served by Head Start?" The funders wanted the report to Congress to be clear and unambiguous, and, as the researchers also learned, they wanted the findings to be complimentary to Head Start.

The story of the Head Start experience illustrates a number of aspects of the qualitative approach to evaluation. These characteristics reflect the qualitative approach in general as discussed in Chapter 1. The data that is collected tends to be descriptive, consisting of people's own words and word-pictures of events and activities. The presentation of findings also employs description. The research tends to be conducted in the places where programs are actually carried out. While usually not as extensive as in basic research, the researcher spends time with those he or she is evaluating on their own territory. The analysis and design proceed inductively. Rather than starting from predefined goals or goals extrapolated from official program descriptions, the researcher describes the program as he or she observes it working. There is an emphasis on process—how things happen rather than whether a particular outcome was reached; and there is a concern with meaning—how the various participants in the program see and understand what happened. Here people at all levels and all positions in the program provide data concerning what the program meant to them. Administrators' views of what was supposed to happen or what went wrong are given neither more nor less weight than what the staff think of what happened. The emphasis is on telling what happened from many points of view, and on the unanticipated as well as the hoped-for consequences of the intervention.

The Head Start example also touches on problems of applying the qualitative perspective to evaluation research. We cover these and other issues in this section.

Getting Funds

Evaluation research is big business these days. In 1964, the Civil Rights Act affected education by appropriating funds to improve the quality of education for racial minorities and the poor. The federal government wanted to keep track of these experimental programs so evaluation efforts expanded. These government funded evaluation research efforts were concerned with the impact and effectiveness of new educational practices. Were changes that were instituted successful? Were the goals as defined by program planners reached? By and large, the large-scale use of evaluation research during the sixties was dominated by techniques employing statistical procedures, pretests and posttests, or other quasi-experimental designs.[2] While quantitative evaluation research still dominates for a number of reasons, the education community has increasingly looked to qualitative methods in search of more helpful evaluation tools.

How do you get to do evaluation research?[3] There are three ways. The first is through the RFP route, as with the Head Start study. You write a proposal to an agency that has requested that some evaluation work be done and compete with other applicants for the contract. A second way is to be asked directly by an agency to provide evaluation services for them. Here you work out a mutually agreeable contract. The third way is to submit to an agency a request to evaluate a program for which they are seeking funding; your evaluation would be funded (subcontracted) as part of the larger grant. Falling somewhere in between the RFP mode and the direct request, the agency and the evaluator work together to write the proposal.

One problem for qualitative researchers seeking funding is research design. Some RFP's that come out of Washington give a clear message: Qualitative researchers need not apply. The research questions are written to exclude the qualitative approach from consideration. Those interested in seeking funding have to spot the signs and know that to pursue these funding sources is futile. Some evaluation RFP's do not give a clear message about whether the potential funders seek a particular research method. In that case, researchers often call to query officials. Although some officers follow strict rules about giving information concerning grant competitions, talking to someone in Washington gives a better sense of their thinking process.

While some agencies are clearly antagonistic to qualitative research, some have expressed a real interest and commitment to the qualitative approach to evaluation. It is to these groups that proposals should be submitted. One problem even here, however, is that proposal reviewers for these receptive agencies may not have had the opportunity to be trained in qualitative approaches and therefore do not understand important aspects of qualitative design. How do you educate such reviewers? How do you go about describing your research methodology and research questions in detail when your inductive approach requires that the specifics of how you proceed evolve in the course of the research? We faced this question briefly in the design chapter by suggesting you might conduct a pilot study before you write a proposal so that your design is clear. Obviously this does not work in evaluation. RFP's have to be responded to quickly. Yet reviewers without extensive training tend to be skeptical if a would-be researcher cannot depict in detail a study's progress beforehand, show his or her command of the technology to be employed, indicate clearly what contribution the findings will make, and assert on the basis of what criteria the treatment will be considered effective. Obviously, you cannot satisfy such a reviewer, but you can address this challenge by conducting a broad-based and substantive review of the literature before you write a proposal, using your review to generate a list of fairly specific questions that you will use to begin your research.

You can discuss how you proceed in relation to those questions, but make it clear that the design may change if the questions lack usefulness. In addition, you can discuss the special problems of rapport and other such issues to indicate to reviewers that you are well aware of problems you may encounter. Be more explicit than you might normally be about data analysis and other such procedures so that the proposal reviewer unfamiliar with the approach can gain a concrete sense of what is entailed. Remember that writing a research proposal to conduct a qualitative study and doing qualitative evaluation call for two separate approaches. The proposal represents a hypothesis on how to proceed in order to give the reviewer an idea of what you will accomplish. It is not a rigid blueprint of how you will conduct the research. When you enter the site, you may want to act as if you know little about schools so that your mind is fresh, but when you write a proposal, you want the reviewer to see you as a competent, knowledgeable person who will make a contribution to improving educational practices.

Thus far we have discussed formal responses to RFP's. In cases where agencies solicit your help, working out a contract in a way where there is mutual understanding concerning what is to be accomplished and how you will proceed is the more likely procedure. In addition, you usually have an opportunity to meet with potential contractors, hear their ideas, and educate them about the qualitative approach.

Relations between the Contractor and the Researcher

What puts evaluation researchers in a different position than most other investigators is that their services are contracted for payment. They are guided not only by the cannons of research, but by the contractor's expectations as well. While not inevitable, and certainly avoidable through careful negotiation and explicit understanding, the researcher's standards concerning rigorous and well-conceived research can conflict with the contractor's expectations. "Hired hands" have an obligation to the contractor that they must balance with the responsibilities of a researcher. Below we sketch some of the areas of disagreement contractors and qualitative researchers often face, and we offer some suggestions on how to avoid or handle them.

1. *Ownership of the data.* If not agreed upon specifically before the study begins, who owns and has access to the fieldnotes and other qualitative data can become a source of disagreement. It is understandable that the agency who has paid you should consider these materials theirs, but research ethics suggest an opposing position. Subjects should be protected from the scrutiny of people who may make decisions about their future, and what transpires between the researcher and subjects is confidential. Contractors may at times want not the data itself, but rather information from you concerning the functioning of particular programs or specific individuals. Whether you give such information, of course, depends on the agreement you have with subjects. But, in order to collect rich data, subjects should feel that what they say to you will not be attributed to them in reports or in your conversations with others. For them to think that what you say will go directly to people in authority will skew what they say.

Qualitative research is rich in subjects' own words. Colloquial expressions, swear words, critical remarks, and even cursing indictments abound in the pages. The nature of the notes may make them particularly blasphemous; consequently, if read out of context, or even in context, grounds exist for strong administrative action against those who uttered them. It should be made clear from the start, to contractor and to subjects alike, that you are a hired hand, but you are not a spy. To act as a spy would violate goals and ethics of research.

2. *Making program goals an object of study.* The cannons of good qualitative research design suggest that research should not be conducted to answer specific questions like, ''Is the program successful or not?'' The contractor who insists that you answer the question ''Is the program working well?'' has to be satisfied with the answer, ''That depends on how you look at it.'' Some contractors feel violated when the goals of the program are questioned. After all, they feel that as the administrators, they establish the goals. They want you to make judgments about their goals because that is why they pay you.

There are several ways to avoid this conflict. First, the best cure is prevention. Make it as clear as possible at the outset of your research that the focus of your work is description or documentation rather than judgments of success and failure. In other words, try to reiterate in your agreement that your goal is not to provide information on whether the program is good or bad (Everhart, 1975). This position will not preclude evaluation of a program's impact, as the following example shows.

One of the authors participated in a study to describe an educational program that took the most violent inmates out of a state institution for the retarded and placed them in a small group home. Was this program successful? From the beginning, discussions with the contractor emphasized that the evaluators would not approach the study with a predetermined definition of what a ''successful'' program would look like. They would not evaluate the program to see if it measured up to some standard. Rather, they started from the position that as outsiders they would not recognize ''success'' if it hit them in the face. As the qualitative evaluators studied this group home for formerly institutionalized people, they realized that participants at different program levels and with different relationships to the men might define success differently. When the researchers walked into a room in the home and saw furniture and lamps in place, they did not see these as cues of success. When they went into a bedroom and saw clothes in dresser drawers, they did not understand that those were also symbols of success. But to the director of the adolescent unit where one of the men, Johnny, had spent so many violent years, these simple facts were clear clues. An interview elicited these observations:

When he was here he spent a lot of time in the disturbed day hall. There were no pictures, few tables, and only indestructible furniture there. At the group home there are pictures and lamps which don't look torn and mutilated, stuffed furniture in which I saw only one bite mark, which I'm sure Johnny made, but which was the only one. We used to be able to tell how bad a time Johnny was having by the scars on the staff, and I didn't see any on the staff there.

When I went to the group home recently, to do the evaluation, I snooped around in the room and Johnny had a drawer full of clothes and that tells me he is not having toileting incidents or ripping his clothes as often. When he was here he never had any clothes in his drawers.

"We often do not understand that we do not understand" what we have seen or what has been told to us (Becker and Geer, 1957). Most apparent accomplishments could easily be overlooked by outside evaluators unaccustomed to the cues of success or who operate only under the definitions provided by the contractor.

3. *The hierarchy of credibility.*   The qualitative researcher, taking all sources of data as important, often shakes up the hierarchy of credibility in an organization. This can be a source of contention between the contractor and the researcher. Sometimes reports juxtapose, say, a high school principal's view of a school with the students' views. Students' perspectives appear as credible as the principal, and often sound as logical. Authority and organizational structure symbolize to some that the words of people at the top are more informative and accurate than those at the bottom, even when those at the top are telling us about those at the bottom. To present the views of the "other side" in a credible way can make authority figures defensive and angry at the messenger with the conflicting news. Qualitative researchers can present views of those holding different hierarchical positions tactfully. Researchers who want their work to be seriously considered, therefore, must monitor how they present their findings, avoiding inflammatory language on the one hand, but not doing a public relations report either.

4. *"All you do is criticize."*   The qualitative approach to evaluation critically examines organizational practices, but that does not mean that it has to be overly negative in its tone. Many times organizations are not doing what they say they are doing, or what their goals indicate they should be doing. What they actually do, however, may be both substantive and laudable. Contractors often get upset with reports that only emphasize what is wrong, with no attempt to present accomplishments. All people perform better with positive reinforcements. You do not have to lie to be helpful, but an optimistic and positive tone is not a compromise.

5. *Contractor-enforced limits.*   Qualitative researchers are dedicated to seeing subjects in context. When they study a program, they want to see how it relates to the larger organization of which it is a part. At times contractors put limits on what can be studied. The limits can sometimes exclude the higher echelons of an organization from scrutiny. When evaluation tasks are narrowly defined to include only the internal operations of a program, the evaluation report can present a distorted view. It may blame the victims of upper-level organizational bumbling. Contractors may become upset when the investigator strays too far from the specific program, but this avenue of investigation may be important. Negotiating broad access to programs when the research undertaking is still under discussion, can protect the researcher from this source of conflict.

6. *Who owns and gets the report?*   Evaluation can be a double-edged sword for contractors. Often they do not want the unintended consequences or actual workings

of an organization to be publicly revealed. Sometimes they want to conceal certain knowledge even from organizational members. Who should get the final report? Does someone own it? This can be a particularly touchy issue. Again, establishing an agreement with the sponsor may forestall later problems. We would advise you, however, not to sell off too many of your rights (to publish, reproduce, and the like).

The reports that evaluation researchers write have political implications and can affect funding, people's livelihoods, and the services they receive. It takes good judgment and a great deal of tact and integrity to conduct such research without making enemies. As veteran researcher J. W. Evans (1970) writes: "It should be clear that the lot of the evaluator is destined to be a harassed and controversial one and those who contemplate a career in this field should be aware of this."

It is important for an evaluation researcher to be aware of potential problems, and to attempt to avoid some of them by careful prestudy planning and discussion. But researchers have a number of needs that make them vulnerable to pressure from contractors and other special interest groups that may lead them awry in their work. The first of these needs is money. Therefore, a good safeguard for keeping your integrity intact is to avoid contract evaluation research if you are (or will become) dependent on the research revenues for a livelihood. To put it another way, you can only afford to do evaluation research if you can afford not to do it.

The Evaluation Site

We have discussed how researchers should handle themselves at the research site in our chapter on fieldwork relations. Our discussion of demeanor, developing rapport, interviewing skills, and such are relevant here. Because the setting is an evaluation site, however, other issues arise.

When you are being paid to evaluate a program, you must evaluate a specific one, and give feedback about the particular program to the agency that hired you. People feel uncomfortable being evaluated. They rightfully feel that there is something at stake. Some subjects may feel more confident about what they do and so participate and share information with you more willingly. Other subjects might feel more threatened in an evaluation and give much more circumspect responses. Informants may fear that you will give them a bad report and that they will loose funding or their jobs.

What are some of the things you can do to reduce discomfort? First, you can communicate clearly to those with whom you spend time that you are there to learn from them—how they feel about what they do, and what they see as strengths and weaknesses. If you are at a particular school to study how their "back-to-basics" program is working, for instance, it is important to know what teachers think about back-to-basics. You must communicate this to the subjects. You are not at the site to decide whether back-to-basics is "good"; you are there to gather subjects' views.

In an evaluation one of the authors did on an audiovisual technology program in the schools, the researcher did not present himself as interested in learning whether different teachers use film strips or movies well or "in the right way." He explained that the team was interested in discovering how the machinery was used, for what reasons, and how these "aids" were perceived. There is a difference between conducting a study *within* the assumptions of the program ideology and taking that ideology *as part of* the subject matter for inquiry. Subjects should know the difference and appreciate that you are not taking a stand.

What may put some people at ease is making it clear that you are not ruled by "the hierarchy of credibility" (Becker, 1970a) in that organization. You take people seriously; you will listen to students as well as teachers, teachers as well as principals, and principals as well as the superintendent. Your demeanor should suggest that you value the perspectives of all.

It is also important to subjects that you are not a spy. They want to know their particular names will not be identified, and that people's identities will in other ways be camouflaged. Problematically in evaluation research, you are at a particular site and your contractor may know which site you are at; thus, your subjects lack a real cover. Camouflaging individual participants is made much more difficult and people will feel less comfortable. There is no way to minimize the difficulty of this situation. Fieldworkers often feel intrusive and vulnerable. You can tell subjects what you will and will not reveal about them, but you may not be able to assure them that they will not be affected by the report you submit. If, for example, you are at a school to look at a particular reading program and you see two teachers behaving inappropriately with a child on the playground, you may not have to give this information to the contractor or to the principal; teachers will feel more comfortable knowing this, but you do have to provide information about the reading program and that will reflect on the school personnel involved. It is most helpful to be clear ahead of time about your role both to the contractor and to those at the site. But there is no way to eliminate subjects' feelings of vulnerability. Worried that their jobs depend on the information they share, they consequently give you guarded information.

Not all evaluation projects need involve such threatening situations. People in agencies hire evaluators not only to assess but to describe and document what is going on. An agency may want just a record of how a particular instance of change is initiated, developed, and resolved. Evaluation of this sort may cause less stress. We contrast two evaluation examples we have already discussed. The Head Start evaluation was tense because many programs worried that their funding would be cut off and the staff would be out of work if they did not meet the mandate's regulations on handicapped children. In the evaluations of technology in the classroom, however, the teachers understood that the evaluators were there to understand how technology and equipment was understood and used. They did not worry that they would be fired for not using the equipment properly.

Feedback

When the qualitative research team studied the teachers using audiovisual equipment, they handed their first report to the teachers at the same time they gave it to the administrators. When the teachers saw that the fieldworkers' intent was to understand their perspective on technology, they became anxious to unrestrainedly share their views. In this situation, the evaluators gave feedback to those at the site during the course of the program. This form of evaluation is called, in evaluation lingo, *formative*. It means that the purpose of the evaluation is to improve an ongoing program through continuous reporting of the evaluators' findings. Information is shared with participants quickly, more informally, and in a spirit of congeniality. The evaluators may meet with subjects on a regular basis, present findings, and discuss the implications for change.

A second kind of evaluation is called *summative*. It has traditionally been the most common type. Here an evaluation is completed and then a final report is issued to the contractor. These reports are used to make decisions concerning reorganization of the program and the allocation of resources. In this sort of evaluation, feedback is rarely provided as the research proceeds. Because it is a more formal kind of evaluation with long-term implications, there are more opportunities for tensions to arise between an evaluator and project participants. For the qualitative evaluator, feedback is an essential methodological concern. Since one purpose of the research is to construct the multiple realities participants experience, the researcher needs to find ways to check out with informants whether or not these constructions reflect the world as they see it. The qualitative approach demands one rely on feedback as a research strategy. The implication is that qualitative researchers may feel more comfortable when engaged in formative evaluation.

Working in Teams

Large-scale evaluation research is often conducted in teams. For the qualitative researcher accustomed to the "lone ranger" approach, this may involve some adaptations, so we turn to look at both the advantages and disadvantages of team research for fieldworkers.

One of the advantages of team work is that it enables a group of fieldworkers to undertake multi-site evaluations simultaneously. Another advantage is that people bring different skills and perspectives to research (Cassell, 1978a). Some researchers may be especially good at establishing rapport, others may write spectacularly, others may be especially persistent in investigating troubling phenomenon, while still others may excel in writing the detailed fieldnotes. While these are skills that all fieldworkers emulate, some of us are better than others at forming relationships, and others are great technicians. Team work allows us to maximize our benefits.

There are disadvantages to overcome as well. A team, like any collection of people, can have problems. People can act irresponsibly, conflicts can develop between different personalities, group leadership can be weak, communication can be unclear. Additionally, as in team sports, if individual team members act too individualistically, the individual players do not cohere. One must work to achieve a balance that helps a team work together but allows each individual enough room to be creative. Foresightedness and good communication from the beginning can help overcome some of these difficulties.

While all groups are different, and while others have developed strategies for handling group situations, we suggest the following guidelines:

1. It ought to be clear from the project's inception what an individual field-worker's responsibilities are. For how many sites will individuals be responsible? Is there secretarial help for reproducing fieldnotes, or is each member responsible for having his or her own typing done? Since it takes much longer to type or write notes than to speak them onto tape, this question is important. Once you know this, you can plan time accordingly.
2. It is very helpful to know the timetable of the project and to be able to roughly lay out a plan of how the final report will be finished. While deadlines may be tough to meet, they lay the groundwork and give people an opportunity to meet project deadlines and individual needs.
3. It is helpful to establish what individual responsibilities are for writing the final report. Will the project leaders be responsible for the actual writing? Will different fieldworkers be responsible for drafting chapters? What role will you play? This knowledge will affect your participation, for example, in meetings called to discuss data analysis and presentation.
4. In spite of busy schedules, regularly scheduled team meetings can help to build group spirit. If a group leader spots discord, the opportunity to resolve it will occur more frequently if there are specific times when teams meet.
5. If at all possible, it is worth hiring someone to research the researchers. This person has responsibility for taking fieldnotes and for being a participant observer of team meetings. The group's oral historian can be invaluable for insights into such concerns as observer bias, group conflict, and the intellectual bent of the group. It is important, if your team undertakes to have such a member, that this role not be construed as the spy for the team leader. Qualitative research groups usually have hierarchies, too, and the researcher should be equally available to all.

Traditionally, as we have said in earlier chapters, fieldworkers went out by themselves into the world to see what they could see. Since some fieldworkers see themselves as artists, they have difficulty reconciling themselves to a group process. The more conscious team members are of these issues, the less likely trouble will arise, and the more likely individual creativity will emerge.

The Audience

Evaluation research, as we have said, is applied because it is used to provide information to practitioners or policy-makers so that they may educate better. As such, the primary audience for the evaluation research report is the group that hires the researcher, whether that be a school, an individual educational program, a federal agency, or a job-training center. Because the written report is supposed to encourage or lead to some kind of action, rather than simply provide more reading, the report must be written in a way that encourages this. It should be short, rather than ponderous, and simply-worded rather than jargon-filled. Though qualitative researchers should have little trouble with most of these suggestions, the nature of qualitative data may mean that brevity does not come easily for those who do not depend on statistical renderings, tables, charts, and lists. Qualitative reports are, of necessity, filled with examples and descriptions. This does, however, tend to lengthen them.

While we discussed how to write a qualitative research report in the preceding chapter, we pass along a suggestion here that facilitates discussion and action by practitioners. The research should include at the beginning of the evaluation report a summary of findings (see Patton, 1980). While you may feel you have discharged your duties by writing your final report and meeting with the person who contracted you, if you are interested in disseminating your research, you may want to write and rewrite your findings to put them in a form for publication. As we said earlier, you can reanalyze data gathered for applied research projects for articles that may appear in professional journals. In order to do this you need to be clear that you have publishing rights for the data. It may seem trivial to mention, but some federal agencies can refuse to allow fieldworkers the right to publish their work or to present findings at conferences. Be sure you are not caught in such a situation.

Timetables

"Ethnography is like fine wine—it needs aging and careful preparation" said Steve Arzivu, an educational anthropologist from California. This perspective has been a dominant one in qualitative fieldwork in education, particularly among people who have used participant observation. Some qualitative researchers have suggested along these lines that one should plan twice as much time to write a report as it took to gather the data (Wolcott, 1975). The qualitative researcher who sees himself or herself as an artist rather than as a technician, needs time to contemplate and muse. But the evaluation researcher is supposed to provide information quickly—findings that are of immediate value.

It is our experience that qualitative research need not always take that long. We have completed evaluation studies from start to finish in less than four months. While our final report was not a publishable monograph of enduring quality, it was well-received and helpful to those who hired us. Research styles in the applied qualitative mode are flexible. It is important to set realistic timetables for your goals, but your goals may be less modest than fine wine. While it is important to be explicit in your research report about the amount of time spent at the site, it is not necessary to make every study a major life-long undertaking. While some have condemned "blitzkrieg ethnography," the practice of rushing through qualitative research (Rist, 1980), at certain times, findings that are reported cautiously and honestly may be useful.

The Future of Qualitative Evaluation

We see the direction for qualitative approaches to educational evaluation as up, but hilly. Some people are still not quite sure whether the qualitative approach fits into "the research paradigm." To school administrators and educational policy-makers, accustomed to wading through statistical research reports, ethnography done in their school does not seem like research:

> Most educational administrators still regard anthropological studies of schools as in-sightful, empathetic descriptions, which they do not trust because they are so under-standable and inevitably they send them on to the social studies teacher for classroom use (Ianni, 1978).

The everyday language of qualitative researchers that actually makes the reports accessible to practitioners sometimes works against them.

Sometimes the individual researcher, feeling alone in the field among subjects who have never heard of the qualitative research approach, may also question its value. A colleague of ours discussed his experiences evaluating one of the early Experimental Schools projects in a southern state. He remembers clearly, several years later, how complex doing an evaluation was, how unlike a laboratory the setting was, and how wearing the continual ambiguity was. To top it off, he had to continually face being labeled a "Yankee." As he discussed the problems of the qualitative approach to the evaluation process, however, his eyes lit up. He told us how the entire direction of the research changed because of the descriptions he elicited. The school district had drastically changed their schooling process, and there seemed to be little change in what had been traditionally one of the pivotal areas for measuring this change—"student outcomes." Researchers generally evaluate student outcomes in terms of the cognitive domain, on the basis of a rise in scores on achievement tests, or improved reading scores, and other test measures. In this district, the reading scores had improved slightly, but nothing dramatic had occurred. "What is happening here?" The question threw itself at the evaluator. And so he began to look toward other sources of information. One teacher said, "Well the test scores may not be rising, but we have noticed so much more going on in class in the affective domain." Black parents said, "Their scores may not be rising fast but our children are no longer on the streets during the school day." Another teacher said, "And the students are taking responsibility for their own learning in ways they did not before. They act in ways that tell us they feel good about themselves."[4]

In this example of evaluating change, the evaluators turned from examining student test scores to talking with teachers, parents, and students about their experiences. Their perspective enlarged.

Other strengths of qualitative approaches to evaluation research have also emerged. Field methods represent an effective approach to researching educational crises because those involved are often so caught up in the immediate situation they cannot step back and sort out differences in how problems are perceived by others.

When values come into conflict, conflicts in perspective always arise. Planning for some situations, for example, should a school be integrated, mainstreamed, or tracked, we are clear that values will conflict. Hence, qualitative researchers are called to the scene because it is expected that they will be able to use their tools to effectively study the conflagrations that might arise. But there are other problems, like financing, staffing, management, and service delivery questions, that do not appear on the surface to be value questions but which are the result of unrecognized and unresolved conflicts (Ianni, 1978). These, too, bear study by the qualitative approach. The field widens.

PEDAGOGICAL USES OF QUALITATIVE RESEARCH

The use of qualitative research in evaluation does not stray too far from traditional definitions of research, but in this section we travel away from the mainstream. What we discuss here is seldom thought about as *research,* and might be better referred to by a different word. While we admit that this is true, we also find an advantage in using it. What we will be discussing is the application of the qualitative approach, the qualitative way of thinking and of collecting data, to the day-to-day lives of teachers and other educational practitioners. We will be talking about how practitioners can use the approach themselves. What use can they make of it as they go about being educators? As we have discussed, "research" emphasizes the rigorous and systematic collection and analysis of data. By using the word *research* in this chapter, we may be stretching the use of the concept, but it does point to our belief in the need for practitioners to be more disciplined and thorough in gathering information in their own settings. Further, it is our belief that all educators can be more effective by employing qualitative research in their work.

As our discussion of the theoretical roots of qualitative research emphasizes, teachers view what is going on in the classroom from a very different perspective than their students. Likewise, the principal sees the school differently than the teacher (or the parents, the custodian, the school nurse, or social worker). Not only do people in different positions in an organization tend to have different views, but there is great diversity among those occupying similar positions. All teachers do not view students similarly; the teacher's particular experiences, background, and out-of-school life flavors his or her particular view. As we go about living our lives, we make assumptions about how other people think (or assume they do not think), and we do this on the basis of scanty or no evidence. Often cliches substitute for real understanding. Thus we hear that certain students are not doing well at the university because "they are lazy," or "they didn't come from a good high school," or "they think they know it already," or "they are used to having it handed to them on a silver platter." Unpopular principals are seen as "too afraid to act," or "more interested in getting promoted than supporting us," or "being over the hill."

When practitioners employ the qualitative approach, they systematically try to understand the different people in their schools as they see themselves. The approach requires that educators be more rigorous and observant in collecting information in order to recognize their own points of view, and to break through the stereotypical images that may govern their behavior toward others. In addition, the perspective calls for noticing patterns of behavior and features of the physical environment so as to be more analytical about regularities that may unknowingly govern their lives.

The belief that practitioners can improve their effectiveness by employing the qualitative perspective is rooted in the way the qualitative approach views change. When approached with an innovation to try in their classes, some teachers say, "It won't work. It doesn't fit the real world." We do not dispute that many innovations do not make sense, and that the teachers are often right. But many practitioners take the "real world" as an unalterable given, as existing out there almost beyond their influence. Many see their situations as nonnegotiable. In this framework, people do not feel they actively participate in shaping and creating meaning. The theoretical perspective that underlies qualitative research takes a different view. Reality is constructed by people as they go about living their daily lives. People can be active in shaping and changing the "real world." They can change, and they can affect others. Teachers and their students define the real world together as they interact each day in their classrooms. While what is possible is negotiated within the limitations of such things as the school hierarchy, availability of resources, and common-sense cultural understandings, how teachers and students come to define each other and what educational environments are like becomes transactional (Sarason and Doris, 1979). Our belief in the usefulness of the qualitative perspective to practitioners is related to seeing all people as having the potential to change themselves and their immediate environment, as well as becoming change agents in organizations where they work. Qualitative research skills can play a part in helping people to live in a world more compatible with their hopes by providing tangible information on what it is like now.

The qualitative approach can be incorporated into educational practice in several ways. First, it can be used by individuals (teachers, instructional specialists, counselors) who have direct contact with clients (in schools the clients are students) in order to be more effective. Second, when the qualitative approach becomes part of prospective teachers' educational training, it facilitates becoming a more astute observer of the total school environment and helps make the process of learning to become a teacher a more conscious effort. Third, qualitative research can be incorporated into the school curriculum so that students go out and actually do interviewing and participant observation studies.

Employing Qualitative Research to Improve Your Effectiveness as a Teacher

How can practitioners incorporate qualitative perspectives in their daily activities? How can they add research to their agenda? Of course, practitioners are busy people; they cannot be expected to keep detailed notes of everything they see or hear, nor do

they have the luxury of pursuing leads and having access to the wide variety of participants that a researcher might have. But teachers can act like researchers as part of
their role. While they never keep detailed fieldnotes, they could be more systematic
in writing down their experiences. Writing notes in a specific notebook helps in collecting materials together. While they cannot interview people like a researcher does,
they can turn the conversations they might normally have into more productive infor-
mation-gathering sessions. Incorporating the qualitative perspective means nothing
more than being self-conscious, actively thinking and acting in ways that a qualitative
researcher does. What are some of the things that you might do differently if you assume this stance?

Incorporating this perspective would mean that you would begin taking yourself
less for granted, and more as an object of study. You become more reflective. Watch
yourself as you go about being an educator. Where do you walk? Where do you
stand? How is your room arranged? With whom do you spend most of your time?
How is your day structured? Who do you avoid? What is your perspective on your
work? What parts of the day do you dread? To what parts of the day do you look for-
ward? How does what you do match what you thought you would be doing or what
you would like to do? What obstacles do you define as standing between what exists
and what you would like to be? Are there particular people with whom you feel particularly ineffective? What do you think about them? What do you think they are
thinking?

What benefits are there for teachers who use the qualitative approach in this clinical manner? Because teachers acting as researchers not only perform their duties but
also watch themselves, they step back and, distanced from immediate conflicts, they
are able to gain a larger view of what is happening. A teacher participated in a study
where she was asked to be a participant observer of one child in her classroom. The
child she picked to observe was one that she "usually had difficulty with." She
observed the child closely and kept a journal on what she heard and saw. By the end
of the project, their relationship had "improved enormously." She came to "like"
the boy, realizing to her surprise that earlier she did not. This feeling, she recounted,
developed because she began to understand what the world looked like to her student and how he made sense out of what he saw. She came to see where their ways of
thinking converged and where they conflicted.

This example reflects one particular problem a teacher chose to confront, but it
represents a good model for using the qualitative approach to improve teaching effectiveness:

Step 1.   Pick a problem on which to focus: a troubled relationship with a student, a particular habit of yours you want to change, or a specific style you want
to nurture.

Step 2.   Keep as detailed notes as you can on the issue, recording observations
and dialogue whenever possible. Attempt to emphasize interactions that happen
around this issue. Record what the student does and says with you and others.

Write down when you exhibit the behavior you want to change and with whom you exhibit it. What are students' reactions to it? Detail class occurrences when the style you want to nurture is in play. Do you notice any students reinforcing this behavior?

Step 3.   When you finish your long-term accounting of events, look through your data for any patterns that emerge. Ask questions about what stands out. Why did I react that way when the student requested information? What was going on in the class when I exhibited that behavior? And so on.

Step 4.   Use the data to make decisions if necessary. Sometimes the research process itself may improve the situation (as in the case of the teacher whose developing respect for her student eased her relationship with him). At other times, however, you may need to use your knowledge to plan. Perhaps you should share, privately, some of what you have discovered about your relationship with a student with that individual. Perhaps you can hold a class meeting with students, or talk with other teachers, or ask a consultant for specific advice. The decision-making is specific to individual circumstances.

The Qualitative Approach and Teacher Education

The qualitative approach requires researchers to develop empathy with people under study and to make concerted efforts to understand various points of view. Judgment is not the goal; rather, the goal is to understand the subjects' world and to determine how and with what criteria *they* judge it. This approach is useful in teacher training programs because it offers prospective teachers the opportunity to explore the complex environment of schools and at the same time become more self-conscious about their own values and how these values influence their attitudes toward students, principals, and others.

We have found that future teachers with whom we worked often were unaware of the values and beliefs they brought to the classroom. Though values influence everyone's work, and can strengthen teaching and interactive abilities, awareness of what these values are helps us see how they help shape our attitudes toward students (and other educators). People become more aware of how they participate in creating what happens to them. As part of a preservice training experience of would-be primary and secondary school teachers, one of the authors used the qualitative research approach extensively.

As part of the training, the students spent time each week in a school. The qualitative approach was employed to help them sort out conflicting perspectives about schooling and to stimulate them to question their own unquestioned assumptions about what schools are like. We trained them in some strategies of participant observation and, as part of their fieldwork, required them to conduct small-scale research in the classroom or school where they were located. We organized their "fieldnotes" by providing a list of general "research" questions. They wrote on one question as a focus for each set of notes. This list of "Observer's Questions" included questions like:

How has the teacher organized the class?

What does the teacher you are observing mean by the term "discipline" and how does he or she act upon this meaning?

How would you characterize the atmosphere in your classroom?

How do teachers in your school feel about their jobs?

What kinds of students are most highly valued in the class you observe?

How are educational problems analyzed by the staff? (These problems may be reading problems, or discipline problems, or the like.) How is blame affixed? Where are solutions sought?

These questions were designed around the particular course content. You can design questions around other foci. The goals of these Observer's Questions were: (1) to increase students' abilities to describe before they evaluated, (2) to create a higher level of self-consciousness about their own values and perspectives, and (3) to encourage them to see more clearly the perspectives of those in different roles in the school.

We found that emphasizing the concept of "perspectives" as a means of looking at school life enabled the students to question the set of assumptions they brought to the teacher's role. Some of these potential educators, for example, assumed that students were difficult for teachers because they came from poor or low-income families or that "cultural" problems caused pupils to become deviants in the classroom. Observations can help university students to distance themselves from the behavior that occurs in the school or classroom.

The qualitative perspective demands that the person whose perspective the student seeks to understand speak in his or her own behalf. It means that students must listen to their words unfiltered through popular educational theories like "cultural deprivation" or mental health metaphors like "hyperactive." Systematic fieldwork enables students to begin to see how power is distributed, the kinds of pressures teachers face, the level of support an administrator provides, or the way students make sense out of school life. We underscore that the purpose here is to help students stand back from their own taken-for-granted notions of school life in order first to examine them, and second to see school through others' eyes.

As the following two examples indicate, the use of the qualitative approach enabled student teachers to broaden their conception about educational "truths." A student observing at an early childhood education center felt at the beginning of the semester that the children were not disciplined. One day she saw Betsy snatch a doll away from another little girl who was playing with it. The little girl who lost her doll started to cry. When the teacher approached the two girls and asked Betsy why she had taken the doll, Betsy replied, "Because I wanted it," and ran away. When the observer tried to stop Betsy in order to get the doll and return it to the child, she was told by the teacher, "Let her go. I'll get another doll for JoAnn." Upset at what she perceived as a lack of discipline, she decided to interview the teacher later about these actions. The teacher explained to the observer that she felt it was not always appropriate to have an adult step in to defend a child's right to some object. By doing this, the teacher explained, she felt the child might become dependent on the teacher to protect his or her rights. "It is very important, I feel, that the child learns that she, rather than the teacher, must defend her own rights. She must learn this or learn to always come up with the short end of the stick. What we need to do is to teach her the skills to defend her territory, so to speak, if the situation calls for it." The observer came to understand the teacher's perspective. Where first she had seen only chaos, she later began to discern method. She may not have heartily approved of this method, but she revised her view of what was occurring. Her perception of reality, in other words, changed.

Understanding a teacher's perspective is only one goal, however; sometimes students learned that relying on their own descriptions clarified for them what the acceptance of the teacher's point of view at face-value could not. In this example, an observer accepted the teacher's comment that the children in her class were "very easily distracted due to their short attention spans." The student's notes at first appeared to lend credence to this evaluation: "I observed the following during lesson time. One of the Indian children wasn't even paying attention to what the teacher was saying. All she did was to look out the window or fidget with her braids." Later in her notes, however, the student commented on another aspect of classroom life: "Some children in the class can't speak any English. They can't comprehend what the teacher says. The Indian girl is an example of this. She just came to the United States a short while ago and does not yet speak any English." The student then documented how her perspective on what was happening in this classroom changed.

We have been describing a way that the qualitative perspective can be employed in teacher education programs. The qualitative method helps educators become more sensitive to factors that affect their own work and their interactions with others. Used pedagogically, the qualitative approach can be incorporated in inservice education, as well as in workshops and informal training sessions. An educational anthropologist, for example, was funded to train Chicano teachers to be ethnographers. The goal of the project was to heighten the teachers' awareness about how cultural factors influence their own and their students' behavior. In order to accomplish these goals, the teachers were placed in field situations very unlike their own. They had to gain entry, establish trust, and go through all the stages a fieldworker usually encounters in their attempt to understand this different "culture." The program stimulated soul-searching and also helped them learn to analyze the agencies and structures that they and their students had to continually confront.[5]

Qualitative Methods in the School Curriculum

When qualitative methods are used as part of the school curriculum, we call this the "Foxfire" approach. *Foxfire,* a magazine started by a teacher and his high school English class in Georgia in the mid-1960s (see Wigginton, 1972a), became the model for many such magazines around the United States. What all these efforts have in common is that students collect folklore in their communities by going outside school, interviewing people about what they do or know, observing them while they are talking and / or working at a chore or craft, and perhaps photographing them as well. Students collect firsthand information from and about people who know the habits, folktales, and crafts of a region. These are usually old people, and so students get to know and become friends with older people in their areas. The students:

> . . . are preserving stories, recording skills and explaining ways of doing things known to the older people in their community, the people whose roots run deeper and whose memories reach back farther than everybody else's (Wood, 1975).

The knowledge about stories, skills, and ways of doing things that the students gather are particular to different regions of the country. The original *Foxfire* magazine, for instance, included reports on making a basket out of white oak splits, moonshining, quilt-making, hog slaughtering, and Aunt Arie's life history (Wigginton, 1972a). But students in Kennebunkport, Maine, learned about fishing and farming the Maine Coast, and students in Washington, D.C., learned about the "black heartland" of their city (Wood, 1975).

In order to accomplish what has been called *cultural journalism,* students need to learn the skills of fieldwork as well as skills to put the information in a magazine. Fieldwork skills include learning how to observe, how to interview, how to use a camera and a tape recorder, how to take notes, and how to gather life-histories (what cultural journalists call "personality stories"); in short, the tools of the qualitative researcher. Putting together the magazine containing these interviews, stories, descriptions, and photographs involves teamwork, writing skills, photographic developing, layout, and countless efforts at decision-making. (For an excellent guide to undertaking cultural journalism in schools, see Wood, 1975.) Again, these are skills qualitative researchers employ when they must write up their data and produce an article, report, or book.

Skills are only one of the benefits gained when the Foxfire approach is included in school curricula. These skills include traditional ones we value, like learning to listen, to write, to do mathematics (involved in getting and spending money to publish the magazine). They also involve skills such as decision-making, organization, and working with others.

There are benefits for those other than students, however, and the principal one is that we are able to preserve knowledge that would otherwise be gone when the grandparents in our communities die. Since in many regions of the country this knowledge has been orally transmitted generationally, it has never been written down. As the Foxfire advisor put it:

> If this information is to be saved at all, for whatever reason, it must be saved now; and the logical researchers are the grandchildren, not the university researchers from outside. In the process, these grandchildren gain an invaluable, unique knowledge about their own roots, heritage, and culture (Wigginton, 1972a).

The Foxfire approach strengthens generational ties and reduces alienation. The Chinese have also used this approach when they have sent students out into the country-side to gather the life-histories of old people who lived through the "bitter past" or participated in the Long March or other historical events. Survivors of the atomic bombing in Hiroshima have also been approached by their children so that their experiences do not die with them. In all these cases, we preserve so as to understand different ways of making sense out of life.

Many teachers may feel that however interested they are in these activities, they do not have the curricular freedom to attempt such projects on such a large scale. The Foxfire approach can be modified for use in classrooms. Students can go out singly or a few at a time to interview different staff members of the school. This must be more than a "one-shot" effort because they need to establish rapport with those they interview. If the principal's secretary has worked in the building for a long time, she might know a lot about how things have changed—or not changed—over the years. Shop teachers, janitors, bus drivers, and neighborhood storekeepers are all good resources. Students will have to work to make their stories come alive.

The qualitative approach, applied pedagogically, is neither therapeutic nor a human relations technique. It is a research method that seeks to describe and analyze complex experiences. It shares similarities with human relations methods in that, as part of the data gathering process one must listen well, question closely, and observe details. But its goals are not therapeutic. The symbolic interactionist emphasis on understanding how many people in a situation make sense out of what is happening to them, encourages an empathetic understanding of different people's points of view. The qualitative researcher's focus on "how things look and feel down under" (Becker et al., 1961) offers the opportunity to bring disparate and often unsought points of view out in the open.

ACTION RESEARCH

When we think of the word *research,* we are often like horses whose master has placed blinders on our eyes to cut out peripheral vision as we travel down the road. One blinder, in this case, is our assumption that only people with years of training, housed in universities, research corporations, or government agencies, can conduct research. The other blinder is that research must always be nonpartisan, serving no particular cause. Action research reflects neither of these premises, and hence, many traditional scholars do not view it as "real" research. From our perspective, research is a frame of mind—a perspective people take toward objects and activities. Academicians and professional researchers investigate questio. s that are of interest to them. They state the purpose of their study in the form of hypotheses or as research questions. They are not only expected to conduct research, but are urged to do so along the lines of established research traditions, whether quantitative or qualitative. While colleagues argue, they share a consensus about what it means to do research. Outside the academy, people in the "real world" can also conduct research—research that is practical, directed at their own concerns and, for those who wish, a tool to bring about social change.

Action research is the systematic collection of information that is designed to bring about social change. Its practitioners marshall data or evidence to expose injust practices or environmental dangers and present recommendations for change. Applied research, we said at the beginning of this chapter, seeks findings that can be used by people to make practical decisions about some aspects of their lives. Action research is a type of applied research in which the researcher is actively involved in the cause for which the research is conducted.

Both qualitative and quantitative methods can be used in action research. Qualitative methods rely on observation, open-ended interviewing, and the use of documents. In this section we look at action research in education and the qualitative approach: its characteristics, the nature of action research data, and its uses.

Research for Action

One afternoon in a suburban elementary school a parent leafs through a textbook while waiting for a conference with her daughter's teacher. The book's descriptions of girls as "no fun to play with" and "sissies," and its pictures of girls standing idly by while boys jump, climb, run, and throw, surprise her. She had no idea that girls still receive such disparaging treatment in schoolbooks. She is so angered by this experience that she calls together a group of community women and explains her experiences to them. The group wonders how widespread this practice is and decides to look systematically at the textbooks of all the elementary schools in their town to see how they depict girls. They decide that they will look at descriptions, pictures, and content relating to girls and women. They examine the textbooks and find that almost all of them repeat the first woman's findings. They make copies of some of the most outstanding examples and write up a report. This report describes what they have found, includes the duplicated pictures, and suggests their recommendations for change. The women give their group a name, and reserve time at meetings of the Board of Education, the Parent-Teachers Organization, the Rotary Club, and the Library Board of Directors to report their findings and present their recommendations for change. After a series of emotional meetings with the school board, a workshop at the YWCA, and a demonstration in front of the superintendent's house, the school board accepts the group's recommendations. This is an example of action research.

Nancy Beth Bowen and nine other children with retardation won the right to an education in 1973 in the famous Pennsylvania Association for Retarded Citizens (PARC) vs. The Commonwealth of Pennsylvania case. Their lawsuit mandated that severely handicapped youngsters were entitled to an "appropriate education" in the least restrictive setting. Good contact between the school program and home was stipulated as an important element of an appropriate education for a severely handicapped child. Several years later, communication between parents and schools seemed to deteriorate so that attorneys worried the students were not receiving an appropriate education. So a group of qualitative researchers traveled to Philadelphia, at the request of the attorneys for the children, to conduct observations in the schools as well as open-ended interviews with the parents of these severely handicapped children. They wanted data on the quality and nature of the children's school program and on interactions between the schools and the parents. The purpose of this research was to gather evidence for consideration by the courts in a case that would show the city of Philadelphia in noncompliance with the law. This is an example of action research.

A college professor and a photographer visited large state institutions for people with retardation in order to document the degrading conditions in which these people live (conditions they had seen on previous trips). On their tour of the institution, the photographer secretly snapped picture after picture on institutional conditions in order that these people's lives would become public. Meanwhile, the professor diverted the guide's attention with conversation and questions. Their photoessay, sold to *Look Magazine,* made it their best-selling issue ever. In book form, *Christmas in Purgatory* (Blatt and Kaplan, 1974) sold over 50,000 copies, raised the national consciousness, and was a prime factor in initiating the movement toward "deinstitutionalization" in America. This is an example of action research.

In all of these examples, the research was undertaken in order to precipitate change on some particular issue. The researchers themselves took an activist, change-agent role, whether they were parents concerned about their children's education, or professional researchers committed to a particular issue.

Action research is always concerned with questions of importance. It may focus on children who are out of school (Children's Defense Fund, 1974), on American prison conditions (Mitford, 1971), on corporal punishment in schools (Center for Law and Education, 1978), or on toxic waste disposal (Levine, 1980b). In its concern with these issues, the action researcher always assumes that the research will reflect his or her values. Scholarly research also reflects values. When scholars employing the qualitative approach are concerned about some social problem, they might study it and write a book expressing the point of view of some powerless group. Some of the best of these include the works of Robert Coles (1964), Thomas Cottle (1976a, 1976b, 1977), and Lillian Rubin (1976). The values of these writers are also clearly reflected in their work, but, while it is valuable research, it is not action research because it is not tied to action for change.

We must make the point here that research always has political consequences. Research derives its meaning from, and its importance in, the purposes for which it is collected and the uses to which it is put. We tend to notice that the research serves some particular goal, however, when the purpose challenges some aspect of the status quo. Many people in bureaucracies also collect data and conduct research with a particular goal in mind: to document how well they are doing in order to obtain continued funding. This is a common function of organizational research. Sometimes the data collected may reveal that some slight reform might be desirable. More funds are therefore needed for the agency so that it can perform better. It is no accident that organizations annually present reasons to show why they need more money and why they accomplished so much with what they had.

You are probably asking: Is action research objective? This question is important to clarify, particularly if you are a graduate student in an academic setting where concern with objectivity in research is high. Objectivity is often defined as giving equal weight to all the information one gathers, or as having no point of view when one undertakes research. In journalism, objectivity has traditionally meant getting both sides of the story (Wicker, 1978). Action researchers believe that objectivity is related to your integrity as a researcher and the honesty with which you report what you find. Let us look at a few examples of how action researchers themselves have discussed it.

An action research manual for people interested in investigating and monitoring state schools for people with mental retardation comments on objectivity in the context of preparing descriptive reports:

> These reports are not intended to yield an ''objective'' view of a facility, if ''objective'' means devoting equal attention to the positive and negative aspects of a facility. Institutional brochures, press releases, and public statements always paint a positive picture of the setting. As a monitoring strategy, descriptive reports should be oriented to violations of legal and moral rights—things that are seldom reported and need to be changed. Given this orientation, the observer should report his or her observations as honestly, completely, and objectively as possible (Taylor, 1980).

While the action researcher in this example is clearly an advocate for the rights of institutionalized people, it is the advocacy role that acts as the stimulus to undertake research on living conditions. But the reportage of those conditions is governed by the concern to be honest, to describe in detail what one has seen, and to be exact.

Jessica Mitford, the famous muckraking journalist, says that she is not objective, *if* objectivity means having no point of view. She strives to be accurate and underscores its importance in her research:

> *Accuracy* is essential, not only to the integrity of your work but to avoid actionable defamation. It can be ruinous to try to tailor the evidence to fit your preconceptions, or to let your point of view impede the search for facts.
>
> But I do try to cultivate the *appearance* of objectivity, mainly through the technique of understatement, avoidance where possible of editorial comment, above all letting the undertakers, or the Spock prosecutors, or the prison administrators pillory themselves through their own pronouncements (Mitford, 1979, p. 24).

Mitford's bias is always clear to the reader, but she never distorts her informant's words or lies in other ways. One must never lie.

Another way of looking at objectivity reminds us of "the hierarchy of credibility" that we have discussed. Tom Wicker conceptualizes objective journalism to be official-source journalism. Until the 1960s, he suggests, journalism that did not rely on official sources was considered subjective. But the experiences of many journalists in Vietnam contributed to changing this view because reporters developed skepticism of what government officials told them. When reporters began to travel among Vietnamese people and low-ranking American officials in the provinces, they did not get the same optimistic picture about how the war was going:

> These reporters began to engage in the most objective journalism of all—seeing for themselves, judging for themselves, backing up their judgments with their observations, often at risk of life and limb, and the government's wrath. Under this scrutiny, the claims of generals, ambassadors, spokesmen began to appear hollow and inflated (Wicker, 1978, p. 8).

From Wicker's point of view, reporters gained in objectivity when they stopped relying exclusively on official sources (what they were told) and began firsthand involvement with their social world. For action researchers, objectivity means being honest, going to the source to gather data, and eliciting the views of those involved in the issue.

What Action Research Can Do

When action researchers collect data for a social cause, they do so to change existing practices of discrimination and environmental endangerment. Action research accomplishes this in several ways:

1. The systematic collection of information can help identify people and institutions that make the lives of particular groups of people intolerable. Geraldo Rivera, for example, exposed the conditions at Willowbrook State School in New York in order to change the way people with disabilities were treated (Rivera, 1972). Critics of services for people with retardation have often noted that institutions are built in isolated spots away from communities to limit public access to them. Rivera used the television camera to increase public access.
2. It can provide us with information, understanding, and hard facts to make arguments and plans more creditable to large audiences and gives points to negotiate when it is time for decisions to be made. Testimonies before legislatures on the dangers of corporal punishment in schools, for instance, are strengthened if details of interviews and observations are included.
3. It can help to identify points in the system that can be challenged both legally and through community action.

4. It allows people to understand themselves better, increases their awareness of problems, and raises commitment. To know the facts firsthand is to have one's consciousness raised and dedication increased about particular issues. Geraldo Rivera, for example, underwent tremendous personal change after covering the Willowbrook story. He never again wants to do the lighthearted stories he once did: "Because of the response to Willowbrook, and the responsibility I feel for the children of state schools, I feel great guilt if I'm not wrestling with some profound issue" (Rivera, 1972).

5. Action research can serve as an organizing strategy to get people involved and active around particular issues. The research itself is an action. Housewives living near the Love Canal in New York, which the Hooker Chemical Company had used for toxic waste disposal, started a Homeowners' Association, and revealed the environmental patterns of poisoning because they were concerned about their children's health in school (located on the edge of the former canal). The process of interviewing neighborhood residents and observing illnesses in homes propelled them to take action to insure the health of their families. Crucial information was provided to identify others experiencing similar problems. As C. Wright Mills (1959) wrote, the first step in social change is to locate others in the same position.

6. It helps you to develop confidence. It is difficult to act forcefully toward some goal when you rely on feelings without data to support your views. Data-gathering helps you to plan strategy and develop community action programs.

Action research strengthens one's commitment, and encourages progress toward particular social goals.

The Action Research Approach to Data

When you conduct action research, you must think about the process as research and you must call the evidence you collect, *data*. If you approach the task as a researcher and ask "research questions," you force yourself into a frame of mind where you undertake your work more systematically. This may sound like a game of semantics, but asking yourself, "What research do I need to do?" makes the job much more serious than asking yourself, "What should I know about this?"

Action researchers are thorough in their search for documentary materials. Much of the material you may need is not secret and can be found in libraries, courthouses, and law offices. If you are working on a corporal punishment case in a community school, for example, you might read through the town's newspapers for the past fifty years to find how corporal punishment was handled in the past.

The facts never speak for themselves. As you look through records and materials, you must continually ask, "What can I do with this material that will make my case compelling?" While all researchers attempt to solidly document their views, the action researcher must also present recommendations for change. Consequently, you must always ask yourself how to make your material compelling enough to encourage others to act.

A particularly compelling kind of documentary material is less accessible to the public. These are documents from the trade journals, newsletters, and magazines of the particular group under investigation (see Mitford, 1979). Advertisements about psychotropic drugs in mental health journals, or school security systems in school administrator magazines, or articles in newsletters of southern private schools may all provide compelling examples of particular points of view. It is firsthand data.

Another compelling kind of data for action researchers is consumer testimony. People who have been gypped or discriminated against or who have suffered can speak forcefully about their concerns. The Children's Defense Fund study of children excluded from school mostly against their will, for reasons like pregnancy, retardation, "attitude," and bedwetting, provided powerful documentation because it let the children's words be heard. Action researchers often build on the qualitative strategy of eliciting consumer perspectives, even when the people are retarded, very old, or very young—people whom we usually assume cannot speak for themselves. These people can become part of the movement rather than objects to be served by it. It is a humanizing process.

When Geraldo Rivera conducted his exposé of Willowbrook, he interviewed for a news broadcast Bernard Carabello, a twenty-one-year-old victim of cerebral palsy who, wrongly diagnosed as retarded when he was three, had spent the next eighteen years of his life at Willowbrook. Rivera recalls his interview with Bernard as the most dramatic moment of the exposé. Difficult to understand, but struggling to communicate, Bernard recounted his desire to go to school to learn to read, and described how much worse conditions got every time there was a budget cut (Rivera, 1972). Bernard symbolized, for the viewers of the six o'clock news, the individual, particular humanity of an institutionalized person. Consumer testimony like this also counteracts the typical administrative stance that outsiders do not know what "it's really like here."

Another characteristic of action research data is that, as we just illustrated, it is often gathered and used to expose. While this is not true of all action research, action research in the muckraking tradition attempts to expose corruption, scandal, and injustice. This strand is particularly noticeable when action research is undertaken on large institutions like schools, hospitals, government bureaucracies, or mental health facilities. In the muckraking tradition, unlike evaluation research, for instance, one does not seek to maintain confidentiality about the site but to expose it. An evaluation researcher is usually concerned with rapport with informants, and does not want to endanger it. In action research, on the other hand, one's goal must be to expose the practice in order to change it. If you want to change the policy of busing in a particular community, affect corporate involvement in curriculum development in a certain school, or affect some other single institution or practice in a specific geographic area, you cannot choose anonymity as a tactic.

If your goals are more nationally-oriented, you must make a more sophisticated tactical decision about revealing names. After you have collected a number of specific instances of a social problem around the country, for example, you may decide to reveal generally where these instances occurred (which parts of the country or which schools), but your focus is no longer on those individually responsible for some injust practice. Rather, you seek to inform people that this national problem occurs everywhere.

In this kind of research stakes can be high. People's lives, jobs, and ways of life are at stake, both those who are subject to injust practices, and those who work in or preside over the bureaucracies that perpetuate them. For these reasons, it is particularly important to be systematic, thorough, and rigorous in your data collection. If it is some practice in a school that is of concern, be certain to visit the site over a period of time to document your concern. Your observations, like any participant observation notes, must be described in detail.

If, as action researchers, for instance, you plan to investigate some incident or pattern of treatment in a residential setting for people with retardation, you can facilitate the systematic recording of fieldnotes if the facility is visited by teams of parents (or other monitoring groups) who collect and compile their notes.

These strategies are not different from those we described earlier in the book; it is just that because many people will find the social-change goals so threatening, it is vital to be honest, accurate, and thorough in accomplishing these goals. While data gathering may take longer, you leave yourself less open to challenges of distortion and libel, and in the long run, you may reach your goals more quickly.

An additional problem that action researchers may face is the charge that they do not have degrees or formal research training and, therefore, their data need not be taken seriously. When Mrs. Gibbs, the housewife who became a leader in the Love Canal struggle, first took the data about environmental patterns of poisoning to doctors, they dismissed it by saying it had only been collected by housewives (Levine, 1980b). If you are systematic, thorough, and grounded in evidence that has been gathered firsthand, like Mrs. Gibbs you will be able to counteract this in the long run.

CONCLUSION: APPLIED RESEARCH AND THE QUALITATIVE TRADITION

Action research, like evaluation and pedagogical research, builds upon what is fundamental in the qualitative approach. It relies on people's own words, both to understand a social problem and to convince others to help remedy it. And, instead of accepting official, dominant, and commonly accepted understandings like "schools educate" or "hospitals cure," it turns these phrases on end and makes them objects of study. Because the primary goals of applied research are action, training, and decision-making, some differences from basic research exist.

The roots of action research are deep. As our chapter on the history of qualitative research in education suggested, qualitative methods arose in a time of social turbulence. Muckraking journalism preceded the social survey, whose goals were to uncover the major problems people faced in the communities of industrializing America, and then to present this data so that people would act to stop water pollution, urban slum expansion, or the tracking of the poor in schools. We find these same efforts emerging again in the 1930s, when photographers like Dorothea Langue and Lewis Hine used photography to reveal the depths of poverty and despair in depression America. In the 1960s, we saw action research again in the form of action research groups such as NARMIC, National Action Research Against the Military Industrial Complex, focusing on American military policies.

Qualitative research has always included both basic and applied work. During some historical periods these stains intertwine; at others, they separate. Recently, a well-known educational anthropologist said that the role of the ethnographer in relation to social change is "to raise to the level of articulated, documented description what insiders and participants feel but cannot describe and define."[6]

In conjunction with others who are concerned about change, whether this change occurs in the evaluation, pedagogical, or action modes, qualitative researchers can help people to live better lives.

ENDNOTES

1. Competition determines who does federally-funded research. Government agencies write RFP's describing research they want accomplished. Various researchers, located in companies and universities, describe their plans, methods, and cost to undertake it. The proposals received are reviewed and contracts are awarded.
2. Evaluation research also enjoyed a short-lived popularity in the late thirties and forties.
3. Of course many people do studies of programs and reflect on how they are working without being paid. There are many excellent studies of this type. They are conducted in the same way that basic research would be conducted, only they have as a particular focus a planned intervention. Our concern in this section is specifically with funded evaluation research.
4. Interview with Joseph Mercurio, 1980.
5. Described by Steve Arzivu in a speech at the meeting of the American Educational Research Association, Boston, May, 1980.
6. Courtney Cazden made these remarks during a speech at the American Educational Research Association, Boston, 1980.

APPENDIX: EXAMPLES OF OBSERVATIONAL QUESTIONS FOR EDUCATIONAL SETTINGS

SCHOOL ENVIRONMENT

Physical Environment

What is the nature of the school architecture?

How large is the building?

Is the building large enough to adequately accommodate the students?

How old is the building?

In general, what is its condition?

Are there fences and walls around the school?

What are the grounds around the school like?

What is the general appearance of the facility?

Are entrances to the building accessible to handicapped students or teachers? Can people in wheelchairs enter the building?

In what section of the community is the school located?

What is the nature of that section?

What transportation facilities are available to and from the school?

Are entrances clearly marked so that new visitors can easily find the office?

What is the temperature like in the school?

Is it adequately heated in the winter and cooled in the summer?

Can the temperature be controlled in individual rooms?

Can windows be opened or are they permanently shut?

What is the nature of the ventilation system?

What doors are present in the school?

How is the space arranged in the school as a whole?

How do teachers define their space?

Do teachers and other staff think of some space as their private territory?

Do students have private, locked places to keep their personal belongings?

Which students are located in the best places in the school?

Are students allowed (encouraged) to decorate the rooms and/or hallways?

What is the nature of these decorations?

Are any parts of the building inaccessible to someone in a wheelchair?

Are there elevators or ramps if the school is on different levels?

Do objects and furniture in the building stay constant so that blind students could find their way around?

Are bathroom doors and cubicles wide enough for a person in a wheelchair to enter?

Are the lavatories clean and free of odor?

Are there soap and towels in the lavatory?

Are there doors on the stalls to ensure privacy?

What is the nature of the graffiti (if any)?

What kind of audiovisual equipment is available?

Where is it stored? How is it procured?

Do some people hoard equipment?

What happens to broken equipment?

Is the equipment used frequently?

Do staff members eat with students?

How much time is given for students and staff to eat?

Is it enough time for a leisurely meal?

What is the dining atmosphere?

How is food served? On what vessels?

What eating utensils do students use?

What kind of food is served? How is it served?

Do staff members talk negatively about students' food in front of them?

Are there any school lunch programs in which certain children do not pay? How is this handled? Is there any stigma attached to getting free lunch?

What are the rules and regulations of the cafeteria?

How is the cafeteria arranged?

What do the children talk about at lunch?

Are children allowed to sit where they wish for lunch?

What do teachers think about cafeteria duty?

What do teachers and other staff members talk about at lunch?

What are the seating arrangements in the teachers' eating place? Is it the same every day?

Economic, Social, and Cultural Environment

What is the reputation of the school in the community (good, tough, dangerous)?

What exactly do people mean when they say those things?

What are some of the major problems the school has faced over the past five years?

How do various staff people react to outside criticism?

What sort of things is the school critcized for by outsiders?

What is the racial composition of the school?

How does the racial composition compare with other schools in the area?

How do teachers, administrators, students, and parents feel about the racial composition?

Has there been or is there pending controversy over the racial composition of the school?

How are minority group students and teachers distributed in the school?

Do classes tend to be balanced or do minority students tend to wind up in the same class?

What is the nature of the relations between different ethnic groups in the school (do groups tend to stick together or is there integration)?

What are the words that members of different ethnic groups use to describe other ethnic groups? Themselves?

What is the socioeconomic composition of the school?

What kind of tax base supports the school?

Semantic Environment

To what extent, if any, do staff members use familiar nouns like *boy, kid, fella, girl,* when talking to students? In what tone are these said and under what circumstances?

Are students ever referred to by some behavioral or mental characteristic (i.e., slow poke, big mouth, Miss pretty)?

What nicknames do staff members give students?

What clichés do staff members use when talking about students? Some examples might be "give them an inch and they'll take a mile," and "spare the rod and spoil the child."

What nicknames do students have for staff?

What nicknames do students use for the various activities, objects and places (i.e., in one school, lunch was known as the "pig out")?

What words do students use in referring to staff in private?

What do kids call each other? Are the nicknames kind or cruel?

To what extent do program titles such as "counselor" or "rehabilitation" actually reflect activities in the school?

What words and phrases are used in the school which you have not heard before?

Are they unique to school?

What is their meaning?

Does the staff use an esoteric vocabulary to refer to activities, behavior, objects, and places instead of more mundane words that might better be used to describe the phenomena?

Can staff members define or intelligently discuss the esoteric vocabularies they employ?

What specifically do staff members mean by "behavior modification," "counseling," and "occupational training"?

How do teachers describe their school?

How do students describe their school?

HUMAN ENVIRONMENT

Teachers

What do teachers complain about?

What do they praise?

How do teachers explain low achievement on the part of students?

How do teachers explain high achievement on the part of students?

Do teachers have favorites? What are they like?

Do teachers distinguish between "my time" and "school's time"?

How do teachers think of sick days and vacation?

What do teachers define as unprofessional behavior?

How are girls treated differently from boys?

Are there assumptions about what boys can do and what girls can do?

What about the images of boys and girls, and men and women in the textbooks?

How does what staff say reflect their assumptions about what is appropriate behavior for boys and girls?

Who are the most popular teachers in the school? What seems to make them popular among teachers? Among students?

Who are the most disliked teachers in the school? What seems to make them disliked?

Other Staff

What are the various titles of the people who work in the school?

What are the jobs of the various specialists?

How can you tell what positions people hold?

What are the specific qualifications for various staff positions?

What training do staff members receive before assuming their responsibilities?

What reasons do staff members give for working in the school (''I like children,'' ''pay,'' ''convenience'')?

What do various staff members think of their jobs?

How are the various specialists (counselor, instructional technologists) thought of by students, teachers, parents, and administrators?

What goes on in the library?

To whom does the librarian define the books as belonging?

What do various staff members consider the most important aspect of their work?

What do various staff members like? Dislike? What are their reasons?

Do any particular staff members ''sit around'' more than others?

What rules and regulations do staff ignore?

Who comprises the janitorial staff?

What do they define as their job?

How does the administration define them?

How do the students define them? The teachers?

What is the nature of the relationship between the janitors and others in the school?

What do the janitors think about various teachers? About student?

Where do the janitors stay? What do they talk about?

Do janitors have any student helpers? Who are the helpers?

Staff Members and Students: Communication

Do staff gossip about students? About each other?

If they do, what is the nature of that gossip?

To what extent are students teased? By staff? By each other? What about?

To what extent are students cursed? By staff? By each other? What about?

To what extent, if any, do students suffer other verbal indignities or put downs?

Is the students' time treated as valuable or do staff members break appointments with them and keep them waiting?

To what extent, if any, do staff members raise their voices when talking to certain students? To what students is this done?

To what extent, if any, are students ignored by staff?

To what extent, if any, are students treated as if they were not there? Under what circumstances?

How do staff and students talk about Fridays (TGIF?) and the other days of the week?

Is the tone of the school different on different days?

What about during different times of the year?

How is the end of the term thought of?

Does the nature of the work differ at different times of the year?

How do staff members measure their success in the school?

How do students measure success?

What are the goals staff members say they are working toward?

How do they see their activities related to these goals?

Are students and various staff members asked if they mind having outsiders observe them or walk through their work areas?

Do staff members knock on doors before entering rooms?

Do you think it would be difficult for you to keep your sense of dignity if you were a student at the school?

How do staff members view the students? As capable human beings? As babies? As dangerous?

To what extent does the staff stereotype students?

To what extent does the staff recognize the students' past experiences and family backgrounds?

How are these things treated?

Do staff members act differently in front of visitors? How?

To what extent do students purposely try to give staff a hard time? How do they do this and what do they think about it?

Do students mock staff members?

If so, what form does this mocking take?

How do students communicate between classes?

Do students approach staff more than the staff approaches students?

To what extent is there free and open communication between the students and the staff?

Do staff hide information from students and vice versa? What sort of things?

What do students think of the staff?

What does the staff think of students?

What are the names used for various achievement groups (bluebirds)?

What type of extracurricular activities are available? Who participates in them? Staff? Students?

What type of achievements are most awarded in the school? Athletic? Academic? Other?

How much decision-making power do students have?

Students

How often and when do students have the opportunity for physical exercise?

Do some students receive more physical exercise than others? What students and why?

What kind of activities do the students enjoy doing? Dislike doing?

What do students and staff wear?

Does dress tell you anything about status systems or informal groups?

What about hair styles?

What do the children in the class fight about?

Who seem to be the most popular children in the class? For what reasons? The least popular? For what reasons?

How do the school monitors behave? How are they selected?

When various children are troubled, whom do they look to for support?

What is the number, if any, of the students on behavior modifying drugs?

What was the role of the school in having the children put on that treatment?

How do various people in the school feel about having modifying drugs?

Is medication ever used as a substitute for a program?

Administration

How long has the current principal been principal and how do people talk about the previous principal?

How do teachers act when the principal enters the room?

What do administrators define as unprofessional?

How do administrators check on teachers?

What are the styles of administrators?

Are there school-wide assembly programs?

What are they like?

How is the administration thought of by the staff? By the students?

How do classes move through the building?

What is the daily, weekly, and monthly school schedule? What are the variations from room to room?

To what extent do student and staff needs rather than the school schedules determine the course of daily life?

To what extent are basic needs like eating and using the toilet done en masse?

To what extent are places provided for students and staff to be alone and not under surveillance?

What are the formal and informal dress regulations for students? For other staff?

To what extent, if any, do students have access to such things as the bathroom, the phone, the outdoors?

Who uses the loud speaker and for what purposes?

What criteria does a student have to meet (age, residence) to be eligible to attend the school?

How are the classes organized—who decides who goes into what classes?

How is the decision made?

How is participation in special programs and events (trips, plays) distributed among students? Equally? As rewards? Does participation in these events reflect class or ethnic destinations?

Who determines the content of these activities? Do students participate in the planning?

How does what is done at each grade level differ?

Are the different grades (rooms) decorated differently? How?

To what extent, if any, are pupils moved from one class to another without being consulted or without their prior knowledge?

What is the nature of student records?

Do records contain a place for parents' grievances?

Do records emphasize idiosyncratic episodes rather than a general picture of the whole person?

Are items entered into the records which are defamatory and discrediting to the student? If so, is the student given opportunities to respond to these remarks?

Are the students' records discussed in public by the staff members?

Do parents have easy access to files containing information about their children?

Parents

What communication occurs between the school and parents?

Are parents consulted in decisions affecting their child?

What rules pertain to visitors?

Is there a PTO?

What does the PTO do?

How many people attend a typical meeting?

What ''kind''of people attend?

What are the programs for the PTO?

How are parents' complaints handled?

What literature or instructions are given to parents and guardians by the school?

What is the nature of that literature?

How often do parents have contacts with the school and what is the nature of those contacts?

What is the extent and the nature of the volunteer program?

Are there any conflicts between the staff and the volunteers? Over what?

What jobs do volunteers do?

What is the school's visiting policy?

Are visitors a common occurrence in the school?

What are the school's open houses like?

Is the view of the school presented during open houses an accurate description of the school on a regular day?

LEARNING ENVIRONMENT

Learning Situation

What decorations adorn the classroom?

Are students interacting with each other? Will they be praised or penalized for such interaction?

What is the ability range of the class as measured by objective tests and past grades?

What are children complimented for?

Are the classrooms spacious or crowded? In good physical condition or run down? Somber or cheerful? Barren or busy?

Which of the students in the class have performed well in terms of past measure of achievement? Poorly? Are these accurate reflections of ability?

What is the average class size?

Is there provision for interest centers in the classroom?

Are all students engaged in the same task at the same time?

Do the students volunteer answers in discussion readily? Do they talk to each other as well as the teacher?

Does classroom procedure optimize cooperation or competition? How often do students work on group projects?

How well do students work independently or on long-range assignments? How much experience have they had in working in small groups?

Are the seats and desks in the class moveable and are they moved?

How do students perceive they will be rewarded for effort? Are all students responsive to the reward system?

Is the class heterogeneously or homogeneously grouped? If the latter, what is the criterion for such grouping?

Teacher-Student Relationships

How many dittoes does the teacher use in class during the day?

Do students have free time when their work is finished?

Has the teacher prepared materials for use during free time?

What kinds of group work activities are provided?

What role does the teacher play during group activities?

Where is the teacher's desk located in the room?

What are the teacher's movements during the day in relation to his or her desk?

What kinds of curriculum materials are used? (i.e., texts, other readings, games, etc.)

Does the main instructional material revolve around the use of texts, with other materials used for "enrichment"?

What kinds of teaching devices are on the walls, ceilings, etc.?

What images of people do they portray?

How are classroom chores divided?

How is the class paced?

What individualized teaching-learning occurs? For whom?

Which students have most contact with the teacher?

Which students have least contact with the teacher?

Which students are touched most and least by the teacher?

Discipline and Control

Can students choose where they sit?

How prominent is control in the day to day operation of the school? Of different classrooms?

What restrictions are placed on students' mobility in the school?

What methods of control are used by staff?

What is the nature of punishment in the school?

How and when are punishments given?

How are requests made by students?

What tone of voice do staff use when addressing students?

What kinds of things do administrators purposely turn their backs on?

What do teachers purposely turn their backs on?

What is the nature and extent of corporal punishment?

Is the physical integrity of students and staff guaranteed in the school?

Is there danger of assault?

Is there an independent complaint system through which students can bring grievances against the staff for problems?

Are threats made to students?

What are typical threats?

How many students express hostility?

What student behaviors elicit punishment?

Which staff members have the authority to discipline students?

To what extent do the punishments and rewards of the school approximate punishment and reward systems in the larger world?

Bogdan, R., & Taylor, S. *Introduction to qualitative research methods.* New York: John Wiley, 1975.

Bogdan, R., & Taylor, S. *The judged not the judges: An insider's view of mental retardation.* Toronto: University of Toronto Press, in press.

Botkin, B. A. (Ed.). *Lay my burden down: A folk history of slavery.* Chicago: University of Chicago Press, 1945.

Bronfenbrenner, U. The experimental ecology of education. *Educational Researcher,* 1976, *5.*

Bruni, S. *The class and them: Social interaction of handicapped children in integrated primary classes.* Unpublished Ph.D. dissertation, Syracuse University, 1980.

Bruyn, S. *The human perspective in sociology.* Englewood Cliffs, N.J.: Prentice-Hall, 1966.

Burnett, J. H. Commentary on an historical overview of *Anthropology and education: A bibliographic guide.* In The Committee on Anthropology and Education. *Anthropology and education; Report and working papers.* New York: National Academy of Education, 1978.

Campbell, D. Qualitative knowing in action research. In M. Brenner, P. Marsh, & M. Brenner (Eds.), *The social contexts of method.* New York: St. Martins, 1978.

Carey, J. T. *Sociology and public affairs, the Chicago school.* Beverly Hills, Calif.: Sage, 1975.

Carini, P. *Observation and description: An alternative methodology for the investigation of human phenomena.* North Dakota Study Group on Evaluation Monograph Series. Grand Forks: University of North Dakota, 1975.

Case, C. A crisis in anthropological research. *Sociology and Social Research,* 1927, *12*(1), 26–34.

Cassell, J. *A field manual for studying desegregated schools.* Washington, D.C.: The National Institute of Education, 1978.

Cassell, J. Risk and benefit to subjects of fieldwork. *The American Sociologist,* 1978, *13,* 134–144.

Cassell, J., & Wax, M. (Eds.). Ethical problems in fieldwork. Special issue of *Social Problems,* 1980, *27*(3).

Cazden, C., John, V., & Hymes, D. (Eds.). *Functions of language in the classroom.* New York: Teachers College Press, 1972.

Center for Law and Education. Corporal punishment. *Inequality in Education,* 1978 (Sept.), #23.

Children's Defense Fund. *Out of school in America.* Washington, D.C.: 1974.

Coles, R. *Children of crisis.* Boston: Little, Brown, 1964.

Coles, R. *Privileged ones.* Boston: Little, Brown, 1977.

Collier, J. Jr. *Visual anthropology: Photography as a research method.* New York: Holt, 1967.

Collins, R., & Makowsky, M. *The discovery of society* (2nd ed.). New York: Random House, 1978.

Cooley, C. H. The roots of social knowledge. *The American Journal of Sociology,* 1926, *32,* 59–79.

Coser, L. Two methods in search of a substance. In W. Snizek, E. Fuhrman, & M. Miller (Eds.), *Contemporary issues in theory and research, a metasociological perspective.* Westport, Conn.: Greenwood Press, 1979.

Cottle, T. *Barred from school.* Washington, D.C.: New Republic, 1976a.

Cottle, T. *Busing.* Boston: Beacon Press, 1976b.

Cottle, T. *Children in jail.* Boston: Beacon Press, 1977.

Cressey, D. Criminal violation of financial trust. *American Sociological Review*, 1950, *15*, 738–743.

Cressy, P. *The taxi-dance hall.* Chicago: University of Chicago, 1932.

Cronbach, L. Beyond the two disciplines of scientific psychology. *American Psychologist*, 1975, *30*(2).

Cronbach, L., & Suppes, P. (Eds.). *Research for tomorrow's schools.* New York: Macmillan, 1969.

Cusick, P. A. *Inside high school: The student's world.* New York: Holt, Rinehart & Winston, 1973.

Dalton, M. Preconceptions and methods in *Men who manage.* In P. Hammond (Ed.), *Sociologists at work.* New York: Anchor, 1967.

Davis, A., & Dollard, J. *Children of bondage.* Washington, D.C.: American Council on Education, 1940.

Davis, A., Gardner, B. B., & Gardner, M. R. *Deep south.* Chicago: University of Chicago Press, 1941.

Davis, A., & Havighurst, R. J. *Father of the man.* Boston: Houghton Mifflin, 1947.

Decker, S. *An empty spoon.* New York: Harper & Row, 1969.

Denny, T. *Some still do: River Acres, Texas.* (Report #3 in Evaluation Report Series). Kalamazoo, Mich.: Evaluation Center, Western Michigan University, College of Education, 1978a.

Denny, T. *Story telling and educational understanding.* Paper presented at meeting of the International Reading Association, Houston, Texas, May 1978b (ERIC Document Reproduction Service No. ED 170 314).

Denzin, K. *The research act* (2nd ed.). New York: McGraw-Hill, 1978. (Originally published, Chicago: Aldine, 1970.)

Deutscher, I. *What we say/what we do.* Glenview, Ill.: Scott, Foresman, 1973.

Devine, E. T. Results of the Pittsburgh survey. *American Sociological Society, Papers and Proceedings,* 1906–1908, *3*, 85–92.

Dexter, L. A. Role relationships and conceptions of neutrality in interviewing. *American Journal of Sociology,* 1956, *62*(2), 153–157.

Didion, J. *The white album.* New York: Simon and Schuster, 1979.

Dollard, J. *Criteria for the life history.* New Haven, Conn.: Yale University Press, 1935.

Dollard, J. *Caste and class in a southern town.* New York: Harper, 1937.

Douglas, J. *Investigative social research.* Beverly Hills: Sage, 1976.

Duster, T., Matza, D., & Wellman, D. Fieldwork and the protection of human subjects. *The American Sociologist,* 1979, *14*, 136–142.

Eddy, E. *Walk the white line.* Garden City, N.Y.: Doubleday, 1967.

Eddy, E. *Becoming a teacher.* New York: Teacher's College Press, 1969.

Eisner, E. *On the differences between scientific and artistic approaches to qualitative research.* Paper presented at the meeting of the American Educational Research Association, Boston, April, 1980.

Erickson, F. What makes school ethnography "ethnographic"? *Council on Anthropology and Education Newsletter,* 1973, *4*(2).

Erickson, F. Gatekeeping and the melting pot. *Harvard Educational Review,* 1975, *45*, 44–70.

Erikson, K. Notes on the sociology of deviance. *Social Problems,* 1962, *9*, 307–314.

Erikson, K. *Everything in its path.* New York: Simon and Schuster, 1976.

Evans, J. W. Evaluating social action programs. In L. Zurcher & C. Bonjean (Eds.), *Planned social intervention.* Scranton, Penn.: Chandler, 1970.

Evans, W. *Photographs for the Farm Security Administration, 1935–1938.* New York: Da Capo Press, 1973.

Everhart, R. Problems of doing fieldwork in educational evaluation. *Human Organization,* 1975, *34*(2).

Everhart, R. Between stranger and friend: Some consequences of "long term" fieldwork in schools. *American Educational Research Journal,* 1977, *14*(1).

Faris, R. E. L. *Chicago sociology, 1920–1932.* Chicago: University of Chicago Press, 1967.

Federal Writers' Project. *These are our lives.* Chapel Hill: University of North Carolina, 1939.

Feinberg, S. E. The collection and analysis of ethnographic data in educational research. *Anthropology and Education Quarterly,* 1977, *8*(2).

Feinberg, W. Educational studies and the discipline of educational understanding. *Educational Studies,* 1979, *2,* 375–391.

Filstead, W. (Ed.). *Qualitative methodology.* Chicago: Markham, 1970.

Fine, G. A., & Glassner, B. Participant observation with children. *Urban Life,* 1979, *8*(2), 153–174.

Florio, S. E. *Learning how to go to school: An ethnography of interaction in a kindergarten/first grade classroom.* Unpublished doctoral dissertation, Harvard University, 1978.

Freedman, P. *Day care as a work setting: An ethnographic description.* Unpublished manuscript, Syracuse University, 1980.

Freire, P. *Pedagogy of the oppressed.* New York: Herder and Herder, 1968.

Fried, A., & Elman, R. (Eds.). *London (Excerpts from Life and labour of the people in London.* C. Booth). New York: Pantheon, 1968.

Fuchs, E. *Pickets at the gates.* New York: Free Press, 1966.

Fuchs, E. *Teachers talk.* Garden City, N.Y.: Doubleday, 1969.

Garfinkel, H. *Studies in ethnomethodology.* Englewood Cliffs, N.J.: Prentice-Hall, 1967.

Geer, B. First days in the field. In P. Hammond (Ed.), *Sociologists at work.* Garden City, N.Y.: Doubleday, 1964.

Geer, B. (Ed.). *Learning to work.* Beverly Hills: Sage, 1973.

Geertz, C. From the native's point of view: On the nature of anthropological understanding. In P. Rabinow and W. Sullivan (Eds.), *Interpretive social science.* Berkeley: University of California Press, 1979.

Geertz, C. Thick description: Toward an interpretive theory of culture. In *The interpretation of cultures.* New York: Basic Books, 1973.

Georges, R. A., & Jones, M. O. *People studying people; the human element in fieldwork.* Berkeley: University of California Press, 1980.

Gerth, H., & Mills, C. W. *Character and social structure.* New York: Harcourt, Brace, 1953.

Glaser, B. *Theoretical sensitivity: Advances in the methodology of grounded theory.* Mill Valley, Calif.: Sociology Press, 1978.

Glaser, B., & Strauss, A. L. *The discovery of grounded theory: Strategies for qualitative research.* Chicago: Aldine, 1967.

Glass, G. A paradox about excellence of the schools and the people in them. *Educational Researcher,* 1975, *4.*

Goffman, E. *Gender advertisements.* New York: Harper, 1979.

Goffman, E. *The presentation of self in everyday life.* Garden City, N.Y.: Anchor, 1959.

Gold, R. Roles in sociological field observations. *Social Forces,* 1958, *36,* 217–223.

Gouldner, H. *Teachers' pets, troublemakers, and nobodies.* Westport, Conn.: Greenwood, 1978.

Greene, M. *Landscapes of learning.* New York: Teachers College Press, 1978.

Guba, E. G. Toward a methodology of naturalistic inquiry in educational evaluation. *CSE Monograph Series in Evaluation,* 8. Los Angeles: Center for the Study of Evaluation, University of California, 1978.

Gutman, J. M. *Lewis Hine, 1974–1940: Two perspectives.* New York: Grossman, 1974.

Hall, D. *Teachers as persons: Case studies of the lives of women teachers* (unpublished). Proposal to National Institute of Education, 1979.

Harrison, S. *The social survey.* New York: Russell Sage Foundation, 1931.

Haskins, J. *Diary of a Harlem schoolteacher.* New York: Grove Press, 1969.

Henry, J. Culture, education and communications theory. In G. Spindler (Ed.), *Education and anthropology.* Stanford, Calif.: Stanford University Press, 1955a.

Henry, J. Docility, or giving teacher what she wants. *The Journal of Social Issues,* 1955b, *11*(2), 33–41.

Henry, J. Attitude organization in elementary school classrooms. *American Journal of Orthopsychiatry,* 1957, *27,* 117–123.

Henry, J. *Culture against man.* New York: Random House, 1963.

Herndon, J. *The way it spozed to be.* New York: Simon and Schuster, 1968.

Herriott, E. Ethnographic case studies in federally funded multi-disciplinary policy research: Some design and implementation issues. *Anthropology and Education Quarterly,* 1977, *8*(2).

Hill, R. J., & Crittenden, K. *Proceedings of the Purdue symposium on ethnomethodology.* Purdue, Ind.: Institute for the Study of Social Change, Purdue University, 1968.

Hollingshead, A. B. *Elmstown's youth.* New York: John Wiley, 1949.

Hughes, E. Institutional office and the person. *American Journal of Sociology,* 1934, *43,* 404–413.

Hughes, E. C. *The sociological eye.* Chicago: Aldine, 1971.

Hurley, F. J. *Portrait of a decade; Roy Stryker and the development of documentary photography in the thirties.* Baton Rouge: Louisiana State University Press, 1972.

Hyman, H. *Interviewing in social research.* Chicago: University of Chicago Press, 1954.

Ianni, F. Anthropology and educational research: A report on federal agency programs, policies and issues. In The Committee on Anthropology and Education (Eds.), *Report and working papers.* National Academy of Education, 1978, pp. 427–488.

Ives, E. *The tape-recorded interview: A manual for fieldworkers in folklore and oral history.* Knoxville: The University of Tennessee Press, 1974.

Jackson, P. *Life in classrooms.* New York: Holt, Rinehart & Winston, 1968.

Jahoda, M., Deutsch, M., & Cook, S. *Research methods in social relations* (Part 1). New York: Dryden, 1951.

Johnson, J. M. *Doing field research.* New York: Free Press, 1975.

Journal of Educational Sociology, 1927, *1*(4).

Journal of Educational Sociology, 1927, *1*(7).

Junker, B. *Field work.* Chicago: University of Chicago Press, 1960.

Kellogg, P. The spread of the survey idea. *Proceedings of the Academy of Political Science,* 1911–1912, Vol. 2, Part 4, 475–491.

Kelly, J. G. Naturalistic observations in contrasting social environments. In E. P. Willens & H. L. Raush (Eds.), *Naturalistic viewpoints in psychological research.* New York: Holt, Rinehart & Winston, 1969.

Kierzek, J., & Gibson, W. *The Macmillan handbook of English.* New York: MacMillan, 1968.

Kohl, H. *36 children.* New York: New American Library, 1967.

Komarovsky, M. *The unemployed man and his family.* New York: Dryden Press, 1940.

Komarovsky, M. Cultural contradictions and sex roles. *American Journal of Sociology,* 1946, *52,* 184–189.

Kozol, J. *Death at an early age.* New York: Bantam, 1967.

Krueger, E. T. The technique of securing life history documents. *Journal of Applied Sociology,* 1925a, *9,* 290–298.

Krueger, E. T. The value of life history documents for social research. *Journal of Applied Sociology,* 1925b, *9,* 196–201.

Leacock, E. *Teaching and learning in city schools.* New York: Basic Books, 1969.

Levine, M. Investigative reporting as a research method: An analysis of Bernstein and Woodward's *All the president's men. American Psychologist,* 1980a, *35,* 626–638.

Levine, M. *Method or madness: On the alienation of the professional.* Invited Address, Division 12, Meeting of the American Psychological Association, Montreal, September, 1980b.

Liebow, E. *Tally's Corner.* Boston: Little, Brown, 1967.

Lightfoot, S. *Worlds apart: Relationships between families and schools.* New York: Basic Books, 1978.

Lindeman, E. C. *Social discovery.* New York: Republic, 1925.

Lindesmith, A. R. *Addiction and opiates.* Chicago: Aldine, 1947.

Lofland, J. *Analyzing social settings.* Belmont, Calif.: Wadsworth, 1971.

Lofland, J. Styles of reporting qualitative field research. *The American Sociologist,* 1974, *9,* 101–111.

Lofland, J. *Doing social life.* New York: John Wiley, 1976.

Lutz, F., & Gresson, A. Local school boards as political councils. *Educational Studies,* 1980, *2,* 125–143.

Lynd, R. S., & Lynd, H. M. *Middletown.* New York: Harcourt, Brace, 1929.

Lynd, R. S., & Lynd, H. M. *Middletown in transition.* New York: Harcourt, Brace, 1937.

Maccoby, E., & Maccoby, N. The interview: A tool of social science. In G. Lindzey (Ed.), *Handbook of social psychology* (Vol. 1). Cambridge, Mass.: Addison-Wesley, 1954.

Maines, D. R., Shaffir, W., & Turowetz, A. Leaving the field in ethnographic research: Reflections on the entrance-exit hypothesis. In W. B. Shaffir, R. A. Stebbins, & A. Turowetz (Eds.), *Fieldwork experience: Qualitative approaches to social research.* New York: St. Martin's, 1980.

Malinowski, B. *A scientific theory of culture and other essays.* New York: Oxford University Press, 1960.

Matthews, F. *Quest for an American sociology: Robert E. Park and the Chicago school.* Montreal: McGill-Queens University Press, 1977.

McAdoo, H. *Oral history and educational research.* Paper presented at the meeting of the American Educational Research Association, April, 1976 (ERIC Document Reproduction Service No. ED 171 831).

McCall, G. J., & Simmons, J. L. (Eds.). *Issues in participant observation.* Reading, Mass.: Addison-Wesley, 1969.

McDermott, R. *Kids make sense: An ethnographic account of the interactional management of success and failure in one first grade classroom.* Unpublished doctoral dissertation, Stanford University, 1976.

McDermott, R. P., Gospodinoff, K., & Aron, J. Criteria for an ethnographically adequate description of concerted activities and their contexts. *Semiotica,* 1978, *24,* 245–275.

McIntyre, D. Two schools, one psychologist. In F. Kaplan and S. Sarason (Eds.), *The psychoeducational clinic; papers and research studies.* Boston: Massachusetts Department of Mental Health, 1969.

McPherson, G. *Small town teacher.* Cambridge, Mass.: Harvard University, 1972.

Mead, G. H. *Mind, self, and society.* Chicago: University of Chicago Press, 1934.

Mead, M. An anthropologist looks at the teacher's role. *Educational Method,* 1942, *21,* 219–223.

Mead, M. *The school in American culture.* Cambridge, Mass.: Harvard University Press, 1951.

Mehan, H. Structuring school structure. *Harvard Educational Review,* 1978, *48,* 32–64.

Mehan, H. *Learning lessons.* Cambridge, Mass.: Harvard University Press, 1979.

Mehan, H., & Wood, H. *The reality of ethnomethodology.* New York: John Wiley, 1975.

Meltzer, B., & Petras, J. The Chicago and Iowa schools of symbolic interactionism. In T. Shibutani (Ed.), *Human nature and collective behavior.* Englewood Cliffs, N.J.: Prentice-Hall, 1970.

Meltzer, B., Petras, J., & Reynolds, L. *Symbolic interactionism: Genesis, varieties and criticism.* London: Routledge and Kegan Paul, 1975.

Mercurio, J. A. *Caning: Educational rite and tradition.* Syracuse, N.Y.: Syracuse University, 1972.

Mercurio, J. A. Community involvement in cooperative decision making: Some lessons learned. *Educational Evaluation and Policy Analysis,* 1979, *6,* 37–46.

Merton, R. K., & Kendall, P. L. The focused interview. *American Journal of Sociology,* 1946, *51,* 541–557.

Metz, M. H. *Classrooms and corridors: The crisis of authority in desegregated secondary schools.* Berkeley: University of California, 1978.

Mills, C. W. *The sociological imagination.* London: Oxford University Press, 1959.

Mitford, J. *Kind and usual punishment.* New York: Alfred A. Knopf, 1971.

Mitford, J. *Poison penmanship.* New York: Alfred A. Knopf, 1979.

Moore, G. A. *Realities of the urban classroom.* Garden City, N.Y.: Anchor, 1967.

Morris, V. C., & Hurwitz, E. *The Heisenberg problem: How to neutralize the effect of the observer on observed phenomena.* Paper presented at the meeting of the American Educational Research Association, Boston, April, 1980.

Musello, C. Family photograph. In J. Wagner (Ed.), *Images of information.* Beverly Hills: Sage, 1979.

N.I.E. *Violent schools—Safe schools; The safe school study report to the Congress.* Washington, D.C.: National Institute of Education, 1978.

North, L. V. The elementary public schools of Pittsburgh. *Charity and the Commons,* March 6, 1909, *21,* 1175–1191.

Odum, H. *American sociology: The story of sociology in the United States through 1950.* New York: Greenwood, 1951.

Ogbu, J. *The next generation: An ethnography of education in an urban neighborhood.* New York: Academic Press, 1974.

Patton, M. Q. *Qualitative evaluation methods.* Beverly Hills: Sage, 1980.

Peters, C. C. Research technics in educational sociology. *Review of educational research,* 1937, *7*(1), 15–25.

Porter–Gehrie, C. The ethnographer as insider. *Educational Studies,* 1980, *2,* 123–124.

Porter–Gehrie, C., & Crowson, R. L. Analyzing ethnographic data—Strategies and results. Paper presented to the meeting of the American Educational Research Association, Boston, April, 1980.

Psathas, G. (Ed.). *Phenomenological sociology.* New York: Wiley, 1973.

Redfield, R. *The educational experience.* Pasadena, Calif.: Fund for Adult Education, 1955.

Riis, J. *How the other half lives*. New York: C. Scribner's Sons, 1890.

Riley, J. J. Sociology and social surveys. *American Journal of Sociology*, 1910–1911, *16*, 818–836.

Rist, R. Student social class and teacher expectations: The self-fulfilling prophecy in ghetto education. *Harvard Educational Review*, 1970, *40*, 411–451.

Rist, R. *The urban school: A factory for failure*. Cambridge, Mass.: Massachusetts Institute of Technology Press, 1973.

Rist, R. On the relations among educational research paradigms: From distain to detente. *Anthropology and Education*, 1977, *8*.

Rist, R. On understanding the processes of schooling. In J. Karabel & A. H. Halsey (Eds.), *Power and ideology in education*. New York: Oxford University Press, 1977.

Rist, R. *The invisible children*. Cambridge, Mass.: Harvard University, 1978.

Rist, R. Blitzkrieg ethnography. *Educational Researcher*, 1980, *9*(2).

Ritzer, G. *Sociology: A multiple paradigm science*. Boston: Allyn and Bacon, 1975.

Rivera, G. *Willowbrook: A report on how it is and why it doesn't have to be that way*. New York: Vintage, 1972.

Roberts, J. An overview of anthropology and education. In J. Roberts and S. Akinsanya (Eds.). *Educational patterns and cultural configurations*. New York: David McKay, 1976, pp. 1–20.

Roberts, J. *Scene of the battle*. Garden City, N.Y.: Doubleday, 1971.

Roberts, J., & Akinsanya, S. (Eds.). *Educational patterns and cultural configurations*. New York: David McKay, 1976.

Robinson, W. S. The logical structure of analytic induction. *American Sociological Review*, 1951, *16*, 812–818.

Rogers, C. The nondirective method as a technique for social research. *American Journal of Sociology*, 1945, *50*, 279–283.

Rogers, C. *Client-centered therapy*. Boston: Houghton Mifflin, 1951.

Rosensteil, A. Educational anthropology: A new approach to cultural analysis. *Harvard Educational Review*, 1954, *24*, 28–36.

Rosenthal, R., & Jacobson, L. *Pygmalion in the classroom*. New York: Holt, Rinehart & Winston, 1968.

Roth, J. *Timetables*. Indianapolis: Bobbs-Merrill, 1963.

Rothstein, W. R. Researching the power structure: Personalized power and institutionalized charisma in the principalship. *Interchange*, 1975, *6*(2), 41–48.

Rubin, L. *Worlds of pain*. New York: Basic Books, 1976.

Sarason, S., & Doris, J. *Educational handicap, public policy, and social history*. New York: Free Press, 1979.

Sarason, S., Levine, M., Goldenberg, I., Cherlin, D., & Bennett, E. *Psychology in community settings*. New York: John Wiley, 1966.

Schaller, G. *The year of the gorilla*. Chicago: University of Chicago Press, 1965.

Schatzman, L., & Strauss, A. *Field research*. Englewood Cliffs, N.J.: Prentice-Hall, 1973.

Schmuck, P. Deterrents to women's careers in school management. *Sex Roles*, 1975, *1*, 339–353.

Schwartz, H., & Jacobs, J. *Qualitative sociology*. New York: Free Press, 1979.

Scott, R. W. Field methods in the study of organizations. In J. G. March (Ed.), *Handbook of organizations*. Chicago: Rand McNally, 1965.

Scott, R. *The making of blind men*. New York: Russell Sage, 1969.

Scriven, M. Objectivity and subjectivity in educational research. In L. G. Thomas (Ed.), *Philosophical redirection of educational research: The seventy-first yearbook of the National Society for the Study of Education.* Chicago: University of Chicago Press, 1972.

Sharp, R., & Green, A. *Education and social control.* London: Routledge and Kegan Paul, 1975.

Shaw, C. *The jack roller* (2nd ed.). Chicago: University of Chicago Press, 1966.

Shumway, G., & Hartley, W. *Oral history primer.* Fullerton: California State University, 1973.

Shuy, R., & Griffin, P. (Eds.). *The study of children's functional language and education in the early years.* Final Report to the Carnegie Corporation of New York. Arlington, Va.: Center for Applied Linguistics, 1978.

Shuy, R., Wolfram, W., & Riley, W. K. *Field techniques for an urban language study.* Washington, D.C.: Center for Applied Linguistics, 1967.

Smith, L., & Geoffrey, W. *The complexities of an urban classroom: An analysis toward a general theory of teaching.* New York: Holt, Rinehart & Winston, 1968.

Snedden, D. The field of educational sociology. *Review of Educational Research,* 1937, 7(1), 5–14.

Sontag, S. *On photography.* New York: Farrar, Straus and Giroux, 1977.

Spindler, G. (Ed.). *Education and anthropology.* Stanford, Calif.: Stanford University Press, 1955.

Spindler, G. *The transmission of American culture.* Cambridge, Mass.: Harvard University Press, 1959.

Spradley, J. *The ethnographic interview.* New York: Holt, Rinehart & Winston, 1979.

Spradley, J. P. *Participant observation.* New York: Holt, Rinehart & Winston, 1980.

Stack, C. *All our kin: Strategies for survival in a black community.* New York: Harper and Row, 1974.

Stake, R. E. The case study method in a social inquiry. *Educational Researcher,* 1978, 7.

Steffens, L. *The shame of the cities.* New York: McClure, Phillips, 1904.

Steffens, L. *The autobiography of Lincoln Steffens.* New York: Harcourt, Brace, 1931.

Stott, W. *Documentary expression and thirties America.* New York: Oxford University Press, 1973.

Strunk, W. Jr., & White, E. B. *The elements of style.* New York: Macmillan, 1972.

Sussmann, L. *Tales out of school.* Philadelphia: Temple University, 1977.

Sutherland, E. *The professional thief.* Chicago: University of Chicago Press, 1937.

Taylor, C. *The social survey. Its history and methods.* Columbia: University of Missouri, 1919 (Social Science Series 3).

Taylor, S. *A guide to monitoring and investigating residential settings.* Syracuse, N.Y.: Human Policy Press, 1980.

Thomas, W. I. *The unadjusted girl.* Boston: Little, Brown, 1923.

Thomas, W. I., and Znaniecki, F. *The Polish peasant in Europe and America.* New York: Knopf, 1927.

Thomson, J., & Smith, A. *Street life in London.* London: Sampson Low, Murston, Searle & Rurington, 1877.

Thorne, B. "You still takin' notes?" Fieldwork and problems of informed consent. *Social Problems,* 1980, 27, 272–284.

Thrasher, F. *The gang.* Chicago: University of Chicago Press, 1927.

Trachtenberg, A. Introduction: Photographs as symbolic history. In *The American image: Photographs from the National Archives, 1860-1960.* New York: Pantheon, 1979.

Travers, R. *An introduction to educational research* (4th ed.). New York: Macmillan, 1978.

Turner, R. H. The quest for universals in sociological research. *American Sociological Review,* 1953, *18,* 604–611.

Turner, R. (Ed.). *Ethnomethodology.* Middlesex, England: Penguin, 1974.

Tyler, R. (Ed.). *Prospects for research and development in education.* Berkeley, Calif.: McCutcheon, 1976.

Vandewalker, N. Some demands of education upon anthropology. *American Journal of Sociology,* 1898, *4.*

Wagner, J. (Ed.). *Images of information.* Beverly Hills: Sage, 1979.

Waldorf, D., & Reinarman, C. Addicts—Everything but human beings. *Urban Life,* 1975, *4*(1).

Waller, W. *Sociology of teaching.* New York: John Wiley, 1932.

Waller, W. Insight and scientific method. *American Journal of Sociology,* 1934, *40*(3), 285–295.

Warner, W. L., & Lunt, P. S. *The social life of a modern community.* New Haven, Conn.: Yale University Press, 1941.

Wax, M. Paradoxes of "consent" in the practice of fieldwork. *Social Problems,* 1980, *27,* 265–272.

Wax, R. *Doing fieldwork: Warning and advice.* Chicago: University of Chicago Press, 1971.

Wax, R. Gender and age in fieldwork and fieldwork education: No good thing is done by any man alone. *Social Problems,* 1979, *26,* 509–523.

Webb, B. *My apprenticeship.* New York: Longmans, Green & Company, 1926.

Webb, S., & Webb, B. *Methods of social study.* London: Longmans, Green & Company, 1932.

Wells, A. F. Social surveys. In F. C. Bartlett, M. Ginsberg, E. S. Lindgren, & R. H. Thouless (Eds.), *The study of society.* London: Kegan Paul, Trench, Trubner & Company, 1939.

Whyte, W. F. Interviewing in field research. In R. H. Adams & J. J. Preiss (Eds.), *Human organization research.* Homewood, Ill.: Dorsey Press, 1960.

Whyte, W. F. *Street corner society.* Chicago: University of Chicago Press, 1955.

Whyte, W. H. On making the most of participant observation. *The American Sociologist,* 1979, *14,* 56–66.

Wicker, T. *On press.* New York: Berkley Publishing Corporation, 1978.

Wigginton, E. (Ed.). *The foxfire book.* Garden City, N.Y.: Anchor, 1972a.

Wigginton, E. (Ed.). *Foxfire 2.* Garden City, N.Y.: Anchor, 1972b.

Wiley, N. The rise and fall of dominating theories in American sociology. In W. Snizek, E. Fuhrman, & M. Miller (Eds.), *Contemporary issues in theory and research, a metasociological perspective.* Westport, Conn.: Greenwood, 1979.

Wilson, S. The use of ethnographic techniques in educational research. *Review of Educational Research,* 1977, *47.*

Wirth, L. *The ghetto.* Chicago: University of Chicago Press, 1928.

Wolcott, H. *The man in the principal's office.* New York: Holt, Rinehart & Winston, 1973.

Wolcott, H. Criteria for an ethnographic approach to research in schools. *Human Organization,* 1975, *34,* 111–127.

Wolcott, H. *Teachers vs. technocrats: An educational innovation in anthropological perspective.* Eugene, Ore.: Center for Educational Policy and Management, 1977.

Wolf, R. L. An overview of conceptual and methodological issues in naturalistic evaluation. Paper presented at the meeting of American Educational Research Association, San Francisco, April, 1979.

Wolf, R. L. *Strategies for conducting naturalistic evaluation in socio-educational settings: The naturalistic interview.* Paper prepared for publication in the Occasional Paper Series, Evaluation Center, Western Michigan University, 1979.

Wood, P. *You and Aunt Arie: A guide to cultural journalism based on Foxfire and its descendents.* Washington, D.C.: Institutional Development and Economic Affairs Service, Inc., 1975.

Ziegler, S. School for life: The experience of Italian immigrants in Canadian schools. *Human organization,* 1980, *39*(3).

Zimmerman, C., & Frampton, M. *Family and society, a study of the sociology of reconstruction.* New York: D. Van Nostrand, 1935.

Znaniecki, F. *The method of sociology.* New York: Farrar and Rinehart, 1934.

Zorbaugh, H. *The gold coast and the slum.* Chicago: University of Chicago Press, 1929.

INDEX

Robert Bogdan received his Masters Degree in Education and Ph.D. in Sociology at Syracuse University. He has studied a range of educational issues using qualitative research techniques. He holds a dual professorship in Special Education and Sociology at Syracuse University. He is the author of books concerned with qualitative research and his articles have appeared in such diverse journals as *Phi Delta Kappa, Educational Technology, Journal of Health and Social Behavior, American Psychologist, Orthopsychiatry, Social Work, Edcentric, Social Policy, Education Digest, Education and Training of the Mentally Retarded,* and *Human Organization.*

Sari Knopp Biklen received her Ed.D. in Education from the University of Massachusetts at Amherst. She teaches qualitative research workshops for graduate students, and is director of the Education Designs Group, a not-for-profit research and consulting firm. She has done evaluation research for the Fleischmann Commission, and has taught in the Department of Education at Syracuse University. She is a recipient of an N.I.E. grant doing qualitative research on women teachers in elementary schools. She is the author of several articles and one other book.